Volume I

The Child Care Professional

Volume I

Karen Stephens

Early Childhood Specialist
Director of ISU Child Care Center
Lecturer in Child Development
Illinois State University,
Normal, Illinois

GLENCOE
McGraw-Hill

New York, New York   Columbus, Ohio   Woodland Hills, California   Peoria, Illinois

Contributing Writers

Sheila Platter
Assistant Principal for Instruction and Curriculum
Garland High School
Garland, Texas

Judy Marks
Child Care Occupations Instructor
North Valley Occupational Center
Los Angeles Unified School District
Mission Hills, California

Technical Reviewers

Bonnie J. Bucher
Director
Proctor Hospital New Horizons Employee
  Child Care Center
Peoria, Illinois

Linda B. Daniels, M.S.
Early Childhood Education Consultant
Ohio Department of Education
Columbus, Ohio

Linda R. Glosson, Ph.D.
Home Economics Teacher
Wylie High School
Wylie, Texas

Constance G. Mueller, M.S., R.D.
Instructor, Foods and Nutrition
Illinois State University
Normal, Illinois

Educational Reviewers

Tanya Benson
Lake City High School
Coeur D'Alene, Idaho

Angela Lattuca Croce
Mira Mesa High School
San Diego, California

Betty Jo Jordan
West Virginia Department of Education
Charleston, West Virginia

Judy Marks
North Valley Occupational Center
Los Angeles Unified School District
Mission Hills, California

Darla Jean Olberding
North High School
Evansville, Indiana

Texanita Louise Randle
Wichita High School South
Wichita, Kansas

Janice Scholz
Office of Applied Technology and Vocational Education
Brevard County
Melbourne, Florida

Glencoe/McGraw-Hill

A Division of The McGraw-Hill Companies

Send all inquires to:
Glencoe/McGraw-Hill
3008 W. Willow Knolls Drive
Peoria, IL   61614-1083

ISBN 0-02-642876-8 Volume I

Printed in the United States of America

7 8 9 10 11 12 13 14   003   02 01

Table of Contents

Special Text Features

Charts and Highlighted Topics

Unit 1

THE CHILD CARE PROFESSION

Reflections

"'These children need a role model.' That's what they told me when I first applied for a job at the child care center in my neighborhood. I was seventeen, needed part-time work, and didn't really care what kind of job I had. Many of the kids in the center didn't have a father figure at home. And they wanted me to be a father figure? What experience did I have for that? Well, I've learned. I help out with all sorts of activities in the center, but the outdoor activities are the best. I like to keep my kids on track (now I think of them as mine). People say I set a good example for them, and they need that. This is the kind of work I want to do after graduation. Men are needed in the child care field. I'm not sticking with it for that reason, though; I'm sticking because I like it."

—Andy

Chapter 1

Families and Child Care

CHAPTER OBJECTIVES

- Explain why the need for child care services has grown.

- Compare and contrast custodial, developmental, and comprehensive child care.

- Compare and contrast the different options in child care.

- Identify factors that promote quality in a child care program.

- Analyze issues in child care.

Terms to Learn

- au pair
- child care
- curriculum
- developmentally appropriate curriculum
- early childhood
- early childhood education
- environment
- extended families
- gender role
- nanny
- nuclear family

Dave couldn't believe the change in his daughter. He watched as four-year-old Holly skipped toward him, holding a special creation that looked like it had been made from part of an egg carton. Holly was beaming. "Look, Daddy!" Holly said with pride as she held out her art project. "I made it for you. Teacher said it has pretty colors. Can we put it on the table when we eat dinner?"

"Of course, we can," Dave replied, drawing Holly close for a hug. "I think it's great." As they left the child care center, Holly chattered happily about her day. She talked about Ms. O'Keefe and Mr. Millen, two of her favorite teach-ers. She also described a musical game that she had played with her friends.

"She's so happy here," Dave thought to himself. "And to think— only a few weeks ago, she seemed like a different child. She had so lit-tle to say when I picked her up, and it seemed like she was always tired and grumpy. I'm so glad I found another child care pro-gram for her. It has made such a differ-ence—for her and for me."

QUALITY COUNTS

Good child care does make a difference. **Child care** is *the broad term that describes any situation in which children are provided with supervision, support, and sometimes training by individuals outside the child's immediate family.* For a parent who entrusts the care of a child to others, the quality of that care is critical. Can you imagine what it would be like as a parent to leave your child with people you don't trust? How would you feel if you thought your child was not happy or not receiving proper care from the people you were paying for child care service? How would you find quality care? These are very real questions that families face. The demand for more and better child care has grown significantly over the last few decades, and it will contin-ue to do so. Identifying and insuring quality child care is a common goal.

THE GROWTH OF CHILD CARE

Throughout the early periods of history in America, child care was uncom-mon. If used at all, arrangements were usu-ally made with nearby family and friends. Since **extended families** often lived together, child care for them was built right into the family setting. These families, *which include relatives other than parents and children,* did not usually need others for child care.

need for child care did surface when parents and other adult family members joined the war efforts. During World War II, for example, many women left their homes to work in the factories, where they helped build defense equipment and supplies. Because of women's presence in the work force, the national government and defense factories created child care centers to care for the children of employed women. Once World War II ended and men came back to the jobs, women returned to their homes, and most of the child care centers closed.

During the 1950s, many families fit a pattern that was typical after World War II. The **nuclear family,** *consisting of a mother, father, and their children,* was common. In many of these families, father went off to work while mother kept the household running smoothly. If you have ever watched a television program from the 1950s, you may have seen images that reflected those times; however, change was ahead.

One of the changes that has affected the way in which families handle child care has been in the extended family. These families have become less likely to live in the same household. Often they have moved far apart, eliminating the convenience of built-in child care. Although some families are returning to this pattern of living, it is still much less common than it was throughout the early years of American history.

Another change evolved during the 1960s as new attitudes about the roles of men and women at home and at work emerged. Ideas about gender roles broadened. A **gender role** is *the behavior and responsibilities expected of a man or woman in the family and society.* Gradually, more women became employed outside the home, a trend that has continued for every decade since the 1960s. Currently over 50 percent of preschoolers have a mother who works outside the home. By the year 2000 and beyond, estimates show that 70 percent of pre-

Child care for extended families who live together is built into the family setting. These families include relatives other than parents and children.

With more women in the workforce, the need for child care services has increased significantly. What special challenges do working parents of young children face?

schoolers will have mothers in the labor force. Although having a parent at home automatically supplied child care in the past, that situation just isn't as common anymore—for several reasons.

The Need for Two Incomes

Many families today depend on the incomes of both parents simply to provide food, shelter, and education for their children. In families with both parents employed, many of the families would live in poverty if one parent stayed home. When both parents are employed outside the home, they usually need help with the care of young children.

More Single Parents

Both mothers and fathers raise children alone today. The number of single mothers, however, is far greater. After divorce, women rather than men more commonly have custody of the children. When unplanned pregnancy occurs and the parents do not marry, the same situation is likely—the mother usually cares for the child. Since the rates of divorce and teen pregnancy are high, so is the number of single parents who have a need for child care while they attend school, look for a job, or go to work.

Career Interests

Some people are highly motivated to have a career. Both family and employment offer them needed fulfillment. Leaving a career to care for children, even temporarily, may result in lost promotions and income as well as other setbacks. Some people who have a career find that they are better parents when they have the outside stimulation of a job.

furnish a place for the child to be supervised while basic needs are met. They may provide food and make sure children get the rest and exercise they need. Activities are limited and informal, with no planned program.

Developmental Care

Many programs go beyond custodial care. An interest in helping children develop properly is the reason. **Early childhood,** *those years between birth and age eight,* is a critical time for development. Children learn so much during the first years of life. Development moves at a fast pace, and personalities are shaped. If developmental delays occur, a child may have trouble catch-

DIFFERENT APPROACHES TO CHILD CARE

As the need to have child care has increased, providers have created different approaches to help meet the need. No two children are exactly alike. No two families are exactly alike. Therefore no one type of care is right for all families. Parents need child care options that suit their situations. They must choose from programs that provide everything from custodial, to developmental, to comprehensive care.

Custodial Care

As you explore the types of child care that are available, you will find some providers who give only custodial care. In other words, they

The early childhood years are important ones. Experiences shape each child's development and personality.

ing up. Problems may continue and become greater over time. How can child care professionals address this situation? Programs that focus on developmental care are the answer. Educational opportunities that promote good development are stressed with this type of care.

Early childhood education is the term applied to those *child care programs that promote development through formal teaching and learning experiences for children up to age eight.* Many of the child care programs you will read about, observe, and perhaps even work in someday include education of the child as part of what they offer. More and more emphasis is being placed on education in the child care setting.

Many parents want programs that give their children educational opportunities. Families are turning to early childhood education to provide their children with a better start toward success in future schooling. Often such programs are used by families who need child care but also want the experience to have educational and social benefits. Some families simply feel their children need the stimulation offered by early education. Such programs are particularly useful to disadvantaged children who need help in catching up developmentally with other children.

Comprehensive Care

Child care programs that supply a range of additional services fall into the category of comprehensive care. These programs meet the basic needs of children and also promote good development. The difference is in what else they provide. Programs may include medical care for children. They may also supply parent education and training. Such classes teach parents about many topics, including nutrition, raising children, infant care, discipline, and caring for special needs children. Some programs even have exercise classes for parents.

SPECIFIC CHILD CARE OPTIONS

The availability of good child care has not kept up with the demand. On the positive side, however, society is recognizing that the need is real. In response, child care programs are increasing in number, kind, and quality.

Before selecting a program, families look for what they need. Whether part-time, full-time, custodial, or educational, they look for places where children will be lovingly and safely cared for. Parents want the right match between child and program. Some options are described below. You will read more about many of these in other chapters.

- *Child Care Centers.* These programs, which often have multiple classrooms, operate all day long but allow parents to use them part-time if necessary. Child care centers usually serve children from six weeks to twelve years of age. Some specialize in certain age categories. Transportation to and from school is generally provided for school-age children. Child care centers may be sponsored by a religious organization, public school, or a private owner. Some are for-profit businesses that operate as a chain in many locations across the country.

- *Family Day Care Homes.* This form of child care usually operates all day, serving children from six weeks to twelve years of age. Some limit the ages they will take. The provider is someone who adapts his or her own residence for the service. Family day care homes tend to be less structured than child care centers. Many parents choose them because they like the homelike atmosphere for their children and the longer hours of operation that some provide.

- *Infant/Toddler Child Care Centers.* Children from six weeks through two

> The family day care provider is someone who adapts his or her own residence for service. Many parents choose them because they like the homelike atmosphere for their children.

years of age are served in these programs. They may be housed in a child care center that serves older children. Full- or part-time service is possible.

- *Before- and After-School Programs.* These programs give school-age children a place to go before and after school while their parents are working. They usually operate from about 6:00 a.m. to 9:00 a.m. and reopen from 3:00 p.m. to 6:00 p.m. Transportation to and from school is often provided.

- *Preschool/Nursery Schools.* Most programs of this type operate for a half day two to three times a week. They emphasize educational services to stimulate children's overall development.

- *Pre-Kindergarten Programs.* Sponsored by both public and private schools, these programs are designed to prevent school failure. Programs

> Most nursery schools and preschools have limited schedules. What might be the advantages and disadvantages of this arrangement?

may be half-day or full-day. Three- to five-year-old children identified as being at risk of academic failure may be enrolled free of charge.

- *Corporate Child Care Centers.* These child care programs are offered by employers for their employees. They may be located in the company's building or in a nearby location. They often charge a lower rate than parents might pay in other programs. As these become more common, studies show that they have many benefits for child, parents, and company.

- *In-Home Child Care.* Some parents prefer to have their child cared for in their own home. Care may be provided by someone trained in child care or someone with no formal training. One option is care by a nanny. A **nanny** is *trained in child care and then employed to come into the home to care for children.* Sometimes nannies live with the family and receive free rent and food as part of their wages. Other times the nanny goes to the child's home in the morning and leaves each evening. Another option is an **au pair** (oh PARE). *This is a young person who comes from one country to live with a family in another country.* Au pairs exchange housework and child care for room and board.

- *Montessori Preschools.* These programs are based on the teachings of Maria Montessori, an Italian physician who worked with children in the early 1900s. Montessori brought new insights into how children learn, supplying materials that enabled children to master tasks in a step-by-step sequence. She promoted independence by emphasizing order and education in the preschool environment. Most Montessori programs operate on a half-day basis.

If you were hiring someone to provide full-time child care in your home, what qualities and characteristics would you look for?

- *Head Start Programs.* Created in the 1960s, Head Start is a federally funded program that primarily serves four-year-olds. It focuses on comprehensive services for low-income families. Although some Head Starts provide full-day care, most provide half-day programs.

- *Early Childhood Programs for Children with Special Needs.* Usually sponsored through public schools, these programs serve children birth to five years of age. Classrooms may include children who

A Positive Attitude

WHAT IS A POSITIVE ATTITUDE?

Whether it's your personal or professional life, a positive attitude makes a difference in how you are viewed by others and what responses you get. With a positive attitude, you look at the bright side of things. You see the good more often than the bad, focus on achievement rather than failure, smile more than frown, build instead of tear down, and believe rather than doubt. Your actions and your words reveal your attitude to others. A positive attitude is often like a magnet, drawing others to you because they like being around you.

A Positive Attitude in Action

"I know we can do it," Delores said to the steering committee at her church. "The children in this neighborhood need it. So many of them are alone after school. Their parents just don't have any options. Why just the other day, a mother told me how scared her five-year-old was when some older kids threatened him and chased him home. The boy's mother was upset. She was angry about what happened and guilty because she wasn't there. This shouldn't be happening to these children. We've got a huge basement that's empty after school. I say let's give it a try."

Delores Jacobs watched as the committee members listened to her words. Soon a lively discussion was going on about what the church could do to set up an after-school program for children in the neighborhood. Repeatedly, Delores chimed in with words of enthusiasm. She suggested names of people who might help them. She was realistic about the problems, but she had answers for those who were negative.

"I think Delores has something here," Robert Lindsey said, "and we seem to be catching her spirit. What are we here for if it isn't to offer support to people who need it?" Delores smiled as she had visions of her dream becoming reality.

Your Analysis

1. How did Delores display a positive attitude?

2. What outcomes may be a result of Delores' attitude?

3. What might have happened if Delores were not a positive person?

4. How do people develop positive and negative attitudes?

5. Do you see yourself as more positive or negative? Describe two examples that support your analysis.

6. What might a person do to become more positive?

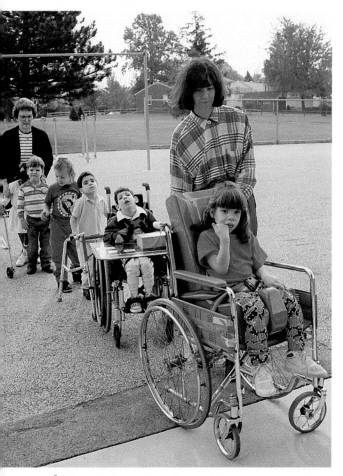

The early years of development are especially critical for children with special needs. Such children may be in specialized programs or may be included in any early childhood program.

have early diagnosis of such disabilities as cerebral palsy, birth defects, autism, behavioral disorders, Down syndrome, and hearing impairment.

- ***Child Care for Children Who Are Ill.*** Staffed with early childhood caregivers and nurses, these programs care for children who are mildly ill. Children who are recuperating from contagious diseases, such as chicken pox, use these programs. Hospitals often provide this care.

- ***Crisis Nurseries.*** Crisis nurseries are provided as a way to prevent child abuse. Parents who feel they are overstressed and at risk of abusing their children may use a crisis nursery. These programs operate on a 24-hour basis. They are usually funded by the United Way and other social service agencies. Crisis nurseries are seldom found in small communities.

- ***Parent Cooperatives.*** Some parents get together to sponsor a play group or preschool of their own. Parents take turns doing such tasks as secretarial work and caring for children.

- ***Other Programs.*** Where specific needs arise, other types of programs are created. Mother's Day Out programs, often sponsored by religious organizations, provide a few hours of child care each week for parents who need a little free time. Malls and health clubs may have drop-off care for their patrons. Respite care provides time off for parents of special needs children. These are a few examples of additional types of care that communities provide.

WHAT IS QUALITY?

Whatever type of care parents choose for their children, they still want it to be high quality. All it takes is one frightening story about a bad child care experience to raise parental concern. Infants and young children can't explain what their lives are like in a child care setting. It is up to adults to make sure that children are safe and happy. This is why an increased effort has been made to bring regulation and quality to the growing child care industry.

Suppose you were going to help your family find child care for a younger brother or sister. What characteristics would you look for to identify a quality program? The rest of

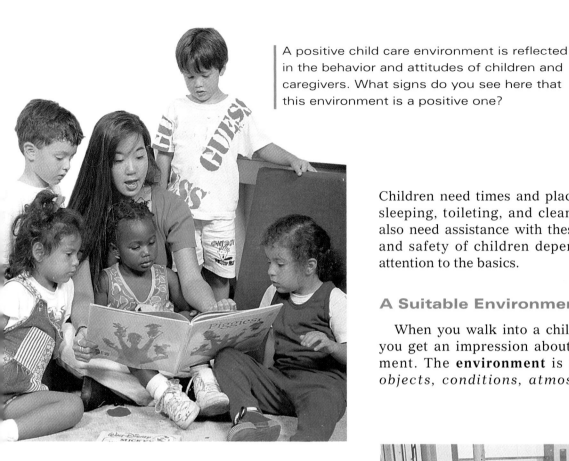

A positive child care environment is reflected in the behavior and attitudes of children and caregivers. What signs do you see here that this environment is a positive one?

Children need times and places for eating, sleeping, toileting, and cleaning up. They also need assistance with these. The health and safety of children depend on careful attention to the basics.

A Suitable Environment

When you walk into a child care center, you get an impression about the environment. The **environment** is *everything—objects, conditions, atmosphere—that*

this text will help you answer that question, but some of the key qualities are introduced here. If you decide to work in the child care field, you will be responsible for learning many specific ways to provide a quality program in all of these areas.

The Basic Needs

It's first things first when taking care of children. Before you can think about entertaining or teaching children, what would you have to plan for? The basics, of course.

A positive child care environment draws children in. The furniture, equipment, supplies, and toys all work together to stimulate the children's senses, invite them to learn, and encourage success. How would you rate this classroom?

makes up the surroundings. In a positive environment, what you see is inviting to the eye. Well-chosen furniture, equipment, supplies, and toys, all in appropriate quantity, make a contribution. The environment is more than just seen, however. It is also felt. A sense of warmth and order comes within a positive environment. A close look at the personalities and actions of employees and children reveals much about a center's environment.

A Well-Planned Curriculum

A well-planned curriculum points to quality. The **curriculum** is *a long-range plan of activities and experiences for children.* Many of the activities help children with their development. Children go through predictable stages of development, but at different rates. For example, Noel's teacher knows that he will learn to tie his shoes. She also knows the age at which he is most

likely to have the skills to do so. What she doesn't know is *exactly* when he will learn. Part of good curriculum planning for Noel and other children his age includes providing activities that allow them to practice the skills they need in order to be able to tie their shoes.

A well-planned curriculum provides many learning opportunities. Research in child development reports that children learn best by exploring with their senses—sight, hearing, touch, taste, and smell. For this reason, activities should give children opportunities to explore with *all* their senses, not just one or two.

The ability to plan appropriate activities depends on having an understanding of how children develop. When *activities include those that are geared to different levels of ability and development,* the program has a **developmentally appropriate curriculum.**

A well-planned curriculum has variety. That is, the planners strive to educate the

Exploration is an exciting as well as interesting part of a child's life. Those who plan curriculums include activities that give children opportunities to explore.

"whole" child. Activities address all areas of development—social, emotional, intellectual, physical, and moral.

An Organized Daily Schedule

In a quality program, the daily schedule provides children with a sense of security. The children can rely on a pattern that stays about the same every day. Although specific activities change daily, a basic schedule that is familiar makes children more comfortable and contributes to better behavior. Daily schedules do vary from one classroom to the next. Infant rooms have separate plans for each individual baby. Gradually, as they grow older, children learn to adapt to a schedule established for the group.

Being in group care for eight to ten hours a day demands a lot of energy from children. A well-organized schedule has time for quiet, as well as active, play.

Appropriate Discipline

"An ounce of prevention is worth a pound of cure." You've probably heard that saying before. How might you apply it to disciplining children? In a quality child care setting, people who work with children avoid many difficulties by taking steps to prevent problems from happening in the first place. What makes them successful? For one thing, they study discipline techniques to learn what works best with children. They use a positive approach with children. They also set up clear and simple rules. They plan schedules and activities that run smoothly. In addition, they think ahead about how to deal with behavior problems that might occur and take action when there is a need.

Parental Involvement

Bridging the gap between home and the child care setting is important to children. The more consistency and cooperation, the better. Although parents are the first teachers of children, they team up with professionals in child care to provide what is needed. Children feel more comfortable when parents and staff members work in harmony. A child care program that avoids contact and input from parents is not a quality one.

Often parents have particular concerns about the care and guidance given to their children. They try to choose a program that fits their beliefs about child care. They may have opinions and requests that the personnel in a good program will want to understand.

A quality program has child care professionals who can help parents. They often

In this corporate child care center, the father is able to spend some time with his child during the day. Parents need to be in touch with what goes on in their children's lives.

Tip
FROM THE
Pros

*S*ome parents may believe that they don't have something special enough to share with their child's class. As a child care profession-al, you can encourage all parents to explore what they have to offer. Then include them. A parent who demonstrates how to hammer a nail so that it goes straight into a piece of wood has something just as interesting to share with children as the parent who is an accomplished artist.

serve as role models when parents watch them guide children's learning and behavior. They can be advi-sors when par-ents ask for suggestions on selecting toys or some other child-related issue.

Good child care profes-sionals bridge home and pro-gram by invit-ing parents to become in-volved. Some ask parents to volunteer in the classroom. Others invite parents into the classroom as special visitors, especially when a particular skill, talent, or interest can be shared with the children. Newsletters and family potluck suppers are just two ways that a good program might use to help build a strong bond between family and staff.

Record Development

New abilities in children develop on a daily basis. Professionals in a quality pro-gram keep notes on each child's develop-ment. Some use checklists to record children's developmental achievements, such as the date when a one-year-old takes that first step.

Note-taking isn't the only way to record children's development. Some centers also save samples of children's work and use

video recorders. The information recorded is used to evaluate development and report to parents. With so much going on in a child care setting, observations cannot be entrust-ed to memory.

A Professional Staff

Research and information on children and child care is not static. In other words, it is always changing, with new ideas and information regularly introduced. A quality child care program has professionals who continue their growth by reading books and journals. They attend conferences and work-shops and share information with other employees. By enrolling in child develop-ment and early childhood education classes, they also promote their professional growth. A well-trained and caring professional staff

Two-year-olds need constant attention and guidance. That requires additional staff and increases the cost of care.

is probably the key ingredient when it comes to quality in child care.

Staff size is important too. When a program does not have an adequate number of staff members, children don't get the attention and care they need. The number of children one person can be responsible for varies according to the ages of the children. For infants and younger children, a larger staff is required.

Learning More about Quality

What you have just read about quality only skims the surface. In each area described, many techniques and efforts can help produce a quality child care program. You will find many ideas throughout this text. Much of what you will read is about preschoolers, those children from ages three to five. This is the age group handled by the majority of child care programs. Information about children who are younger and older, however, is also important. You will find specific discussions on these other age groups—infants, toddlers, and school-age children—featured throughout the text.

A LOOK AT THE ISSUES

*T*he subject of children and child care is sometimes emotional. That's because certain questions concerning child care are controversial. People want what is best for children, but they don't always agree on the right approach to take. Answers are not easily reached when you look at both sides of the issues. Can you see varying points of view on the issues described below? What compromises and solutions can you offer to these questions?

- ***Does the creation of child care programs promote the breakdown of the family?*** Some people believe that it does, saying that child care programs allow parents to turn away from their responsibilities. For example, they would criticize parents who put their children in child care when they have a career by choice rather than economic necessity. Other people say child care services help many single parents and dual-income families who would otherwise struggle to give their children adequate care when they have to be employed. Hoping for a return to the 1950s style of family life doesn't seem to be realistic. Today's world is different and requires new approaches to managing as a family. Most people would agree that the strength of families is a serious concern in society. What they don't always agree on is the methods for keeping families strong and healthy.

- ***What price, if any, is paid by placing children in child care at a very young age?*** Research is contradictory on this issue. Some people believe that children can thrive even with early placement in child care. Others believe that a child needs the ongoing presence of a parent for a period of time during the early years. Such factors as the quality of a program, the condition of the family environment, the time involved, and the child's age and personality probably influence the answer to this question. Research also shows that the consistent presence of one individual as the primary caregiver in a program makes a significant difference in the child's well-being.

- ***When and how should a child's formal education begin?*** The demand for child care has created pressure on public and private schools to provide longer kindergarten programs, pre-kindergarten, and programs that extend the day. Some people are concerned that such programs put too much pressure on children. Others believe that children can benefit from programs that are well planned and provide what children may not be able to get otherwise.

• *How can families get the quality child care they need?* Quality programs have been slow in coming. Some child care situations are still inadequate. The number of quality programs is growing. Quality child care, however, usually comes with a high price, making it inaccessible to many. Often the people who need it the most can least afford it. Creative ways of funding child care may be the answer, including grants to private businesses as well as other methods.

Controversial problems are not easily solved in society. It takes time, experience, and the sharing of ideas. People who care about children, including parents and child care professionals, will be at the forefront, looking for solutions that make sense.

CHILDREN, THE FUTURE, AND YOU

*I*f you decide to work in the child care field, you will be in charge of the most valuable resource society has—children. Properly raised and cared for, children are able to raise their own families someday in that same caring manner. When children have positive experiences as they develop, they grow into adults who make contributions to society rather than tear it down. People who love children and want to insure a good future for them are needed in the field. What better reason can there be to aim for a career in child care? If you want to help children get a good start, then the child care field may be just the place for you.

Not everyone agrees about the impact of child care on children, families, and society. There is agreement that children in child care deserve and need the best care possible.

Chapter 1 Review

Chapter Summary

- Parents who need supplemental care for their children often use child care services.
- Economic and social changes have caused an increased need for child care services.
- Efforts are being made to improve the regulation and quality of the child care industry.
- Early childhood professionals have many responsibilities when providing quality child care.
- Child care professionals continually further their growth by keeping up-to-date on research and information about children and child care.
- Parents and child care professionals look for solutions to the emotional and controversial subject of children and child care.

Reviewing the Facts

1. What is child care?
2. Why is quality child care important?
3. Give three reasons for the increased need for child care services.
4. Compare and contrast custodial, developmental, and comprehensive child care programs.
5. Which type of child care program would be most suitable for the child in each of the following situations: (a) a child with a strep infection; (b) an eleven-year-old child whose single parent gets home at 5:30 p.m.; (c) a three-year-old with Down syndrome; (d) a child whose parents choose to employ someone to provide care in their own home?
6. What are the fundamentals of quality child care?
7. What are the ingredients of a well-planned curriculum?
8. Describe a developmentally appropriate curriculum.
9. Identify four controversial issues concerning child care.

Thinking Critically

1. Have you read or heard about any child care situations that were not favorable for children? If so, share the examples with the class. Were the situations resolved? How?
2. Describe a good child care situation with which you are familiar. What gives it quality?
3. Do you or any of your classmates have memories of child care experiences? Describe what these situations were like and any impact they had.
4. Share your point of view on each of the issues described in the chapter.
5. Suppose you were talking to an employed parent who feels guilty about having to use child care services. What would you say to the parent?

Activities and Applications

1. **Resource File.** Begin a resource file of brochures from different early childhood programs.
2. **Interviewing Parents.** Interview several parents who use child care services. What do they like about their child care arrangement? What would they change?
3. **Volunteering.** Volunteer to work in an early childhood classroom for a day. Record your thoughts and feelings at the end of the day. Was it what you expected? What did you like? What surprised you?

Your Professional Portfolio

From school to work. What does that mean? It means that you have an important transition ahead. Moving from the school world to the world of work takes adjustment. It also takes good preparation. The work you do in school not only helps prepare you for future jobs, but it can also be used to help you land the job that you want. Many students today build portfolios, or collections, of the work they do in a class. One way they use these is to show their capabilities to a prospective employer. You will discover more about portfolios and how to build one as you complete this course. Pay particular attention to the portfolio project ideas in the box like this one at the end of each chapter. If you do, you will be better prepared to make your own transition from school to work in the future.

Observing and Analyzing

First Steps to Observing

How often do you look at what is going on around you without really seeing? It's easy to do. Your thoughts may be elsewhere, or you simply might not have the habit of noticing things. As you begin this course, now is the time to check up on your skills in this area.

To learn about children, you need to observe them. Later in this text you will read about conducting formal observations of children. For now, just take some first steps. Watch children whenever opportunities arise. For practice, watch any situation, even when children are not involved.

Your early observations in this course can be casual ones. Use the ideas that follow to help you begin polishing this skill:

- **Make the decision to watch.** You are probably not in the habit of watching for the sake of watching. In other words, events go on around you all the time, but you may not make a conscious decision to pay close attention. Try that now. Notice a situation that is going on and decide to focus on all aspects of it.
- **Look for details.** It's easy to come away from an event without remembering exactly what you saw. Did you notice clothing? What expressions did the people display? What gestures were used? What was the setting like? Check yourself later to see what you remember.
- **Listen as well as look.** Participating can make observing more difficult. If possible, step back from what is going on and keep quiet. Then you can focus on listening. Learn to concentrate on what you hear without feeling that you have to get involved.
- **Ignore distractions.** Distractions can be the downfall when you want to be observant. It's like running out to the concession stand during a movie and missing some key scenes. When you return, you've lost track of what is going on. You need a complete and accurate understanding of what you see in order to make your observation useful. Practice watching without letting other people, noises, and events get in the way.

As you become a more disciplined observer, you may find that this skill is useful to you in many ways, not just in learning about children. You might perform better on tests. You might learn to see and appreciate simple things. What other possibilities are there?

Chapter 2

Your Role in Child Care

- List the rewards and drawbacks of working in the child care field.

- Describe qualities people need to be an early childhood professional.

- Identify career possibilities in the child care field.

- Determine what the training and education requirements are for careers in the child care field.

- Explain what the CDA credential is.

- Assess your own suitability for a career in the child care field.

Terms to Learn

- CDA advisor
- child care resource and referral specialist
- child development associate (CDA) credential
- child development consultants
- compassion
- director
- early childhood professionals
- home visitor
- portfolio
- resourcefulness
- spontaneity

think this might be it," Maria thought as she left the job fair. "I think I've figured out what I want to do." A feeling of excitement swelled inside her as the thoughts began to run through her mind. Her feelings of uncertainty were quickly slipping away. Resolve was setting in.

Maria loved children. As a babysitter, she was always in demand. She never *just* spent time with the children in her care. She got involved with them, leading them in games and teaching them. That's why the children always begged their parents to call Maria when they needed a sitter. Working with children was not only fun for Maria, but it was rewarding too. "This makes sense," she thought.

As Maria headed for home, the job possibilities shown in the child care display at the job fair ran through her mind. Would she like to take care of children? What if she obtained more education? She might even become a teacher. The feeling that she had a direction to follow was a good one. She had some thinking to do and questions to explore with her counselor, but the possibilities excited her.

WORKING WITH CHILDREN

*K*nowing what you would like to do when you enter the work world *is* a good feeling. Through the job fair, Maria's thoughts about her future became clearer. The fact that you are reading this text may indicate that you have some interests similar to Maria's. Do you think you might like to work with children? As with any career, there are rewards as well as drawbacks to consider.

The Rewards

Above all else, just being around children can be rewarding. Children make you feel needed and special. They accept your faults and draw upon your strengths. Children are open-hearted and affectionate. Forgiveness comes easily to them. Children usually don't hide what they are thinking or feeling. Their honesty and directness is endearing to most adults—and sometimes amusing as well as embarrassing. After all, the little boy who innocently asked why the teacher's teeth were crooked wasn't aiming to hurt the teacher. He just wanted to know.

As a child care professional, you can make a real difference in the lives of young children. Through your efforts, children can learn skills like independence and cooperation. You can help build a strong foundation from which children develop into healthy, well-adjusted, caring adults. Children face

Young children find delight in their world and share it with the adults who care for them.

writer, actor, and storyteller, all rolled into one. You are a trusted counselor and nurse as you comfort hurt feelings and tend to bruised knees.

Each child care professional chooses the field for his or her own reasons. Most would agree, however, that a love of children is at the top of the list.

The Drawbacks

As with any job, you have to be realistic. Examining the drawbacks helps you figure out what you can accept and what you can't.

Working with young children can be draining, emotionally and physically. Anticipating and meeting so many needs may cause stress. Some of the responsibilities are not glamorous. Wiping noses, changing diapers, and cleaning up spills are simply part of the daily routine.

People who work with children are exposed to many minor childhood illnesses, such as colds, flu, and chicken pox. On the plus side, most caregivers eventually build strong resistance to the diseases that can be caught from children.

Not all child care programs are adequately funded. For this reason, wages tend to be low and fringe benefits minimal. Money for classroom materials may also be limited. Many efforts are being made in the field to improve the wage situation. To attract and keep quality employees, salaries must be reasonable. At the same time, services cannot be so costly that the parents who need them cannot afford the fees.

Working with young children often requires long hours. People who work directly with the children spend about eight hours per day on the job, with two fifteen minute breaks. Staff members may eat lunch

some tough situations today. Some come from families that are troubled by problems connected with alcohol, abuse, divorce, or economic difficulties. These children, perhaps even more than others, need the support of skilled caregivers. People who work with children feel proud when they contribute to a better future by addressing the needs of society's children.

Working in an early childhood program helps you stay young. Have you ever taken a glimpse of the world through a child's eyes? You will take less for granted if you do. To a small child, the discovery of a butterfly, an insect, a flower, or a pebble is a wonder. Any of these could create new interests in you, too, as you rediscover them through a child's eyes and mind.

Working with children is seldom boring. Although there is a consistent daily schedule, creative teachers make sure no two days are just the same. Teaching allows you to use many talents and skills. As you prepare and conduct activities, you are an artist, scientist, musician, mathematician, dancer, with the children. Planning and preparation is usually done in the evenings or on weekends. Time off must be planned carefully, since children must be constantly supervised, and substitutes are not always easy to find.

At times children and their families go through crisis. Illness and death in the family are examples. Resulting behavior problems may pose an extra challenge. Worry about a child may last well beyond the end of the work day. The strain, however, is diminished by the good feelings that come when you are able to help a child get through difficult times.

Many of the responsibilities you have while caring for children may not be especially fun, but they are necessary. As on any job, less pleasant tasks, such as cleaning up spills, are handled best with a positive attitude.

PORTRAIT OF A PROFESSIONAL

When thinking about a career in child care, you need to think about whether the job appeals to you, but there's another question to ask. Do you fit the job? To be a child care professional, you need certain qualities. As you read on, think about how well suited you are.

Appreciation of Children

From what you've read so far, you can see that no one could work well with children without having an appreciation for them. Spending time with children means communicating on a different level than you do with adults. Although you have contact with parents and other child care employees, much of your time as an employee in the child care field is spent with children. You have to want that.

Working with children every day requires real enjoyment of being with them. You will learn from them as they learn from you.

THE MULTICULTURAL CLASSROOM

Every early childhood program is a multicultural one. That means the children who enroll are from differing family origins. They represent many cultures and ethnic groups. To get along in society, children must first get along with each other. This is where you come in. As a child care professional, your mission in promoting multiculturalism has two components.

First, you must create a classroom that has a multicultural perspective. The objects children see and the activities they participate in can often have a multicultural base—if you plan that way.

Throughout this text, you will find many suggestions for promoting understanding among all people. You will also learn ways to help children be proud of their heritage.

Second, you must set an example for the children. Children mimic the attitudes and actions of adults. When you are tolerant and open-minded about people of all types, you help children adopt these attitudes. When you accept a child, the other children are more likely to be accepting also. There is room for nothing less as you prepare children for the future.

Appreciating children means participating in activities *with* them, not just watching. Physical contact, such as holding hands and having a child sit on your lap during a story, is part of the job in an early childhood program. Warm relationships are built with children as you listen to their ideas and feelings.

Energy

Children have a high energy level. That means that early childhood professionals need good physical and emotional stamina in order to keep up with them. Caregivers have to stay one step ahead of children, or a classroom quickly gets out of control.

Sense of Humor

A sense of humor is useful in many situations. With children around, humor is common. Their antics and laughter match their level of development. Children love it when you are ready and willing to laugh and be a bit zany with them. You need a serious side that takes care of business and gives steady support, but children also appreciate a more casual side that lets loose and has fun when the occasion is right.

A child care professional is careful, of course, to laugh *with* children, but never *at* them. Children often do and say things that are funny from an adult point of view, but the children don't understand why. Laughter at times like this can hurt a child.

Your sense of humor comes in most handy with children when the unexpected happens. When things don't turn out as you planned or mistakes are made, a willingness to laugh and enjoy the turn of events makes you and the children feel at ease.

Patience

What could be more important to someone who works with children than patience? Children make mistakes. They are often slow at doing things because they haven't perfected their skills yet. Acceptable behavior may not have been mastered. They are

Most children love to giggle, laugh, and have fun. The better able you are to understand children's sense of humor and to join in once in a while, the better you will be at working with them.

still learning self-control, and following rules requires new understanding and effort. You have to be prepared to repeat directions frequently and give many reminders. You will also be continually asked to give explanations. As any parent will tell you, "why?" is a young child's favorite question.

Compassion

Compassion works together with patience. A person with **compassion** *recognizes when others are having problems and wants to be of help.* Children need adults who try to understand and accommodate them. What may seem like a trivial fear or worry to an adult may be critical to a child. Compassionate adults calmly and gently help children with problems that arise.

Many problems are routine ones. A child who hits may simply need help with learning to handle anger more appropriately. A shy child can be shown how to ask to join in a game. Other children need more compas-

sion. As you work with children, you might meet a child who has a serious disease, developmental delays, or a traumatic family life. Special compassion and skills are needed in such situations.

Flexibility

Because children are so different and unpredictable, they can surprise you. Children have spontaneity. **Spontaneity** (SPAHN-tuh-NAY-uh-tee) is *acting impulsively, or without taking time to use thinking and reasoning skills.* Since you never know what will happen next with children, you need to be flexible. A person who can't stand disruptions in routine would have a hard time working with children.

Creativity

People who think creatively are needed in child care. The activities you plan and the way you carry them out will be much more interesting and effective if you are creative. Children don't want to do the same things in the same way over and over again. They enjoy creative experiences, and they learn from them.

Resourcefulness

Resourcefulness is *an ability to find the ways and means to do something.* Just

Understanding the intensity of a child's feelings is a key to compassion. Brian shed these tears when his favorite leaf was torn. As a caregiver, how would you have reacted?

Children learn more and enjoy life in the child care setting more when their days include interesting activities. It takes a creative person to come up with new ideas that bring pleasure as well as opportunities to develop skills.

of these problems? The resourceful person finds opportunities where others give in to obstacles. Resourcefulness enables people to make things happen and get things done.

Sociability

Working in a child care program is a very social job. The schedule allows you little time to be by yourself. In addition to the constant interaction with children, you also work with parents and coworkers. A person who relates well to others, using good communication skills, does better than one who prefers to be alone.

think about what you might need if you were working with children. A low budget could mean that you need supplies and equipment that you can't afford. A child with special problems might need professional help. If you work with disadvantaged children, you might see a need for warm winter coats and mittens. If you were planning a special event, you might need volunteers. How would you solve all

A successful child care program depends on every employee working well with children, parents, and other staff members.

Building Professional Skills

Dedication

WHAT IS DEDICATION?

Devotion, loyalty, and self-sacrifice are words that are often linked to the word dedication. When you are dedicated to a job, you have strong feelings about the value of the job and your desire to do it well. A dedicated person tries not to settle for second best and often contributes personal time, energy, and resources in order to do a job right.

Dedication in Action

Karl took a long look around the room. The walls were covered with rows of pages from coloring books. "Is this *all* the children have been doing?" he wondered. The children in the center had certainly done plenty of coloring. He saw no evidence of other art projects, nothing that would have called for more creativity.

It was Karl's first day on the job. "Things are going to change," he said to himself. Karl's predecessor was gone, and Karl was eager to get to work. "They seem bored," he noticed as he watched the children. "Maybe that's why there is so much bickering. With some

work, we can turn that around too."

In the evening Karl pored over some activity books. He found ideas that would be good for the week and put aside others to include in his plans for the future. After gathering some materials together, Karl headed for the store to buy a few additional items. As he drove, his thoughts were on the center and how he might make improvements. He remembered reading about a particular early childhood course in the university catalog. "I'll check into that on the weekend," he thought. "I need all the help I can get."

Your Analysis

1. List examples of Karl's dedication.

2. Compare Karl's approach to his job with what his predecessor's seemed to be.

3. How will the children be affected by Karl's dedication?

4. How would you have to feel about a job in order to be dedicated to it?

Commitment

Every child care professional should feel a sense of commitment. This means that you are dedicated to doing your best for the children in your care. You *don't* settle for doing the job halfway. You *do* take classes, read related journals, attend conferences, and share ideas with coworkers. You *do* research, plan, and prepare well. Most of all, you care about the children and are dedicated to having a positive effect on their lives.

CAREER OPPORTUNITIES

*I*f you and child care are a good match, why not explore the opportunities available in the field? There may be more of these than you realize.

As a group, *people who work in early childhood programs* are called **early childhood professionals.** Children usually view anyone who spends time with them in the center as a teacher. Actually, all the people who make up the child care team may have any of several titles. They may be called teachers, caregivers, child care workers, teacher's assistants, and teacher's aides. Different levels of training, as defined by each program, are generally required for specific titles. The people who work with children must be able to communicate effectively and work well together. Although there are many other jobs related to the child care field, the focus in this text is on working directly with the children in a preschool setting. You will see the term "teacher" used often throughout the text in that connection.

While the majority of the people in the child care field work directly with the children, some have other positions. A key person in most child care settings is the director. The **director** of a program *may work with children but has the primary*

Those who choose the child care field as a career can expect to spend considerable time working directly with children. To a preschooler, anyone who works with them is likely to be thought of as a "teacher."

Many people combine an interest in children with other skills in choosing a career. A pediatrician, for example, must be an expert in both child development and medicine. A lawyer might specialize in cases related to children.

Where the Jobs Are

Where might you find a job in the child care field? Here are some ideas:

Battered women's shelters

Child care centers

Child care centers on Native American reservations

Child care law centers

Child care resource and referral agencies

Children's activity coordinator for cruise ship

Crisis nurseries

Departments of human services

Early childhood professional organizations

Elementary schools

Employer-sponsored child care programs

Family education agencies

Head Start

High school lab schools

Homeless shelters

Hospital pediatric units (child life therapy)

Hospitals with sick bay child care services

Mental health agencies

Migrant worker programs

Montessori preschool programs

Nurse/nurse practitioner

Nursery schools

Parks and recreation programs

Phone-a-Friend (hotline for children alone before and after school)

Prisons with in-house child visitation

Programs sponsored by religious organizations

PTA

Salvation Army

State boards of education

United Way

University lab schools

U. S. military bases

Visiting Nurses Association

YWCA, YMCA

---

responsibility of management. The director manages daily operations and guides the staff. Large programs may have a **home visitor**, *a parent educator who goes into a child's home to teach the parent how to guide the children's learning and to answer parents' questions.* A **child care resource and referral specialist** *works mainly on the telephone as a counselor with parents.* Referral specialists assist parents in choosing child care arrangements. Companies that create and market toys, clothing, and equipment for young children employ **child development consultants.** These individuals *give child development advice to people who create children's products.*

Child care is a fast-growing field. There is a need for lawyers who specialize in child care law and architects who specialize in designing child care center buildings. Publishing companies employ people with child development background to edit and review child care textbooks.

These are not the only opportunities for you in child care. A look at the lists above and on page 48 will give you a sampling of the kinds of places that employ people in child care and some ideas about positions.

Making Your Schoolwork Count

Suppose you were an employer interviewing people for a job. The first candidate, Terry, interviews well. Terry describes several work experiences, giving you details about projects developed on previous jobs. Chris also interviews favorably, having projects to talk about too. During your conversation, Chris opens a binder, revealing neatly displayed photographs and actual examples of completed work. You notice how well organized and neat the binder is. You are impressed by the projects shown, observing that they are thorough and creative. It's time to decide who you will hire. Based on what you know, what is your decision?

Employers make decisions like this regularly. When they don't know applicants personally, they look for every clue that will help them choose the right person. When interviewing for the job, Chris stood out because of something extra—a portfolio.

A **portfolio** is *a collection of actual examples of a person's work, put together to show his or her capabilities. The examples are assembled in a binder, folder, or some other type of container that allows for simple, attractive presentation.* You can present a portfolio to a potential employer, as Chris did, or use it to help gain entry into an education or training program.

What goes into a portfolio is not the same for everyone. A journalist could clip his or her best articles and mount them in a binder. An artist might take photographs of certain works to place in an album. As a potential employee in the child care field, you can use the work you do in this course to create a portfolio. At the end of the chapters in this text you will find suggestions for projects that are suitable. You may find other activity ideas there that would also make good portfolio entries. Follow the instructions of your teacher, and include ideas of your own if you like.

Building a portfolio is an ongoing process of evaluation and refinement. To build your portfolio, save your work during the course. As the work you do is evaluated by you and your instructor, make improvements. Sometimes even good work can be better. By continually examining your efforts, you can eliminate some items and include others in order to shape your portfolio.

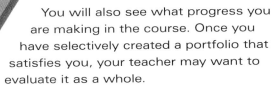

You will also see what progress you are making in the course. Once you have selectively created a portfolio that satisfies you, your teacher may want to evaluate it as a whole.

Start now to develop a portfolio of your best work in the child care field. If you do, you will make your schoolwork count when you move into the work world.

What Could You Include?

Awards
Achievements
Examples of community service
Certificates
Photos of projects
Actual projects
Lesson plans
Examples of activities
Bulletin boards
Written personal analyses
Self-evaluations
Summary descriptions of projects
Videos
Tapes
Evaluations by teachers
Reports
List of books read
Diagrams
Charts
Graphs
Designs
Computer printouts

What Could You Be?

Not everyone who has a job associated with children is a teacher. Have you ever thought about any of these alternatives?

Adoption counselor

Amusement park guide

Architect specializing in child care settings

Art, music, or dance instructor

Athletic coach or assistant

Author of children's literature

Child care law attorney

Child custody mediator

Child development specialist for toy corporations

Children's librarian

Children's museum staff member

Children's photographer

Children's television programmer

Family life educator

Family therapist

Illustrator of children's literature

Newspaper or magazine columnist writing about children

Owner of children's clothing store

Pediatric dentist

Pediatrician

Textbook author

Writer for children's magazines

EDUCATION, TRAINING, AND EXPERIENCE

*I*f you decide to work in the child care field, how will you prepare for the job? The answer depends on which job you seek and where you live. In the United States, there is no uniform standard required for education, training, and experience. Each state establishes its own requirements. As you would guess, different job titles have different requirements. To find out about the requirements for your state, contact the local agency that licenses or regulates child care centers. (Programs in the public schools usually have higher requirements.

How Much Education Is Needed?

HIGH SCHOOL DIPLOMA	TWO-FOUR YEARS OF COLLEGE*
Teacher's aide	Nanny
Teacher's assistant	Teacher in child care center
Bus driver	Home visitor
Cook	Center director
Custodian	Assistant director
Receptionist	Child care resource and
Secretary	referral specialist
Bookkeeper	
BACHELOR'S DEGREE* **(Four Years of College)**	**MASTER'S DEGREE*** **(Four Years of College Plus Graduate School)**
Parent educator	University or college instructor
Educational coordinator	Author of professional journal articles
Dietitian	Legislative lobbyist
Nutritionist	Social worker
Family and consumer sciences instructor	School psychologist
University lab school instructor	Child care consultant
Parent involvement coordinator	Music therapist
District manager of child care center chain	Researcher
Play therapist in pediatric hospital program	Attorney in child care law firm
Representative for child and adult care food program	Architect with firm specializing in child care settings
Licensing specialist	Director of play therapy in hospital
Director of child care resource and referral agency	

* Specializing in Early Childhood and/or Child Development

The CDA Credential

*I*n some professions, people can earn credentials that show they are qualified for the work they do. The child care field has a credential that may be of interest to you. It was developed in the 1970s when people became concerned about the quality of child care programs. They wanted to make sure that people who care for children have the education and training they need to make them competent caregivers.

The **child development associate (CDA) credential** is *awarded to an applicant after the person demonstrates competency skills in specific areas of child care*. These six areas are listed and described in the Appendix at the back of your text. Both on-the-job experience and course work are required as part of this national credentialing process. A CDA advisor *counsels candidates and provides specific training for the credential.*

Many states now require that certain employees have a CDA credential in order for a program to be licensed. You may not need the credential if you plan to obtain a four-year college degree, but you should check to see if it would be useful in connection with whatever goals you set for yourself.

You can apply for a CDA credential once you become eighteen. You must also have a high school diploma or the equivalent. Information about the CDA credential can be obtained from the Council for Early Childhood Professional Recognition, 2460 16th Street, N.W., Washington, DC 20009-3575, Phone: 1-800-424-4310.

These requirements can be obtained from your State Board of Education.)

Few, if any, jobs in child care accept less than a high school degree. For specialized positions, advanced education (beyond high school) is required. For teachers, at least two years of college education, specializing in child development, is usually necessary. Two to four years of college may be required of directors. Programs that employ an educational or program director may require a master's degree for the position. The chart on page 49 gives you an idea about the education needed in some states for certain positions in early childhood.

As you plan for your future, remember that better jobs and better pay are definitely linked to education. In addition, you can work more effectively with children when you have the knowledge that education provides. Setting educational goals is worthwhile. Having something to aim for is the first step to achievement and the rewards it brings.

While formal education and training in high school and college are very valuable, firsthand experience with young children is also an excellent way to learn how to teach and care for young children. By serving as a volunteer or teacher's aide, your training can begin today.

Tip FROM THE Pros

*A*re you interested in volunteering to work with young children? Check to see if there is a social service hotline in your area. They can give you ideas about who needs volunteers.

Education and training are keys to success in a child care career. They can help you work more effectively and open doors to opportunities.

Answering these questions will help you decide on a direction. What follows then is action. Talking to people who are knowledgeable about the child care field can provide you with information and ideas. Making plans for any education and training that you need will set you on the right path for your goal. Learning more about children should always be your aim. The rest of this text is a good place to start as you explore your role in child care.

It's your future. Isn't it worth taking the time to do the research needed to make the right career choice?

GETTING READY

*T*he child care field awaits you if you are interested. As the need to serve children and their families grows, the opportunities also grow. The course you are now taking can be a foundation for you, leading toward further education or training and eventually a career.

In her book, *Careers with Young Children—Making Your Decision*, published by the NAEYC (National Association for the Education of Young Children), Judith Seaver advises those who are serious about a child care career to ask themselves:

- Why do I want to work with or for young children?
- What are my skills and abilities?
- What degree of involvement with children is best for me?

Chapter 2 Review

Chapter Summary

- Working with young children has rewards as well as drawbacks.
- Successful child care professionals require special personal characteristics.
- Working with children means more than just supervising them. You have to value the contact and communication that takes place in warm relationships with children.
- Child care professionals should be committed to having a positive effect on children in their care.
- People who work in early childhood programs are called early childhood professionals.
- Opportunities for employment in the child care field may involve direct or indirect contact with children.
- Positions in the child care field require varying degrees of education and training.

Reviewing the Facts

1. List four rewards and four drawbacks of working with young children.
2. List six personal characteristics of successful child care professionals.
3. Why is a sense of humor important when working with young children?
4. Define spontaneity. How does being flexible help when working with young children?
5. What is resourcefulness? Describe a resourceful person.
6. Describe at least four positions in the child care field that *do not* involve direct contact with children.
7. What are the training and education requirements for each of the following: (a) teachers; (b) directors; (c) educational or program director?
8. How is a CDA credential earned?
9. What are three questions you should ask yourself when deciding on a child care career?

Thinking Critically

1. Could some aspect of a job be negative to one person and positive to another? Explain.
2. Of all the qualities a person needs for working with children, as listed in the chapter, which one do you think is most important? Why?
3. Suppose the child care field employed many people who did not really enjoy children. What might the impact be on families and society?
4. What do you think would be most enjoyable about working with children?

Activities and Applications

1. **Newspaper Research.** Read the classified section of your newspaper. What opportunities in the field of early childhood are listed? What requirements for education and training are identified?
2. **Career Analysis.** Make two columns on a sheet of paper, labeling them "Reasons Why the Career Is Right for Me" and "Reasons Why the Career Is Wrong for Me." Then under each column list as many reasons as you can think of why a career in the child care field would work for you and why it wouldn't. What do you conclude?

3. **Preparing Questions.**
Make a list of questions
you would like to have
answered about working
in the child care field.
Then as you complete this
course, collect the
answers you are looking
for and keep a written
record of them.

Your Professional Portfolio

Choose three qualities
you have that would
help you work effec-
tively with children.
How could you present
these? You might sim-
ply write an explanation
of each one. You could
make a poster or take
snapshots that illus-
trate how you display
these qualities. You
might even ask respon-
sible people who know
you well to write
descriptions of how
they see the qualities in
you. When your project
is finished to your satisfaction, save it for pos-
sible inclusion in your
finalized portfolio.

Observing and Analyzing

Observing Careers

Even if you have narrowed down your career choice to knowing you want to work with children, you may still have some decision making to do. This chapter has shown you that there are many specific job possibilities in the child care field. How will you decide which direction is the right one for you?

This is where observation skills can come in handy. From week to week, you will find yourself in many circumstances where people are working with, or for, children. These are perfect opportunities for you to observe what the jobs are like. You can explore your own interests by noticing the actions of others. Pay attention to what you see. Ask yourself the questions below in order to discover whether or not the career is one you might enjoy:

- What is the work setting like? Is it appealing to you?
- What responsibilities do you see employees performing? Are they ones you would enjoy?
- What problems or difficulties do you see occurring? Would you mind encountering them? Given the right skills, could you handle them?
- How would you describe employee attitudes toward the job? Analyze both positive and negative situations to determine what is causing them. What would your reaction be under the same circumstances?

Choosing the right career requires more exploration than just observation. On the other hand, that's a good place to start. When you make it a point to take notice, you may discover many possibilities that are worth a second look.

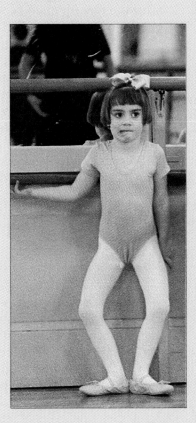

Meet Ella Simpson, a child care referral specialist at a child care resource agency. Her primary job is advising parents on how to find and select quality child care. Based on information gathered from parents, she refers them to area child care options that would best meet the family's needs. In this interview, Ella describes the importance of her job and why she finds it rewarding.

Why did you choose this career?

"I find great satisfaction in helping parents make sure their children are cared for properly. The referrals I make are based on individual families' needs, such as the age of the children, how much money parents can afford to pay for child care, and the need for public transportation. I also respond to special requests and situations. For instance, some parents prefer child care in a person's home; others prefer center-based care. Parents may have a disabled child who needs child care providers with specialized training. All of this information is taken into account before I provide referrals."

What education and skills do you need?

"Most referral agencies require specialists to have at least a two-year associate's degree in a field related to children. Many require a four-year bachelor's degree in social work, child development, or early childhood education. In my position understanding how children grow and develop is important. I also need to be aware of the child care programs that are available. Parents trust me to match their child to the appropriate service.

"Communication skills are necessary in my job. I need to be an alert listener. The ability to communicate clearly with people from all different backgrounds is a real asset. I find the ability to speak both English and Spanish very helpful.

"I've always been a 'people person,' so talking with parents is a pleasure. I understand the hard choices they face when making child care arrangements. Some parents call our agency when they are unhappy with their child care provider. I'm sympathetic to their concerns, which helps them relax and calmly plan ways to solve their problem.

"Most referral agencies use computers to organize and maintain information about local child care programs. My computer skills are very valuable."

What is a typical day on the job like?

"I work mornings and afternoons three times a week. Two days a week I work afternoons and evenings until 8:30 p.m. This is so parents who work daytime hours can use our services.

"Most days begin with listening to our answering machine. Then I return calls to parents who left requests for services. Between callbacks I accept new phone calls, which can last up to half an hour. While doing this, I take detailed notes on the type of care parents want. During our conversation, I give tips on what to look for in quality care, stressing that the child care choice is their personal decision. After the conversation, I enter the information into the computer. The computer matches available options with the family's specific needs. Then I mail out a list of child care options, including brochures and educational literature on the importance of quality child care.

"I spend about four hours a day on the telephone. The other hours I may spend organizing our lending library of toys and books, developing new brochures for parents, or speaking to civic groups on opening new child care programs. Like other professionals, I attend staff meetings, complete paperwork, and participate in child care conferences."

What is most challenging about your job?

"The hardest part is not having enough child care enrollment slots for all the children who need care. Finding care for infants and school-age children is especially challenging. With more parents working outside the home, the demand for child care services is growing. Telling parents that there are no available child care spaces for their child is very hard."

What do you like best about your work?

"It's gratifying when a parent calls to say I helped find just what they needed for their child. Quality child care is a big worry for families; it's good to ease their anxiety."

SHARE YOUR THOUGHTS

1. If you were a referral specialist, how would you describe quality child care to parents?
2. What questions would you ask parents to determine the type of child care they need or prefer?
3. Why is it important for a referral specialist to have good communication skills?
4. What part of being a referral specialist sounds most interesting to you? What part would you like the least?

Unit 2

CHILD GROWTH AND DEVELOPMENT

Reflections

"Even though classes and textbooks teach lessons about children, sometimes the best ones are learned through real-life experiences. That happened to me one morning during my first week on the job. Clarissa, who looked to be about age five, was not happy. I watched as she obstinately refused to take off her coat, repeatedly saying 'no' to the teacher. A picture started forming in my mind about Clarissa, and it wasn't a complimentary one. I even made a comment to another teacher about Clarissa's behavior. 'Do you know how old Clarissa is?' the teacher asked me. As I shook my head, she replied, 'She's almost three.' I know my eyes widened and my mouth dropped open. Clarissa's behavior didn't match her appearance at all, but it did match her age. I vowed then and there that I would never again be so quick to judge. That's one decision that has helped me greatly in my work with children."

—Ming

Chapter 3

Basic Principles of Development

CHAPTER OBJECTIVES

- Explain why understanding child development is important.

- Identify child development theorists.

- Identify and briefly explain the areas of development.

- Describe some principles of development.

- Analyze the impact of heredity and environment.

- Explain how self-esteem affects development.

- Recognize and be able to make objective observations.

Terms to Learn

- cephalocaudal
- child development
- cognitive development
- emotions
- maturation
- motor skills
- proximodistal
- self-concept
- self-esteem
- sequence
- values

Kendra Taylor glanced at the faces of the children in her story group. All the children were close in age. Their attention was focused on Kendra. She was holding a surprise box, from which she was about to pull a special item that would introduce the story she planned to read. The children were eager to discover what would emerge from the box—all except one child.

Even though he was the same age as the rest, Jackson just didn't react as the others did. "Why isn't he interested in the story?" Kendra wondered. Again, she had lead him to the story group, while the rest of the children quickly moved there on their own. Jackson often seemed only remotely interested in the stories Kendra read. What was humorous to the other children had little effect on him. Something just didn't seem right. Of course, each child had his or her own personality, habits, and characteristics, but the picture of Jackson that was forming in Kendra's mind was causing her concern. It was time to talk to the rest of the staff. They would compare observations and explore whether or not Jackson needed some special help. Kendra knew that taking action now could mean a great deal to Jackson in the future.

UNDERSTANDING DEVELOPMENT

Kendra Taylor is a teacher in a child care program. One of the things that makes her especially effective in her job is her understanding of children. If you were in Kendra's position, how would you decide whether Jackson has a problem that needs diagnosis and treatment? Coming to such conclusions is not easy, but Kendra uses her knowledge and understanding of child development to help her.

Child development is *the pattern of change that occurs as children grow from birth to adolescence.* The study of child development includes descriptions of how, when, why, and in what order changes occur. When you understand what a child's capabilities should typically be at different age levels, you know what to expect from the child. You notice when a child is developmentally ahead and needs extra challenges. You also notice when something is not right.

For example, someone who isn't aware of the age at which children usually put complete sentences together may not notice that a child is having language problems. Undiagnosed, the problem gets worse. Other problems arise, and the child suffers further developmental difficulties. An alert observer, on the other hand, sees what is happening and seeks help that enables the child to improve his or her language skills and move forward developmentally.

The people who work in child care today have an especially large responsibility for monitoring the development of children. With so many parents employed, more children than ever before are spending time in group care settings. A caregiver may spend more waking hours with a child than the parents do. For this reason, child care professionals must keep a sharp eye on how children are progressing. Knowledge helps provide the confidence they need to handle children correctly.

THE CONTRIBUTION OF THEORISTS

Much of what is known about children and their development is the result of years of study by many researchers. Hundreds of years ago children were

thought to be miniature adults. Few realized their special needs and characteristics. As interest in children and a desire to make their lives better grew, so did the need for information about them. To learn more, researchers developed and tested theories, a standard method of scientific research. They observed children and reached conclusions. Attitudes toward children have been shaped by what people discovered. The way society handles children has been strongly influenced by those who study child development.

Many researchers, or theorists, have contributed to the body of knowledge about children that exists today. As might be expected, the impact of some research has been greater than that of others. The conclusions reached have not always been accepted by everyone. Over time some theories have been replaced by newer ideas. The result over the years, however, has been an increased understanding and appreciation of children.

Certain theorists stand out when it comes to the study of children. Take a look at the chart on pages 62-63. There you will find information on several past and present theorists. You might even recognize some of the names. As you read further in this text, you will learn more about the work of some of these individuals. Keep in mind that these people are just part of the picture. Researchers at universities and elsewhere are continually exploring topics that relate to children. Through the efforts of all, people learn more and more about enriching the lives of children and the families that support them.

In 1921 Swiss researcher Jean Piaget began to study how children learn. His 50-year effort in this area has made a significant contribution to what is understood about intellectual development.

AREAS OF DEVELOPMENT

*I*n order to study children effectively, researchers look at specific topics. You, too, will be able to understand child development better if you look at the parts that make up the whole. Child development is often broken down into these areas of development: physical, intellectual, emotional, social, and moral. In this unit of the text, you will see how children change at different ages in each of these areas.

Physical Development

Physical development includes the growth of the body as well as its abilities. Growth in height and weight is an obvious aspect of physical development. Growth is most dramatic during infancy and adolescence. As children develop physically, they gain new abilities. *Those abilities that depend on the use and control of muscles* are called **motor skills.**

Coordination and balance accompany physical development. Learning them poses many challenges for children. Think what it would be like if you tried to walk a tightrope for the first time. Would you be shaky and

In what ways can reading to children help their intellectual development?

insecure? Would you fall? Children experience these sensations over and over again as they try out new physical skills and work toward mastering them.

Intellectual Development

Intellectual development, which is often called **cognitive development,** *occurs as children learn to think, understand, reason, and use language.* Although the learning process is still not fully understood, research has provided much knowledge about what takes place. Infants enter the world

Physical skills develop with age and practice. Why is this toy a good choice for improving motor skills?

Child Development Theorists

Jean Piaget (1896-1980) Swiss psychologist, biologist, and educator	Piaget believed that human cognitive development is a result of adaptation to the physical environment. This adaptation results in organized patterns of behavior and perception. Through observation of children, Piaget identified how the development of a child's thought processes and intellect proceeds through a series of stages.
Lawrence Kohlberg (1927-1987) Cognitive development theorist	Kohlberg's theory describes stages in the development of moral reasoning. Each level of development reflects the relationship between the self and society's rules and expectations. The lowest level relates to obedience and avoidance of punishment, and the highest level relates to conscience and ethical principles.
Erik Erikson (1902-1994) Psychoanalytical theorist	Erikson studied the development of personality by dividing life into stages of psychological crisis. Erikson believed that personality characteristics are developed according to how each individual adapts at each stage.
Alfred Binet (1857-1911) Psychologist; devised first intelligence test	Binet believed that intelligence increases with age, and is reflected in how children make judgments, understand the meanings of words, and solve problems. Binet's test showed the relationship between chronological age and mental age. A revised version of this test is called the Stanford-Binet Intelligence Scale, an IQ test.
Urie Bronfenbrenner (1917—) Developmental psychologist and professor at Cornell University	Bronfenbrenner believes that behavior and development should be observed in natural settings over long periods of time. Bronfenbrenner defines the ecology of human development as a reciprocal relationship between the self and a complex ecological environment.
Benjamin Bloom (1913—) Psychologist	According to Bloom, 50 percent of adult intelligence is achieved by age four, making early childhood education the most important time in a child's life. Bloom's Taxonomy ranks thought processes from the least to the most difficult cognitive levels and gives examples of tasks at each level.
Maria Montessori (1870-1952) Italian physician and educator	Montessori believed that children actively construct their own knowledge by using their senses. The Montessori method of teaching stresses that children learn at their own pace and level of development. Montessori preschools use specially designed materials that encourage individual learning through stimulation of the five senses.

Lev Vygotsky (1896-1934) Psychologist, socio-cultural theorist and researcher	Vygotsky studied intellectual development and children's social interactions with peers and adults. He believed that the combination of biological development and cultural experience influenced the ability of children to think and learn. His socio-cultural theory indicates that children's language and problem solving abilities are closely tied to social contacts. Only through social contact can children develop intellectually. Vygotsky believed that dramatic play was one of the best ways to promote symbolic thought and social competency in children.
Rudolf Dreikurs (1897-1972) Family educator and child psychologist	Dreikurs maintained that an attempt to understand why a child misbehaves is important when providing guidance. Parents and caregivers must learn to observe a child objectively rather than seeing their own difficulties. Dreikurs developed techniques that allow children to experience the actual consequences of misbehavior.
Haim Ginott (1922-1973) Psychologist	Ginott believed that children should be allowed to express their feelings, so they can recognize and face their emotions. In his book *Between Parent and Child*, Ginott gives specific suggestions on how to help children become aware of their feelings and to handle emotional outbursts.
B. F. Skinner (1904-1990) Psychologist and behavioral theorist	Skinner's research of operant conditioning used a number of experiments to illustrate how learning is influenced through positive and negative reinforcement. Skinner believed that in order to achieve desired behavior from children, parents should reward or punish existing behavior.
Sigmund Freud (1856-1939) Psychoanalytical theorist and founder of psychiatry	Freud believed that personality develops through a predictable pattern of psychosexual stages. As children move through each of these stages, the source of pleasure moves to different areas of the body. Freud believed that emotional or psychological problems in adulthood are related to a child's satisfaction or dissatisfaction with how basic needs are met in each stage.
Anna Freud (1895-1982) Daughter of Sigmund Freud and analyst for Erik Erikson	Freud's work with mentally disabled children was influenced by the psychoanalytic theorists. She believed that all children go through normal stages of psychological development, and psychoanalysts must fully understand these stages through direct observation of children. In London in 1938, Freud established the Hampstead Child Therapy Course and Clinic, which treats children with mental disabilities and trains workers in childhood therapy.

ready and eager to learn, relying mostly on their senses—sight, hearing, taste, smell, and touch. The early years bring rapid changes in a child's knowledge and thinking abilities. Throughout childhood, complex intellectual processes are gradually developed, including the ability to analyze, evaluate, and solve problems.

Emotional Development

As children develop emotionally, they acquire *feelings about themselves, others, and the world.* These feelings are called **emotions.** Some emotions are associated with positive (good) feelings and others with negative (bad) feelings. Happiness and contentment, for example, are positive, and anger, fear, and frustration are negative. Both positive and negative emotions are experienced by everyone at one time or another.

When emotional development is at its best, children experience more positive emotions than negative ones. Positive emotions indicate that children feel good about themselves and what is going on in their lives. Children who have plenty of positive feelings are likely to be emotionally well adjusted.

Even though part of living means having negative emotions, children learn to understand and manage them as they develop. They discover that negative emotions are acceptable, and sometimes expected, under certain circumstances. For example, sorrow over a loss and anger over mistreatment are justifiable. What children need to learn is how to handle such emotions appropriately and recover from them.

Good emotional development depends heavily on the treatment a child receives. For example, children learn to give affection when they receive it. They learn to think favorably of themselves when people around them are supportive and loving. They learn to treat others well when they are treated well. Emotional development is very complex. As you learn more about it, you will see how important the role of a caregiver is in this area.

Very young children express their emotions—both positive and negative—very openly. Older children have better emotional control.

Social Development

As children discover how to relate to other people, social development takes place. They learn the skills they need to get along with people and to fit into society. Many interpersonal skills are part of social training. Children learn to play together, share, and trade. They discover how to settle fights with words, rather than hitting, kicking, pushing, or biting.

When children develop socially, they begin to understand that society has rules to live by. Getting along well means identifying and obeying the rules. Children also learn to care about the feelings and thoughts of oth-

| Group play activities give children a chance to develop and practice social skills.

ers as they try to see issues from different points of view.

Proper social development serves children well. With it, they are liked and accepted by many people. Without it, they may feel isolated and different.

Moral Development

Moral development is closely linked to social development. Moral development comes as children begin to understand and act according to what is right and wrong. They develop *beliefs and attitudes about what is important.* These are called **values.** Families teach many values, and religion and society teach them too. In any case, what children learn has social impact

because it affects how they interact with other people.

In most child care settings, moral guidance is based on such widely held values as respect, sharing, and friendship. Families and religions don't necessarily agree on all moral issues and values. Learning basic societal values, however, is an important part of moral development in early childhood. With a sensitive approach, the child care professional can handle this aspect of development effectively.

| Part of moral development is learning values. Certain basic values can be promoted in the child care setting. A child who learns to care and become involved when someone else is hurting is adopting the values of respect and compassion for others.

Knowledge

WHAT IS KNOWLEDGE?

You must have knowledge in any field in order to succeed. In child care you cannot recognize progress, encourage development, and identify problems unless you know how and when development takes place. Through study and experience, people gain the knowledge they need. Knowledge is a necessary resource for making decisions and taking action.

Knowledge in Action

"Never overlook the simple solutions." This statement from her nursing school days always seemed to pop back into Minda Rahami's mind. As a nurse, she divided her time among several schools in the community. As she completed some paperwork on nine-year-old Bernadette, that often remembered thought momentarily came to her again.

Bernadette's father Luke had come in personally to see her a few weeks ago. He was very concerned about the changes he was seeing in Bernadette. "She used to be a good student," Luke had explained to Ms. Rahami, "but now it takes her all night to finish a simple homework assignment, and she complains that her teacher doesn't

give them enough time to finish their work. Bernadette says the other children tease her about being a 'slowpoke.' She's been complaining about headaches, and now she doesn't feel good enough to go to school on some days. I don't know what the problem is, but I am worried. She used to love school, and now she dreads it."

"Let me have a talk with her," Ms. Rahami suggested to Luke, "and then I'll get back to you. We may want her to have a physical exam."

Later, as Ms. Rahami talked with Bernadette and watched her carefully, she had a thought. "Bernadette, we're going to give you a little eye test. I'm going to have you look at some shapes on the wall, and you can tell me what you see."

Several weeks later, with a new pair of glasses, Bernadette was again enjoying school. Her headaches and unhappiness had disappeared. Luke was happy, too, and grateful that he had found someone capable to turn to for help.

Your Analysis

1. Why does Ms. Rahami need to be knowledgeable in her work with children?

2. What knowledge did Ms. Rahami use to help solve Bernadette's problem?

3. Explain how this situation illustrates the concept that growth in one area affects the development of other areas. Give specific examples.

DEVELOPMENTAL PRINCIPLES

*T*o understand development, you need to be aware of certain principles. As you observe children, you will see examples of all the principles described here.

Development Is Interrelated

You can study the different areas of development separately, but you can't isolate them in real life. Inevitably, one area has impact on another.

Suppose you were helping a young child learn self-feeding skills. This is a physical skill that requires the use of small muscles in the hand. How successful would the child be without intellectual skills too? With each attempt at self-feeding, the child uses trial and error to learn a little more. Gradually, thinking abilities combine with physical skills to help the child master the goal of self-feeding.

As you think about other specific examples, you will see how all areas of development fit together. Because the different areas stimulate and reinforce each other, problems in one area can affect others. Likewise, promoting development in any area has a positive effect on total development.

Development Is Similar for All

Development follows a similar pattern for everyone. Whatever a child's background, development occurs in approximately the same way for all. Even children from different parts of the world go through the same stages. For example, all children sit before standing, and stand before walk-

Skills in Action

Physical Development. Jason and Joe utilized physical skills to place each block precisely.

Intellectual Development. The building process—from planning to choosing appropriate blocks—depended upon intellectual skills. How are they using the structure?

Social Development. The boys worked together to plan, make, and use the building. They may also have learned their building skills by playing with other children.

Emotional Development. Persistence is needed to finish a project, especially if problems arise.

Although you will learn what an "average" child of a certain age can do, in reality each child develops at his or her own rate. These children are all the same age. What variations in physical growth can you identify?

ing. Unless there are problems, such as a physical or mental disability, everyone eventually develops similar skills and behaviors. *The gradual process of development as each stage unfolds* is called **maturation.**

Rates of Development Are Individual

The interesting thing about development—and the challenging part for caregivers—is that it doesn't occur at exactly the same rate for every child. All children experience growth and develop new abilities at a pace that is unique to each individual.

If rates of development are different, then how can a caregiver tell when a child should be learning a new skill or reaching a new growth level? Researchers have found that patterns of development are predictable, especially during early childhood. They report on the abilities of the "average" child, but what does "average" mean? In mathematics, when you average the numbers 5, 6, 8, and 9, what do you get? The answer is 7, a number that is not even in the original list. If these were children's ages, the average age of the group would be seven, yet not one child is seven. An average, therefore, gives information, but it is not exact.

Labeling Developmental Stages

*O*ften when you read about children and child development, terms like "infant," "toddler," and "preschooler" are used to identify developmental stages. The problem with such labels is that not everyone uses them in the same way. You may find, for example, that "toddler" refers to ages twelve to twenty-four months in one reference and twelve to thirty-six months in another. In this text, the labels for developmental stages refer to these age ranges: infants—birth to twelve months; toddlers—twelve to thirty-six months; pre-schoolers—ages three to five; and school-age children—six to twelve years.

These stages provide an organized way to study child development. Because children change so much at each stage, however, the descriptions you will read in the chapters ahead are often tied to specific ages within each range.

As you study children and their development, be alert for variations. The labels you find in other references may differ somewhat from the ones used in this text. That doesn't matter. What does matter is the ages that are described. What matters even more is understanding that the descriptions and guidelines are only general ones.

As an example, child development researchers have noted that the "average" child walks at twelve months of age. This means that at least half of the children researchers observed had accomplished this skill by twelve months. The other half did so after that age. Children who walk at ten months of age are not abnormal. Neither are children who walk at fourteen months. Knowing that most children walk around the age of twelve months is simply a guidepost to help you assess whether children are developing properly. When a child is significantly outside the average pattern and possibly other problems are noted, investigation is in order. The child may need assistance with development.

Sometimes the same child may experience different rates of development in different areas. For example, in one family the decision was made to wait an extra year before their child entered kindergarten. The child had strong abilities intellectually but didn't seem ready socially for a school experience. A year later the child's social development had caught up, and the child was much better prepared to enter school.

Researchers have found that boys tend to develop more slowly than girls. Generally, boys' development lags from two to six months behind girls of the same age. The causes of this difference in rate of development are still unknown. Understanding the difference, however, helps caregivers react more appropriately to children of both genders (male and female).

Avoiding Comparisons

People who care for children need to guard against evaluating development in a judgmental way. Children who develop certain skills more quickly than others are not superior, just as those who lag a bit behind are not inferior. Eventually, most children catch up and master the same skills. Comparing children or making them feel inadequate or better only leads to trouble.

Development Is Ongoing

Although development is emphasized in the early years of life, it does not stop at a certain age. Sometimes the pace is slower than at other times, but development still continues. Because people change throughout life in many ways, the process is often referred to as *life-span development*. You have seen examples of this—a young adult who becomes independent; an adult who seeks a career change; an older person who gains wit and wisdom. All of these, and more, are part of the total picture that makes up development. There can be no denying, however, that helping a child get off to a good start developmentally sets the stage for satisfying development over a lifetime.

Development Is Sequential

Could you spell a word if you didn't know the letters of the alphabet? Of course, the answer is "no." In the same way that you learned the alphabet before you learned to spell, the skills that children learn during development build upon those acquired earlier. Development follows an orderly **sequence**, or *step-by-step pattern*. Several principles describe in general the sequences of development as shown in the illustration below.

Sequences of Development

From Center to Outside ▼

Children develop from the center of their body outward. Development progresses from the spine to the arms and legs and then to the fingers and toes. This is called the **proximodistal** (PRAHK-suh-MOE-DISS-tull) principle of development. Children can use their shoulders and swing their arms in large circles before they can coordinate and maneuver their wrists and fingers.

From Top to Bottom ▲

Children progressively master body movement and coordination from the head downward. This is called the **cephalocaudal** (SEF-uh-luh-KAWD-ull) principle of development. First children can lift their head and then the trunk of their body. Eventually they coordinate their whole body in order to walk.

WHAT AFFECTS DEVELOPMENT?

You only need to look at the children you know to see that development doesn't bring about the same results for each one. What reasons can there be for all the differences that occur in how children develop? Sometimes circumstances of birth have an effect. A child may be born with abnormalities. Problems during prenatal development or the birth process itself may result in developmental difficulties. Injury or illness during the early years of life may also interfere.

While these situations do not occur with all children, two factors do: heredity and environment. Each has a strong impact on how children develop. Together, they bring up a question that has fascinated researchers for a long time. Which has the greater influence on children, heredity or environment?

Heredity and Environment

Children are born with a biological makeup that defines what they are like. This biological makeup, called *heredity*, is received from parents at conception. *Environment* also shapes what a child is. Environmental influences include such things as people, surroundings, and experiences. While heredity provides

From General to Specific ▼

Development progresses gradually from general to specific. Attempts to acquire new abilities start out simple and become increasingly complex. For instance, children jump up and down with both feet before being able to hop on one foot. Running comes first and skipping later. Babies make sounds before learning to form specific words.

From Large to Small ▲

Children develop control over large muscles before small muscles. For example, children can run and jump before they are able to throw or catch a ball accurately.

children with a foundation for development, researchers have found that environmental experiences affect growth, too. Both could limit potential; however, early nurturing experiences have been found so powerful that they can cause physical changes in the development of a child's brain. Researchers have described the physical changes as creating networks in brain wiring.

These networks begin developing at birth. They are sensitive to environmental influences during the first months of life. The networks become more complex as children receive appropriate nurturing. The more intricate the networks become, the better able children are to learn and develop.

Brain researchers have confirmed what experience, and good early childhood programs, such as Head Start, have suggested for years. Good nutrition, proper health care, consistent and loving nurturing, and developmentally appropriate intellectual and social stimulation improve a child's ability to grow in all areas. Consider these developments in brain research as you think about your role in caring for children. These benefits can last a lifetime.

Tip FROM THE Pros

Sometimes you help build self-esteem in children in little ways that you are hardly aware of. Self-esteem builders can become habits if you consciously make the effort until they are automatic. Try these: smiling at children; making eye contact; giving a pat on the head or shoulder; using positive words, like "great try" or "good job"; listening one-on-one whenever possible.

Self-Esteem

Suppose that a new toy has been placed on the playground at a child care center. It is a colorful, heavy-duty bicycle with two wheels. Jarod sees the bicycle for the first time, and he can't wait to try it out. He jumps on and makes several clumsy attempts to ride. He laughs at his mistakes and forgets about the spills, determined that he will master this new challenge. Bill also sees the bicycle. Inside he yearns to ride it, but something tells him not to try. He is sure he will fall. Instead of taking a turn, he stands back to watch. Eventually he walks away, with a feeling of disappointment inside.

In this situation, Bill and Jarod illustrate a principle that should be foremost in your thinking: children need a good self-concept and high self-esteem in order to develop and function well in the world.

Self-concept is *the picture individuals carry in their mind of who they are, what they can do, and what they are like.* Self-concept is developed through interaction with people and surroundings. Many

Positive interactions help children build a positive self-concept. With very young children, parents and other caregivers have the greatest influence.

researchers believe a child's self-concept is basically formed by age six.

Self-esteem is *how much people do, or do not, like the picture they have of themselves.* It is a sense of self-worth. Self-esteem may be high, low, or anywhere in between. When people feel good about themselves, they are said to have high self-esteem. Children who are developing high self-esteem are positive and optimistic. They enjoy trying new things and meeting new people.

When children think negatively about themselves, they have low self-esteem. They avoid trying something new because they expect to fail. If they don't try, however, opportunities for the positive input they need from caregivers are limited. If they try and do fail, low self-esteem is reinforced. Sometimes children don't work very hard in school because they think too poorly of themselves. Success isn't consistent with their self-concept or self-esteem.

Throughout this book, ways to build self-esteem will be identified. How children are cared for, parented, educated, and disciplined affects self-esteem. Providing experiences that build high self-esteem is the best gift you could ever give a child. It is a key factor in fostering good development.

OBSERVING CHILDREN

All that you learn about children and their development comes to life when you see the principles in action.

Practice promotes your observation skills. Now is the time to start. As you progress through this course, look for opportunities to watch children in a more thoughtful manner than you ever have before. Begin in little ways, looking for the signs of development that you will read about in this unit. You will have observation assignments, but you can practice on your own. Every effort you make in this area will contribute toward making you a more effective child care professional in the future.

THE MULTICULTURAL CLASSROOM

Are individuality and confidence traits that you would encourage children to develop? Very likely your answer is "yes." Like many others, you may believe that these qualities are part of high self-esteem. Not everyone agrees.

In some Asian countries, for example, children are taught that conformity is better than individuality. Not conforming can mean defiance or not fitting in. A sibling who strives to be "like" a brother or sister rather than "different" gains respect. Not drawing attention to yourself is preferred.

Likewise in these cultures, a child who demonstrates confidence may seem lacking in modesty. Since modesty is highly valued, confidence is not.

As a child care professional, you need to be sensitive to the viewpoints of other cultures. Children can be confused by contradictions. Learn about the cultures represented in your classroom. You may want to modify the way you handle some situations. Talk with parents. Invite them to observe the program, where they can see your methods in action. When both sides develop understanding, everything goes more smoothly.

wrote objectively and one, subjectively. An *objective* expression uses facts without the interference of personal feelings or prejudices. A s*ubjective* expression, on the other hand, reflects personal judgments. Which of these terms describes the way Rachel handled her observations? If you said "objective," you are right. Rachel described what happened without interpreting and evaluating. Note how Todd conveyed his opinion, not just what he saw, when he reported on the scene.

When you observe children, use Rachel's example. You should write objectively. Objective observations do not reach conclusions. They simply record facts that can

Rachel and Todd were watching the children in a center from a corner of the room. As they observed, a scene involving two children unfolded. Later, Rachel and Todd finalized their notes on what they saw. Study carefully what each of them said:

Rachel: "Sherise got angry and stood up. Her face became red. She turned to Felipe and said in a harsh tone, 'Those are my crayons! You can't use them.' She grabbed a crayon from Felipe's hand and sat back down to continue working on the picture she was drawing. Felipe walked away without a word."

Todd: "Sherise suddenly displayed aggressive behavior as she confronted Felipe over the use of materials at the art table. Felipe was pretty meek about it. Sherise showed that she is a domineering child."

Todd and Rachel wrote in very different ways about what they observed. One

Objective or Subjective?

Can you recognize objective writing? Analyze each of the following pairs of statements, deciding which ones are objective and which are subjective:

- Tim was afraid to enter the child care center.
- Tim had a look of fear on his face as his father led him through the door of the center.

- The children walked in several directions around chairs, tables, and toy shelves in order to get to the story circle.
- The furnishings in the center were poorly arranged.

- Lee grabbed the clay from Marta's hands.
- Lee showed his nasty nature while sitting next to Marta during the art activity.

- Two samples of children's artwork decorated the walls of the center.
- There wasn't enough artwork displayed in the center.

- Bethany was too frustrated to finish her project.
- Bethany tried to apply glue to the paper airplane three times before giving up.

later be interpreted by professionals who have the necessary expertise. Often professionals, those well trained in child development, medicine, psychiatry, or psychology, use many observations to reach conclusions about a child. Only when they have carefully documented observations that are truly objective can they reach accurate conclusions.

As you build your observation skills, learn to be objective. Like the professionals, you may eventually be called upon to analyze and reach conclusions about the behavior of children. With objective observations, you will be better able to build a true picture of a child and provide the right support.

Chapter 3 Review

Chapter Summary

- To guide and care for children appropriately, knowledge of child development is required.
- Many theorists have contributed to knowledge about children and their development.
- Child development can be divided into different areas of study.
- Development includes many changes in the way children look, act, feel, and function.
- The different areas of development affect each other as children grow and change.
- Even though development follows a similar pattern for everyone, children have individual styles and rates of development.
- Children develop in predictable step-by-step sequences that build on each other.
- Heredity and environment influence development.
- Self-esteem affects development.

Reviewing the Facts

1. Why is it important for those who work with children to understand child development?
2. Name three theorists and briefly describe their contributions to the body of knowledge about child development.
3. List and briefly describe the five areas of development.
4. List five principles of development.
5. Can you accurately predict when a child will accomplish a developmental skill? Explain your answer.
6. Should the child who develops at a slower pace than others be considered inferior to the rest? Explain your answer.
7. Explain four principles that describe the sequential nature of development.
8. Is potential limited by heredity and environment? Explain your answer.
9. Why do caregivers need to help children develop high self-esteem?
10. Explain the difference between objective and subjective observations.

Thinking Critically

1. If a child care professional has limited knowledge of child development, what impact might this have on the children under his or her care?
2. How are multiple areas of development related to each of these skills: (a) walking; (b) grasping objects; (c) speaking; (d) learning independence.
3. Which do you think has greater impact on a child, heredity or environment? Explain.
4. Could the self-esteem level of a child care professional have an effect on the children in his or her care? Explain.

Activities and Applications

1. **Theorists.** Choose a theorist to research. Prepare a paper or give an oral report to the class.
2. **Values.** Work with a partner to list values that might be acceptable to teach to all children in a child care setting. Compare your list with those of others.
3. **Self-Esteem.** Observe young children in a public

setting, such as a mall or park. Make a list of specific behaviors that show high self-esteem.

4. **Analyzing Heredity and Environment.** Make a list of traits and abilities you believe you have inherited from your parents. Then write down any traits and abilities that you believe have been influenced by your environment. Do any items fit in both lists? Summarize your observations.

SCHOOL TO WORK

Your Professional Portfolio

Develop a self-esteem checklist for evaluating the self-esteem of preschoolers. You might use a question format, including such items as: Does the child participate willingly in activities? Does the child play with other children? Is the child able to complete tasks regularly with reasonable success? Refine the checklist as you complete this course and include it in your portfolio.

Observing and Analyzing

Studying Children's Development

The study of children's development is not limited to the classroom. Sometimes simple, everyday situations provide a spontaneous opportunity to observe the concepts you have studied in your classroom. Here are some ideas:

- **A Trip to the Park.** Observe the playground area designated for young children. Look at the types of equipment and watch how children use each one. What motor skills are demonstrated by children of different ages as they use the swings? If there is a large climbing apparatus that has multiple functions, such as a jungle gym, crawling tubes, climbing net, and slide, describe the difference in mastery of motor skills between the youngest and oldest participants. Do they all use the jungle gym and slide the same way?

- **Restaurants.** When you visit restaurants, fast food or other types, note what provisions are made for children. What accommodations does the restaurant offer for children who are too small for the chairs? Booster seats and high chairs? Why do the younger children create more spills and messy areas? What motor skills does the child need to eat the meals sold specifically for children? If there is an outdoor play area, why are some areas age- or size-restricted? How does the design of the tables, chairs, and play area relate to the children's development?

- **Watching Television.** Observe commercials shown during children's programs. What kinds of products are advertised? What appeals are used? How might self-esteem be influenced when children see items they want and later get? What if they do not get what they see and want?

- **The Toy Store.** Observe a selection of toys in a toy store to identify those that promote different types of development. Which toys focus on these different areas of development: physical, intellectual, social, and emotional? In what ways do some toys promote multiple areas of development? Which toys, if any, have very little value in promoting development?

Chapter 4

Understanding
Infants

CHAPTER OBJECTIVES

- Identify and define reflexes infants have at birth.
- Identify signs of physical, intellectual, emotional, and social development in infancy.
- Describe the sensorimotor period as presented by Piaget.
- Describe three types of temperament and explain how temperament affects personality development.

Terms to Learn

- attachment behavior
- bonding
- egocentric
- eye-hand coordination
- infancy
- nurture
- object permanence
- perceptual motor skills
- reflexes
- sensorimotor period
- stranger anxiety
- temperament
- vocalizations

For ten-month-old Jacob, a shopping trip to the supermarket was an adventure. It was also an opportunity for development.

First, his nanny Andrea held his hands while she walked him to the front door of the house. Then she swooped him into her arms while he squealed with delight. Jacob loved the feeling of walking, although he couldn't quite manage it on his own yet. Even at his young age, he was eager to move in the direction of independence.

As they drove to the supermarket, Andrea talked animatedly to Jacob. She pointed to objects outside the car and asked him many questions that he didn't yet have the ability to answer. At the supermarket she strapped him into the child's seat in the shopping cart and pushed him up and down the aisles, all lined with brightly colored boxes and cans. He grasped at the smooth paper labels as Andrea held up two cans and asked, "Which shall we buy, Jake—these dark red kidney beans or these bright green peas?" He liked her smile of approval as he tried to imitate some of the sounds she was making.

Jacob's senses were called into action as they roamed the supermarket. In some parts of the store, he could feel the colder temperatures. In one section he smelled some unusual but interesting aromas. He was fascinated by the cashier's face as she leaned over the counter to coo and smile at him, but he was happiest when Andrea picked him up and held him again.

On the drive home, Andrea peeled a banana and let Jacob gnaw on a small piece as he watched the passing scenery from his car seat. The banana tasted good, he decided, and it was soft and sticky between his fingers. That, too, was a wonder. The world, it seemed, was full of wonders.

THAT AMAZING FIRST YEAR

To many caregivers, the conversion of a helpless, crying newborn to an active, inquisitive, babbling one-year-old happens so fast that they hardly have time to enjoy each momentous step along the way. The process occurs in twelve months, but so much goes on that people often look back and wonder how much they missed noticing.

Infancy is often defined as *the time between birth and twelve months of age*. The remarkable changes that take place make up the most concentrated period of accelerated growth and development in a person's life.

Frequent feedings and plenty of rest help infants grow rapidly.

PHYSICAL DEVELOPMENT

Rapid growth and development require energy. To help sustain them, very young infants sleep up to seventeen hours a day and require frequent feedings. Generally, infants come into the world weighing between six and ten pounds (2.7 and 4.5 kg). They are usually about 20 inches (51 cm) long. By the end of their first year, most babies weigh about 22 pounds (10 kg) and are 30 inches (76 cm) long. Of course, inherited qualities from a mother and father influence this growth.

An infant's head grows rapidly. Open spaces in the bones of the infant's skull, called *fontanels*, allow for the growth of the quickly developing brain. The bones of the skull gradually grow together, and the open spaces are usually closed by eighteen months.

At six months, baby teeth begin to appear. By two years of age, all twenty baby (or *primary*) teeth are usually present.

Presence of Reflexes

All humans are born with **reflexes**, or *instinctive, involuntary reactions to a stimulus, such as a noise or touch.* Infants have

Insuring Safety

The largest fontanel on an infant's skull is located on the top of the head. It is often called the "soft spot." Until this area becomes covered by the bones of the skull, the possibility of injury is present. Although the overlying skin is tough, any sharp or hard blow to the head could cause internal injuries. Caregivers need to be especially cautious about protecting an infant's head during the time that this "soft spot" exists.

*A*s new teeth push through an infant's gums (a process called *eruption*), the child is said to be teething. This is very painful for babies and usually difficult for their caregivers as well. Infants may cry and become cranky during eruption, which lasts from two to ten days for each tooth. They may even run a slight temperature. Caregivers can ease teething by giving infants teething biscuits and teething rings filled with ice water. The gnawing action and ice water help relieve the pain. During teething, caregivers need extra patience and understanding.

Tip FROM THE Pros

certain reflexes that function only for the first months of life. After that, intellectual and physical growth allow for voluntary action.

Reflexes that infants have are:

- Startle reflex—throwing out the arms and legs in response to a loud sound or sudden movement.
- Rooting reflex—turning toward a touch on the cheek or lips and beginning to suck.
- Grasping reflex—automatically closing the hand when the palm is touched.

- Babinski reflex—fanning the toes when the bottom of the foot is stroked.
- Other reflexes—making a walking motion when held up with the feet touching the floor, and appearing to swim when held horizontally in water.

To understand how reflexes work, suppose that you are working in an infant care center. You are preparing to feed three-week-old Elisha her formula when you accidentally drop the bottle on the floor. Elisha responds with the startle reflex. She throws out her arms and legs when she hears the

What purpose might the rooting reflex serve?

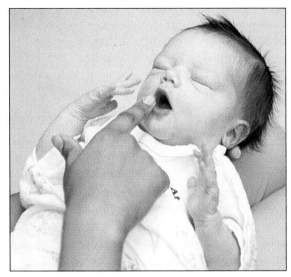

How would you feel, as a parent, if your newborn firmly grasped your finger? What effect might this have on your emotional attachment to the baby?

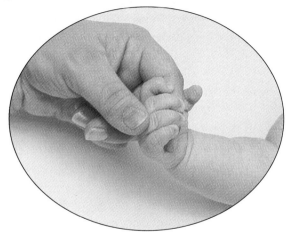

loud sound. As you pick Elisha up, the touch of the blanket on her face triggers the rooting reflex. She turns toward the blanket and begins to suck. Then while feeding her, you touch the palm of her hand, and her hand automatically closes. Within just a few minutes, you have seen three common reflexes present in infants.

Sensory Development

At birth, babies are equipped with all of their senses. They can see, hear, taste, feel, and smell. Within the first week of life, these senses quickly become more refined.

Newborn babies hear well enough to distinguish the voices of those caregivers who spend the most time with them from the voices of others. Vision is not clear at birth,

but it improves within weeks. Soon, infants prefer looking at a human face, or picture of a face, that is held about 12 inches (30.5 cm) from their eyes. They enjoy brightly colored objects and patterns with contrasting colors. Their visual *perception*—learning about something through the senses—is not yet developed enough for them to follow objects with their eyes or to reach for objects.

Babies sense differences in taste. They prefer sweet over plain tastes. Limiting sweet food and drinks is necessary, however, as part of a caregiver's interest in providing healthful meals and snacks. When solid food is offered at about six months, babies often spit out the new food simply because the taste and texture are new.

Within the first two weeks of life, babies can recognize the unique scent of their mother. They gradually learn the scents of other family members as well.

Babies feel differences in texture. In fact, some babies are so sensitive that they become cranky and cry if dressed in clothing of a texture they dislike.

Motor Development

At birth, babies are completely dependent on others. They cannot lift or hold up their own head, roll over, sit up, or stand. Physical strength and movement improve quickly, however. Muscular development eventually gives infants *mobility*, allowing them to move from one place to another. The chart on page 83 lists major motor developments during the first year of life.

Motor development influences, and is influenced by, other types of growth. Curiosity, a sign of intellectual growth, motivates infants to become increasingly mobile. Sitting up allows babies to make eye contact, which encourages social growth.

Even in the first months of life, infants need sensory stimulation for normal development.

Improving eye-hand coordination gives an infant additional ways to explore the world. These blocks, for example, are seen, touched, and tasted.

Walking and self-feeding have a similar effect.

As babies progress physically and intellectually, they acquire **perceptual motor skills**—*skills that require the coordination of vision, intellect, and movement.* Climbing up a step is a perceptual motor skill. The child must see the step, judge the height, and lift his or her hands and knees. A related skill is **eye-hand coordination,** *the ability to move the hands and fingers precisely in relation to what is seen.* Infants begin to develop eye-hand coordination around three or four months of age. They can see a toy, reach for it, and grasp it successfully. Eye-hand coordination continues to develop throughout childhood.

Motor Development during Infancy

AGE	MOTOR DEVELOPMENT
Two months	Lifts head and chest when lying on stomach
Four months	Sits erect in arms of adult; reaches for objects
Six months	Grasps objects; rolls self over
Eight months	Thrusts arms and legs out and squirms to push self forward; pulls self up
Ten months	Crawls on hands and knees; walks with help of adult
Twelve months	Stands, sometimes walks alone; picks up small objects between thumb and forefinger; begins self-feeding

INTELLECTUAL DEVELOPMENT

*H*ow do people acquire thinking skills? Much research has gone into this question. The work of cognitive theorist Jean Piaget has provided much insight into how children learn. He identified four periods that people go through as they develop intellectually from infancy through adulthood. The chart on this page shows these. Additional explanations of these periods will be found throughout the chapters in this unit. The first one, the sensorimotor period, is described here, since it applies to infants.

The Sensorimotor Period

Piaget used the term **sensorimotor period** (sents-ree-MOH-tur) to describe the time frame during which infants develop their intellect. *During this period, from birth to age two, infants and one-year-olds learn by using their senses and motor abilities to gain information about the world.* As you can see in the chart on page 85, the sensorimotor period is subdivided into stages. Children learn by touching, tasting, smelling, and hearing. For instance, the principle of cause and effect is learned when an infant sees that pulling a string on a toy will make the toy move. If the child moves forward while pulling the string, the toy follows. This and similar types of learning usually begin between seven and eight months of age.

At around nine months, Piaget found, most children acquire an intellectual ability called **object permanence.** *This is the understanding that an object continues to exist even when out of sight.* Children discover that although a person or object disappears from view, it will be back. Before object permanence develops, you can cover a child's toy with a scarf and the child's interest shifts to something else. After object permanence develops, the child deliberately removes the scarf to find the toy.

Piaget's Periods of Cognitive Development

PERIOD	DESCRIPTION
Sensorimotor Period Birth to age two	Babies learn primarily through their senses and their own actions. Behavior is primarily motor.
Preoperational Period Age two to seven	Children start to think symbolically and imaginatively. They rely less on motor abilities and more on thinking to direct behavior.
Concrete Operations Period Age seven to eleven	Children use logical thinking, relating it to actual (concrete) objects and experiences.
Formal Operations Period Age eleven through adulthood	Children think logically, but now with the ability to apply it to ideas that are abstract and hypothetical (unreal).

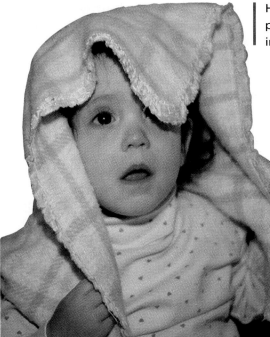

How is playing peek-a-boo related to object permanence? How would a very young infant react?

As intellect increases, children begin to analyze, make associations, and form predictions. At one year, for example, Dane learned that the rattle of keys in the front door lock meant that his mother or father had come home. His smiles and excitement at seeing his parent strengthened the bonds between them, aiding Dane's emotional development.

The Role of Language

Language plays a large role in developing intellectual abilities. Children understand language long before they can speak it well

Stages of the Sensorimotor Period

STAGE AND APPROXIMATE AGE	CHARACTERISTICS
1—Birth to one month	Practices inborn reflexes; does not understand self as separate person.
2—One to four months	Combines two or more reflexes; develops hand-mouth coordination.
3—Four to eight months	Acts intentionally to produce results; improves eye-hand coordination.
4—Eight to twelve months	Begins to solve problems; finds partially hidden objects; imitates others.
5—Twelve to eighteen months	Finds hidden objects; explores and experiments; understands that objects exist independently.
6—Eighteen to twenty-four months	Solves problems by thinking through sequences; can think using symbols; begins imaginative thinking.

THE MULTICULTURAL CLASSROOM

The point has been made that language is an important part of intellectual development. What happens, then, to the infant who comes to a child care program where the language spoken is different from the one heard at home? Such situations are easier to manage than you might think.

Children are amazing. They learn quickly that there are two ways of saying things. Because they are ready to absorb anything new and because they haven't had time to get used to handling only one language, accepting two ways of saying "me," "cup," and "cracker" is often easy for them. Many caregivers make it a point to learn certain words and phrases in the child's own language. This helps insure that important messages get through. Obtaining a bilingual dictionary with an English pronunciation guide helps ease communication with the child and family.

themselves. By six months of age, children can understand some spoken words, such as "mommy" and "daddy." By one year, children can usually speak several words. By eighteen months, two-word sentences are common; by age two, complete sentences can be formed.

Even very young babies benefit when you talk to them. Although they do not understand the words, they soon make **vocalizations**—*sounds that imitate adult language.* When adults respond to vocalizations, infants begin to learn that wants and needs can be expressed through language. Eventually, they learn specific ideas. Understandable spoken language isn't far behind.

EMOTIONAL DEVELOPMENT

*I*nfants experience such emotions as discomfort, distress, and happiness. As children develop, feelings become more specific. Excitement, joy, frustration, and anger are evident. These emotions are much easier to identify and manage after an infant learns language skills.

Bonding

Throughout a baby's first year of life, almost from the minute of birth, an important emotional development is taking place—bonding. **Bonding** is *forming a strong attachment to, and preference for, the primary caregivers.* This is usually a parent or parents. Secondary bonding can take place with other caregivers. A sign that bonding has occurred is **attachment behavior.** *The infant shows signs of pleasure when the caregiver appears and signs of distress when that person leaves.* Babies who smile and gurgle with delight when their caregivers enter the room and cry or fuss when these individuals leave are testimony to attentive, involved caregivers.

Bonding is necessary for development of good self-esteem. According to theorist Erik Erikson, children develop a sense of trust or mistrust based on the quality of early experiences with caregivers and with their environment. If needs for food, warmth, and comfort are met consistently, infants devel-

A baby who is cuddled during feeding gains a sense of security and trust, as well as the food needed for physical health. How else can caregivers foster self-esteem in infants?

op a sense of trust. If these needs are not satisfied consistently, they develop a sense of mistrust. They see the world as a threatening and unpredictable place. The earlier children develop trust in others and in their environment, the better their emotional health. Responsive, reliable, and stable caregivers in the earliest months of life are critical for the development of trust. Positive social development cannot take place until babies experience a trusting relationship that allows them to bond with their primary caregiver.

Development of Personality

How children develop personality characteristics is a fascinating topic. While the process is not completely understood, research has given clues to the mystery.

Personality begins during infancy. Hereditary traits form the basis for personality, which continues to be influenced by experiences with the environment. Reactions from caregivers in a child's life affect personality. Interactions with people

Starving for Attention

An extreme example of how development in one area affects growth in another is failure to thrive, which is also called *marasmus*. Babies with this condition fail to grow normally. While the condition can be caused by physical problems or poor nutrition, it can also be due to a lack of social and emotional interaction. The infants have not been held, played with, or spoken to, even though their physical needs have been met. When older, these children may be unable to care for others and form lasting personal relationships. As a caregiver, you need to be able to identify infants with health problems so that help can be sought. Although failure to thrive is relatively uncommon, knowing that it can occur will enable you to take action if necessary.

and the environment, however, do not completely explain how personality develops.

From the day they are born, children have distinctively different ways of approaching the world. *A person's inborn style of reacting to the environment* is known as **temperament.** Temperament has a strong impact on personality.

Identifying Temperaments

The work of doctors Stella Chess and Alexander Thomas in the 1960s and 1970s resulted in the identification of three categories of temperament: difficult, easy, and slow-to-warm-up. These temperaments contribute to the development of different personality traits.

According to Chess and Thomas, easy children adjust quickly to changes in their routines. They are responsive to stimulation, tend to be sociable, and smile frequently. They have few problems with eating or sleeping. Their relaxed outlook on life often makes them easy to care for.

Slow-to-warm-up children can also be outgoing and sociable, but they usually need more time to adjust to new people and new situations. Often these children are prematurely labeled as "shy." Slow-to-warm-up chil-

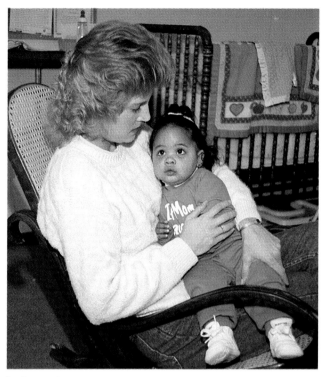

Caregivers can help children who are slow-to-warm-up prepare for changes and experience success with new situations. Such children need frequent reassurance.

dren require notice when changes are made. They may be hesitant to begin new activities. With time and experience, this hesitance lessens.

Difficult children can be more challenging, but they are *not bad.* They simply have an approach to the world that requires more patience from caregivers. Difficult children often have digestive and sleeping problems. They do not adjust well to changes in routine. They can be negative, and they need lots of support when trying something new. Difficult children become overstimulated

A nurturing caregiver can make real contributions to children's lives.

and frustrated easily, often causing them to withdraw from contact. Caregivers may misinterpret withdrawal as dislike. These children also often have a high activity level. They experience emotions intensely and sometimes unpredictably.

While no child is completely one temperament or the other, children do exhibit a general pattern of behavior that is consistent with one category more than another. Knowledge of temperament does not allow you to change a child, but it does help you better understand children's behavior. Individual temperament helps explain why children raised in the same family can develop very different personalities.

As you work with children, remember that the terms for temperament used by Chess and Thomas are only tools to use in objectively analyzing children. Remove judgment from your thinking as you use them. For example, "difficult" in this use only describes a set of characteristics. A "difficult" child may very well turn out to be an outstanding attorney or a competitive athlete. You can provide positive support to a child of any temperament when you understand that these terms help you learn how to work with children, not how to feel about them.

How can labeling a child as "difficult" be harmful to the child? How can understanding a child's temperament be helpful?

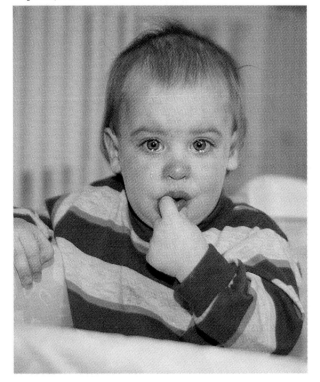

SOCIAL DEVELOPMENT

Do babies have friends? Can infants love their parents? In the strictest sense, babies are not capable of these types of relationships, any more than they are capable of walking or adding numbers. As with other areas of growth, however, the foundations of social development—the ability to form relationships with others—are laid during infancy.

Piaget believed that during the first year of life, children's thinking is **egocentric** (ee-go-SEN-trick). *They see everything only from their own point of view.* During infancy, for example, children do not play cooperatively with each other. They may show interest in another baby but only as they would another object. They do not perceive the baby as another person. It is impossible for them to understand how anyone else thinks or feels.

It takes several years of social experiences to help children grow beyond egocentrism. Emotional development is linked to this process. When infants learn to trust caregivers, they learn to value a social relationship. They discover that they can depend on others for assistance. They become secure in their relationships. Positive social skills are further developed when such routines as feeding, diapering, and bathing are pleasant experiences.

Stranger anxiety is a sign of intellectual growth. If an infant experiencing this fear is in child care, what steps might the staff take to minimize the baby's anxiety?

Stranger Anxiety

The fear of unfamiliar people, usually expressed by crying, that many infants develop is called **stranger anxiety.** It becomes common as object permanence develops, usually around nine months of age. By then, children are able to distinguish between strangers and caregivers. They may scream if a stranger tries to pick them up.

Children usually grow beyond stranger anxiety by twelve or fifteen months of age. Because of this fear, parents are advised to avoid placing children in a new child care setting when they are between the ages of eight and fifteen months.

TAKING TIME TO NURTURE

As you reflect on all the development that takes place during the first year of life, you can see that the changes are remarkable. Infants have so many challenges to meet. Imagine what would happen to an infant who is often ignored. Will he or she build muscles and become skilled at using them if left lying in a crib all the time? Will the child learn sounds that are seldom heard? Will the child feel loved when touching and holding are limited?

Obviously, developmental problems are likely when caregivers do not nurture a child. To **nurture** (NUR-chur) means *to provide love, support, attention, and encouragement.* Caregivers who are generous with their time and willing to take the extra steps that are needed give a child the best possible start in life.

How Can You Recognize Good Health?

While growth rates vary, all infants show certain signs when they are in good health. To help you identify healthy children, look for these signs:

- Clear, bright eyes.
- Steady increases in height and weight.
- Smooth, soft skin.
- Glossy hair.
- Appropriate muscular control for the age.
- Doesn't tire easily.
- Quick, definite movements.
- A generally happy, active, and curious disposition.

Building Professional Skills

Good Judgment

WHAT IS GOOD JUDGMENT?

Good judgment is the ability to make wise decisions. Using intellectual skills, such as reasoning and thinking about consequences, is part of good judgment. A person develops good judgment through experience and increased understanding of individuals and their abilities. You don't acquire good judgment overnight. It comes with practice as you continually refine your decision-making skills. With good judgment, you can resolve any number of challenging situations.

Good Judgment in Action

Rosa walked through the park, pushing eight-month-old Jerome in his stroller. The two four-year-old girls that she cared for in her family day care home were walking beside her. As they strolled, Rosa recognized a group of older women from her neighborhood, who were out for their morning walk.

"Rosa!" they called. "Is that the Sandburg boy? Can we see him?" They gathered around the stroller and bent down to see Jerome. Jerome began to fuss and whimper.

Rosa took a step forward, moving herself into Jerome's line of vision. "He's a little shy with new people. I think he wants a little room."

"Oh, are you sure?" asked Mrs. Atherton.

"When my granddaughter was that age, she loved to be held and cuddled. Everyone remarked that she was such a sweet baby." Mrs. Atherton reached out to stroke Jerome's cheek. Jerome shrieked and thrashed his arms in front of his face.

"I'm sorry, Mrs. Atherton," Rosa apologized, "but like I said, he's not comfortable with strangers. He'll probably be a little friendlier in a few months. I'm sure you'll understand if we go on with our walk today."

A few seconds later, Rosa stopped in a quiet spot beneath a tree and squatted down with the girls beside the stroller. "You're okay, little guy," she soothed Jerome. "You just don't want to be passed around like a hot potato, do you? You've got your own way of dealing with people, and that's just fine."

Your Analysis

1. How did Rosa show good judgment? Give specific examples.

2. What might have been some consequences if Rosa had not used good judgment in this situation?

3. Identify some everyday situations that you face in which good judgment helps you.

Chapter 4 Review

Chapter Summary

- Infancy is a time of rapid growth.
- Infants are born with certain reflexes.
- Senses are quickly refined during infancy.
- Greater mobility comes as infants develop motor skills.
- Intellectual development takes place when babies are allowed to explore their environment with senses and motor skills.
- Bonding and the development of trust are needed for emotional health.
- Studies show that children are born with different temperaments.
- The foundation for future social relationships is built during infancy.
- An infant who is nurtured gets a good start in life.

Reviewing the Facts

1. What is infancy?
2. Briefly describe physical growth during infancy.
3. What are reflexes? Describe three reflexes infants have when they are born.
4. Describe how infants gradually gain mobility.
5. At approximately what age can an infant: (a) sit erect in the arms of an adult; (b) reach for and grasp objects; (c) begin self-feeding with finger foods?
6. Describe sensorimotor learning. What well-known theorist developed research on cognitive development?
7. Define and give an example of object permanence.
8. Explain the meaning of bonding. Why is bonding important?
9. Briefly describe the three types of temperaments identified by Chess and Thomas.
10. What is stranger anxiety? When is it most intense?

Thinking Critically

1. A baby enjoys trying to grasp objects. What types of toys allow the baby to practice this skill? What could you make that would serve this purpose?
2. Why might a talkative person be good at working with infants?
3. What could a child care professional do to help when parents miss out on certain "firsts" in the child's life?
4. How do you explain a baby's sensitivity to different tastes, smells, and textures? What purpose might it serve?
5. What dangers might there be in labeling a child as difficult?
6. How would you handle situations that involve stranger anxiety?

Activities and Applications

1. **Motor Development.** Observe and compare the motor skills of a two-month-old and a six-month-old. What physical progress has the older infant made?
2. **Judging Ages.** With a partner, find magazine pictures that show infants. Try to judge the ages of the infants pictured, applying your knowledge of development.
3. **Nurturing.** Videotape a parent (or a child care student) playing with an

infant. Review the tape several times. Cite specific examples of ways that the parent's involvement stimulates the child's physical, intellectual, emotional, and social development.

4. **An Important Point.** Complete the following sentence in writing. "I believe a very important point to remember about infant development is . . ."

SCHOOL TO WORK

Your Professional Portfolio

As an addition to your portfolio and for your own personal use, begin a resource list to develop as you complete this course. Include resources that would be useful to you as an employee in the child care field. You might include the names of books, magazines, newsletters, companies that provide toys and equipment, and agencies. Include reviews of selected resources.

Observing and Analyzing

Studying Infant Development

To understand how infants develop you need to observe them. Although your classroom experiences will provide excellent information, to observe infants up close is to really understand how complex and fascinating they are.

Observing infants requires considerable concentration. Although infants may appear to be accomplishing little in their day-to-day experiences, their minds and senses are taking in everything in their environment. You will need to watch carefully to see what is going on. Through observation, the differences and similarities between infants will be more apparent.

- **A Newborn Nursery.** If your local hospital will allow visitors, look for the name labels on each crib and record the heights and weights of the infants. What is the range?
- **A Look at Proportions.** Observe a sleeping newborn and compare the size of the hand in relation to the face. How large is the hand when placed on the cheek? Place your own hand on your face to see the difference in proportions as compared to the infant. How long is the infant's arm in relation to the head? If you raise your arm above your head, how far does your elbow reach? Observe a child who can walk and see if the head-body proportions are the same as those you have seen in younger children.
- **Bonding.** Look for opportunities to observe the relationship between infants and their caregivers. What signs of bonding do you see? What kind of voice is used? How is a crying infant comforted? How does the caregiver interact with the infant during feeding, diaper changing, and playtime?

Chapter 5

Understanding Toddlers

CHAPTER OBJECTIVES

■ Describe major physical developments in toddlers.

■ Identify significant signs of intellectual, emotional, and social growth in toddlers.

■ Explain the impact of role models on children.

■ Explain why the two-year-old stage can be particularly trying for children and adults.

■ Describe an environment that promotes sound emotional development.

■ Explain the impact of play on social development.

■ Identify ways to promote responsibility in toddlers.

Terms to Learn

- accommodation
- assimilation
- attention span
- autonomy
- concepts
- fine motor skills
- gross motor skills
- parallel play
- preoperational period
- role model
- self-help skills
- solitary play
- toddler

This was the part of the afternoon that Barbara Taylor enjoyed the most. On days when the weather was nice, she got out the special wagon that was equipped to hold four children from her child care center. It had high sides, small benches with backs, and seatbelts to hold the children in place.

As she snapped the belts closed, she gave each child a quick hug. She got several in return. The children loved these outings too. The fresh air felt good, and it was an opportunity for a change of pace.

Barbara walked casually, pushing the wagon in front of her. As they traveled along, she talked to the children and pointed out things they saw on the way.

When they got as far as the park, she unloaded the children from the wagon, so they could do some exploring. "Let's look at this," she said to them. "What do you think we might find under this rock?" The children crouched down beside the rock, ready for discovery. From experience they knew Barbara could find interesting things. "Are you ready?" she asked, building a little suspense for what she hoped to find. Her fingers gripped the side of the large rock as she began to lift it gently. All eyes were on the rock.

CHANGES AND CHALLENGES

What an exciting time for learning is presented by the toddler stage. Whether it's the hidden surprises under a rock or the textures and flavors of new foods, children at these ages are ready to absorb all the information they can.

Toddler is the term commonly given to *a child between the ages of twelve and thirty-six months*. Toddlers are in a transition stage. They are no longer infants, but they are eagerly beginning to increase their skills so they can be more independent. This can be a confusing and frustrating time for children—as well as the adults who care for them.

PHYSICAL DEVELOPMENT

Watch a fifteen-month-old walk and you'll see why children this age are called toddlers. Learning to stand erect, they often appear a bit bowlegged. Their stomachs stick out, and they "toddle" from side to side. By eighteen months, they are much improved at the art of balance. Once they reach age two, their bodies begin to slim down and take on the appearance of a more mature child.

Building Professional Skills

Flexibility

WHAT IS FLEXIBILITY?

Having flexibility means that you can change plans easily. You are not set in a rigid way of doing things. Flexibility can also be a mental quality, when you are able to see a situation from a different viewpoint and with a different attitude. Flexibility is an important quality for getting along with others and resolving conflicts.

Flexibility in Action

Carolyn had the scene set up perfectly. Eighteen-month-old Tobias sat quietly on the table in front of a pale blue background. He babbled happily at his mother, who stood just out of the camera's range holding up Tobias' favorite doll. Suddenly his expression changed. His lip curled down, and he began to squawk and then wail. "Mama!" he cried, as he shifted to his hands and knees.
"I don't understand," his mother said helplessly. "He loves this toy. It always makes him happy."

"That's okay," said Carolyn cheerfully. "These things always take longer than you planned." She had been a professional child photographer for a long time, and she was prepared. She showed

Tobias items from a big box of toys and stuffed animals. Nothing held his attention. Then he caught sight of one of her photography magazines.

It was the latest issue. Carolyn hadn't read it yet, but she decided to let Tobias hold it anyway. Gleefully, he latched onto the magazine and patted the pages. Several pages tore as he pulled on them. He was so amused that he hardly noticed when Carolyn snapped his picture.

"I can always buy another one," she chuckled to herself later, picking up the scattered pages, "or tape this one back together." Tobias's expression that she had caught on film was worth much more than the price of a magazine.

Your Analysis

1. How did Carolyn show flexibility in her job?

2. Why do you think flexibility is an important quality for child care professionals?

3. Can a person be too flexible? If so, what might be some negative consequences of this?

4. How might a caregiver's flexibility affect a child's social and emotional development? Would the effects be mostly positive or mostly negative? Explain your answer.

Average Heights and Weights of Toddlers

AGE	HEIGHT	WEIGHT
One Year	30 in. (76 cm)	22 lbs. (10 kg)
Two Years	34 in. (86.5 cm)	28 lbs. (13 kg)
Three Years	38 in. (96.5 cm)	32 lbs. (14.5 kg)

Physical Growth

After infancy, growth in height and weight slows for toddlers. The chart above shows approximate heights and weights for children from one to three. These numbers can vary greatly for individual children.

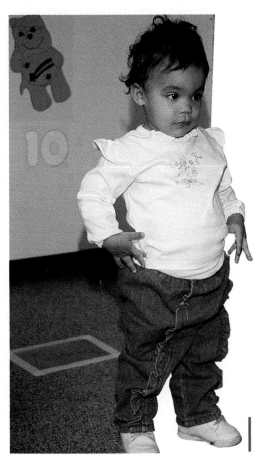

The toddler stage is one of dramatic changes and development.

Body proportions gradually change along with height and weight gains. An infant's head is relatively large in comparison to the rest of the body, and arms and legs are short. With physical growth, children take on more mature proportions.

Because less fuel is needed for growth, appetites decrease during the toddler years. Two-year-olds can feed themselves with a fork and spoon but often show less interest in eating and may dawdle over food. Likewise, although teeth come in rapidly between eighteen and twenty-four months of age, children do not always chew their food properly. Instead they may gulp their food to finish meals as quickly as possible. For safety reasons, food should still be served in very small pieces to prevent choking.

Motor Development

Motor development and coordination advance quickly during this time of life. Improving **gross motor skills**, *skills that use the larger muscles of the back, legs, shoulders, and arms*, gives children new physical abilities. Learning to walk gives them greater independence.

From twelve to eighteen months, children begin to climb. At first, climbing up stairs is easier than climbing down them. By age two, however, this skill is mastered as well. Older toddlers love to climb over, around, on top of, and through obstacles in their path. They become more skilled at running, hopping, and jumping.

Between eighteen and twenty-four months of age, children begin to push themselves on wheeled toys. By the end of their second year, they are able to pedal a tricycle or similar pedal-type vehicle.

Toddlers are also refining their **fine motor skills**, *those that require use of the smaller muscles of the fingers, wrists, and ankles.* These skills contribute to improved eye-hand coordination and other perceptual motor skills. Children learn to stack blocks, string beads, and put together simple puzzles. Twelve- to eighteen-month-olds can stack two to four blocks and join a two-piece puzzle. Between eighteen months and thirty-six months, children become adept at doing simple six-piece puzzles and can build towers of about eight blocks.

Development of small muscles and increased eye-hand coordination also enable

Fine motor skills improve throughout the toddler stage. Caregivers need to provide both opportunities for play and appropriate toys.

toddlers to turn the pages of a book one at a time and to scribble with a crayon. By age two, they can turn doorknobs and even work a television remote control, as well as feed themselves.

Insuring Safety

Toddlers may try to practice their climbing skills even when it is unsafe. Be careful that children do not make "stairs" from pieces of furniture, from chairs and tables or countertops, or from drawers and cabinets.

Toilet Training

Children around age two are physically and intellectually ready to begin toilet training. Most are gaining control of the muscles that stop as well as start elimination. Intellectually, they are learning to recognize bodily sensations that precede elimination and to understand the use and purpose of a toilet or potty chair.

Children are generally able to use a regular toilet by the age of two or three. Some children are trained by eighteen months, but this is rare. Girls tend to master the skill earlier than boys.

INTELLECTUAL DEVELOPMENT

*D*iscovery is a big part of intellectual development. For example, Corey was walking with his two-year-old nephew Ozzie around the neighborhood when Ozzie became excited. He pulled Corey over to a huge oak tree and pointed at the small objects scattered beneath it. Ozzie squatted down and gazed at one. He picked it up and held it close to his eyes, fingering the smooth exterior and rough cap. He pressed it to his nose and wrinkled his nostrils. Finally he looked inquiringly at Corey, holding the puzzling object up to him.

"Acorn," Corey said slowly. "That's an acorn."

Like Ozzie, other toddlers continue to grow intellectually through sensorimotor development. Because they learn by doing and by using their senses, they need many hands-on experiences. They need freedom to explore their environment. In order to develop their thinking skills, they need time to satisfy their curiosity. Children have a keen sense of wonder and are fascinated by the simplest things. A child's desire to explore can easily conflict with an adult's desire to follow a tight schedule. That's why adults have to be sure they provide adequate time for a child's investigations. Observing the wonders of the world stretches a young child's mind. Adults who patiently respond to "Why?" and "What's that?" are rewarded with an enthusiastic learner.

Knowledge develops through other means also. Children use trial and error, repetition, and imitation. They observe adults closely and copy their behavior. They even begin to adopt attitudes that adults have. *A person whose behavior and attitudes are imitated*

Toddlers want to try. They may be slow and they may make a mess, but they need opportunities to test and practice their skills. The patient adult builds self-esteem and helps skills develop by allowing the child to try.

by others is called a **role model.** Caregivers are especially powerful role models for children. If you were working with children, what kinds of attitudes and behavior would you want them to learn from you? How would you make sure the children learn them?

Unlike infants, older toddlers do not often explore objects by putting them in their mouth. For this reason, the health and safety concerns that go along with this habit are reduced.

Attention Span

Toddlers are slowly developing an increased **attention span,** which is *the ability to focus on a specific activity for a period of time.* Attention span generally increases with age. It is also affected by the child's interest in the activity and the activity's developmental appropriateness. Think of the last time you read a dull story or attempted to solve a problem that was beyond your abilities. Was it easy or difficult to stay

focused on what you were doing? Children, likewise, are more apt to stay with an activity that provides a reasonable challenge without boring or frustrating them. This helps make the experience a positive one and encourages learning.

Memory

At about nine months Nadia began to look for objects that were removed from view. She realized that the objects still existed even though she couldn't see them. You will recall that this concept is called object permanence. What ability do you think Nadia needed for this understanding? The answer is memory. Memory is the ability to recall images and information. Without memory there would be no learning. If an experience left no impression, it could not affect or improve future thoughts and behavior. When Nadia could remember what she saw, she was better able to understand that the objects out of view still existed.

Memory begins to develop in infancy and grows rapidly over the next two years. Toddlers begin to have memory of actual events. Two-year-olds can remember a parent who has been absent for several weeks. They can repeat bits of favorite rhymes and stories and tell about experiences after returning from a walk.

Symbolic Thinking

Once a child has the ability to remember, the stage is set to develop a more advanced thought process—symbolic thinking. With symbolic thought, children understand that one thing can stand for something else. They learn to use images, art, and language as symbols to represent objects, events, and concepts.

Why is attention span considered such a key skill for intellectual development?

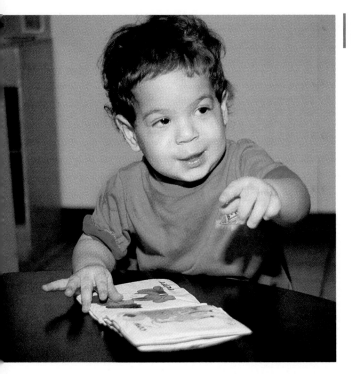

As symbolic thought develops, toddlers become more interested in simple books.

ing and creating. The development of symbolic thought is a significant milestone in intellectual development.

Language Development

Command of more refined language skills fosters incredible intellectual development from ages one to three. Children who at twelve months said only a few words quickly acquire vocabularies of up to 50 words. Babbling continues as children gradually grasp the meaning of their native language.

Eighteen-month-olds respond to questions that are answerable with a "yes" or "no." They identify parts of the body by pointing to them when named. They follow simple directions, such as "Hand me the ball." Communicating with signals that use

Symbolic thought is characteristic of Piaget's second period of intellectual development—preoperational. The **preoperational period** *covers ages two to seven. In this period children start to think symbolically and imaginatively. They rely less on motor abilities and more on thinking to direct behavior.* Intellectually toddlers are beginning to move out of the sensorimotor period and into the preoperational one. A two-year-old may show signs of symbolic thinking, although this ability develops much more fully after toddlerhood.

Because they are starting to think symbolically, many older toddlers enjoy make-believe play. It's not unusual to see a two-year-old holding "conversations" with the use of a wooden block "telephone" or sitting inside a cardboard box that has become a vehicle.

Imagination and creativity are natural outgrowths of symbolic thought. When children begin to think symbolically, they show first signs of the human potential for invent-

"Where is your ear?" Toddlers understand more words than they can speak.

THE MULTICULTURAL CLASSROOM

Regardless of cultural background, most children provide certain widely understood clues that give messages about their needs. A drowsy child needs a nap. A crying child needs attention, perhaps a dry diaper or a hug. A child who is tugging on his or her pants may need to go to the bathroom. Not all messages are as easily communicated.

When children come from different ethnic backgrounds and if they speak another language, caregivers need information that will enable them to respond appropriately to children. A home language survey can help. Parents fill out this form along with other enrollment forms. On it they explain how the family refers to common terms, such as sleep, eat, look, hit, milk, doll, urinate, and bowel movement. Phonetic spellings are helpful. Even in a preschool of all English speaking families, two dozen different words might be used in connection with toilet use, plus a variety of words used to describe the related body parts. A home language survey can help prevent frustration for children and caregivers as they communicate.

the hands, arms, head, or face—gesturing—begins at this age.

Many two-year-olds have a growing vocabulary of 50 to 300 words. They can name familiar objects. More understandable speech includes three- to four-word sentences. Their ability to follow increasingly complex directions, such as "Put the ball inside the box," shows they have begun to understand prepositions as well as nouns.

Conceptual Development

The ability to understand **concepts**—*general ideas formed from other information*—increases rapidly with emerging language skills. Concept development and language development build on each other. The more concepts children encounter, the more words they need to label them. The more words children understand, the more concepts they are able to identify and label.

When labeling concepts, children usually begin by using broad generalizations. One word, to them, has a wide variety of meanings. As their experiences increase, they gradually learn that concepts have limits.

Piaget used two terms to help explain how children absorb information and attempt to make sense of it. Through **assimilation**, children *take in new information and try to make it fit with what they currently know and understand*. When the information doesn't fit, another process takes place—accommodation. With **accommodation**, children *change their thinking to make the new information fit*. Cognitive development is a continual process of balancing new information with existing concepts in order to reach more accurate understandings. In the following example, you can see how this process was used by Anwar to expand his thinking.

Two-year-old Anwar was watching a neighbor's new pet. He observed that the animal was covered with white fur that had black spots. It had four legs, two eyes and ears, a nose, and a long tail swinging from side to side. As Anwar petted the animal, his father repeated, "Doggie. Pet the doggie gently."

The next day, Anwar and his father were driving past a farm. Anwar saw a black-and-white cow in the field. He pointed and exclaimed, "Doggie! Doggie!" Anwar was using assimilation to try to incorporate something new with what was already familar to him.

"That's a cow," his father explained. "Look how big the cow is."

Anwar was confused. After all, the animal was spotted. It had four legs, two ears and eyes, and a nose. There was even a long, swishing tail at the end.

"Doggie!" he repeated.

Given time and experience, Anwar learned to identify cows. He observed important differences, such as shape, size, and other features, that distinguish a cow from a dog. Through the process of accommodation, Anwar altered his thinking to make the new information fit.

By age two, children begin noticing similarities and differences. They match and sort very simple items that look alike. Children begin to recognize shapes and sizes. For example, many can work a puzzle with four pieces that have different shapes. This abili-

ty is a critical early step that precedes learning to read language symbols.

Toddlers also begin to understand opposite concepts. They start to see the relationship between such terms as hot and cold, hard and soft, and up and down.

Cause and effect continues to hold fascination for them. When playing hide-and-seek games, they become more methodical as they think about where and how to look for the hidden person or object. This means they are learning to solve problems, a complex intellectual skill.

EMOTIONAL DEVELOPMENT

Toddlers are only beginning to develop emotional control. They are still prone to impulsiveness and quick mood swings. You may have heard people talk about the "terrible twos." Some children try adult patience more at this age than at any other. Children may be cheerful one minute and screaming dramatically the next. Understanding what a child may be like and knowing that the stage will pass can make working with children of this age easier.

For the most part, when the basic needs of toddlers are met, they are very pleasant and cooperative. Sudden shifts in mood and behavior are more a result of individual temperament. Problems may stem from frustration. The child is struggling to learn and

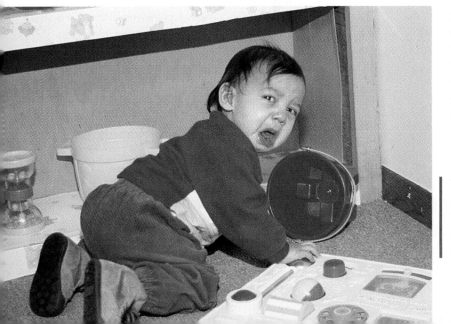

Toddlers are often frustrated by their limited abilities. Parents and other caregivers need to be understanding and patient.

do more, but not all the abilities are present yet. When their grasp of language is inadequate, children may resort to whining and crying. As their language skills improve, toddlers are better able to communicate their wants, needs, and feelings. Some of the frustrations they have are eliminated. They also gradually learn to identify and manage their feelings more appropriately. When there is stability in home life and the caregiving environment, any trying emotional times of the two-year-old stage are likely to subside.

Development of Autonomy

According to Erikson, toddlers are developing a sense of **autonomy** (aw-TAHN-uh-mee), or *independence*. They start to see themselves as separate from their caregivers. They want to be self-governing. Indeed, they need to learn this task in order to overcome doubts about themselves and move forward with their personal development.

You will see children take many opportunities to assert their independence. Frequently they exclaim "No!" to what seems like everything and everyone. They often resist cooperating in routines they used to enjoy, such as eating and bathing. They are sensitive about being bossed, shown, helped, or directed. Doing exactly the opposite of what is wanted happens frequently. If you ask a child of this age to give you something he or she is holding, the child will often run off with the object instead.

By showing patience and offering as many reasonable choices as possible, caregivers can make the progress toward autonomy easier for child and adult alike. Watching them practice their reasoning and decision-making skills can be a fascinating, and even humorous, study.

Appearance of Fears

Looking back on your own childhood, do you recall having fears that were very real but now seem ridiculous and irrational? Perhaps it was water, spiders, or monsters. This is a common experience for toddlers. Their fears may range from storms to birds to being alone in a room. They are often frightened by strange figures dressed up in larger-than-life costumes, such as Santa Claus and the Easter Bunny.

Fear arises for several reasons. Some are very good ones. You wouldn't want children to be unafraid of jumping from a high wall or petting a wild animal. Healthy fear contributes to children's safety.

Fear may develop from lack of experience. For a young child who has never been in a wading pool,

Animals intrigue toddlers but may also frighten them. How are this child's parents handling the situation?

stepping into water a foot deep may be very frightening. Some fears are irrational or stem from misconceptions. Others are learned from other children and adults. For example, Marco's older brother cringed and turned away whenever he saw a spider. What do you think Marco's reaction to spiders was?

For toddlers, some fears are partially a result of intellectual as well as emotional development. As children become more aware of the outside world, they realize they are vulnerable to danger. Life is scarier away from the shelter of the family. In addition to causing fears, this realization can also produce mixed emotions about becoming an independent being.

When fears do arise, toddlers are usually calmed when caregivers are close at hand. Children overcome fears with patience, understanding, and emotional support from caregivers. It often helps to talk with children about fears. If a child fears storms, explain that rain is needed for flowers to grow. If an older child fears climbing, *gradually* introduce the child to different heights on climbing structures. Pushing children to overcome fears all at once usually backfires. It results in a more— and not less—fearful child. Most fears pass with time and experience if handled in a supportive, understanding manner.

Importance of Security

A sense of security continues as a primary emotional need for toddlers. Stable routines and rituals help fulfill this need. As creatures of habit, children feel more secure and relaxed when their daily schedule and environment are reliable and predictable.

Tip
FROM THE
Pros

*T*oddlers find rules and limits especially frustrating. Wherever possible, create a "can-do" environment that encourages children's participation. Use nonbreakable tableware, and allow children to take turns helping to set the table for meals. Let them help sort and put away toys. Such tasks also strengthen intellectual skills.

Only when they experience this sense of security are they free to take chances with exploration. In this way, emotional development affects intellectual development.

SOCIAL DEVELOPMENT

Social development in very young children progresses more slowly than other areas of development. It takes time for children to establish social relationships with *peers* (people their own age) and those who are not primary caregivers.

Beginning at age two, children can participate in groups of up to eight, but only for short periods. They may enjoy group singing for five minutes or listening to a short story with others in a group. The primary focus of social interaction, however, continues to be parents, siblings, and other caregivers. In the child care setting, children are most comfortable sharing time with a caregiver in a small group that includes only two or three children.

At age two, children begin making friends. They often show kindness when someone is hurt or crying. From this age, children increasingly like snuggling with a buddy in a cozy space. Friendships bloom after the age of three.

Play and Social Development

For children, play is the primary mode for interacting with the world. It is their "work." Through play, they stretch their abilities and expand their understanding of concepts. They spend hours poking, prodding, and

How can brief group activities benefit toddlers?

dren. They are interested in other children, but more out of curiosity than a desire to form friendships.

Between twenty-four and about thirty months, children engage in **parallel play**. You will see them *playing near each other but not with each other.* Two children of this age might investigate a toy together at the same time, but each acts independently of the other. A small group of toddlers might all play with the same caregiver at the same time. The interaction, however, is taking place primarily between the caregiver and each separate child, not among the children.

As they approach age three, children gradually begin interacting with other children of about the same age, usually for limited periods of time. Parallel play continues to be their main style of interaction. Two or three children of this age may play dress-up in the same area but only occasionally join in each other's play theme.

Learning Social Rules

Toddlers are beginning to understand the concepts of limits and rules. Not until age

manipulating objects. They engage in delightful banter with caregivers. Play is the best method of learning throughout the early childhood years.

From eighteen to twenty-four months, children still engage mostly in **solitary play**. They *play alone rather than with other chil-*

Let's Pretend

Pretend play and make-believe can make important contributions to the intellectual, social, and emotional development of toddlers. Through make-believe, children practice symbolic thinking. They "see" tea in empty plastic teacups and cookies on empty plates. A sheet

"becomes" a cape or dress. They also learn social skills, even before cooperative play begins. By assuming the roles and feelings of their make-believe characters, children teach themselves empathy. They learn to look beyond themselves and into the lives of others. Pretend

play also satisfies children's emotional need for security by allowing them to be in control. When they "heal" a stuffed animal patient or "teach" a class of dolls, they feel a sense of power and competence not usually experienced in their real lives.

three do these concepts become part of everyday behavior.

By age two, language has developed well enough for caregivers to set a few, very simple rules for children and offer very brief reasons for them. Rules should relate primarily to safety.

Social skills, such as using table manners, sharing, and cooperating, develop slowly. Plenty of opportunities to develop these skills should be provided, but remember that the process is slow. The best way to teach positive social behavior is to provide good examples.

Developing Responsibility

Even at this early age, children are forming a sense of responsibility. You can encourage responsibility (as well as independence) by allowing children to develop **self-help skills.** *These are skills that allow children to help take care of themselves and their personal needs.* Self-help skills that are appropriate for toddlers include getting dressed, putting away toys, washing hands, and brushing teeth.

Responsibility, of course, is more than just self-care. Children need to learn how to take on responsibility as they interact with others too. When approached properly, toddlers take pride in what they do to be helpful. Setting napkins around the table, for example, may seem like a small job to you, but a two-year-old takes it seriously and is proud when given recognition for the accomplishment. If the napkins are crooked, that doesn't matter. Adults have to react with sensitivity. Self-esteem grows when you say something like "Chelsea put the napkins on the table all by herself." Self-esteem suffers when you do the job over again because it isn't up to adult standards.

A patient adult takes the time needed to encourage responsibility. When children become responsible for themselves and learn to be helpful to others, they develop a sense of belonging and importance. Thus, social development contributes to emotional development.

A NOTE OF UNDERSTANDING

*T*oddlers may seem like human bundles of contradictions. For every time they are cheerful, spontaneous, enthusiastic, and helpful, there is likely to be a time when they are negative, argumentative, and obstinate. Knowing how they grow can help you understand their moods and behavior. You can then help them deal with the challenges of this stage, channel their budding abilities, and take a positive step toward maturity.

Learning self-help skills can build a toddler's self-esteem. Think about how you might go about teaching one specific skill. How could you make it fun to learn?

Chapter 5 Review

Chapter Summary

- The rate of physical growth for toddlers slows.
- Curiosity fosters intellectual development.
- Toddlers can remember actual events, and they have an increasing attention span.
- Symbolic thinking, creativity, and imagination are important intellectual developments that begin at this age.
- Toddlers strive to develop autonomy.
- Seemingly irrational fears are common to toddlers.
- Toddlers need a sense of security.
- Toddlers engage in solitary and parallel play.
- Children this age can begin to understand simple rules and to develop a sense of responsibility.

Reviewing the Facts

1. Give the age at which the average child is likely to do each of the following: (a) begin to climb; (b) pedal a tricycle; (c) stack three blocks; (d) stack eight blocks; (e) scribble with a crayon; (f) turn a doorknob.
2. What three things must occur before a child can be expected to learn to be toilet trained? At what age do children become toilet trained?
3. What is attention span? Identify three factors that affect attention span.
4. What is symbolic thinking? Explain how symbolic thinking is related to play toddlers enjoy.
5. Explain why a toddler might say "doggie" when looking at a cat.
6. What is autonomy? Describe the behavior of a child who is trying to achieve autonomy.
7. What types of fears do toddlers experience? What are some possible causes of these fears? Should they be made to face their fears? Why or why not?
8. What can be done to help give toddlers a sense of security?
9. Describe solitary and parallel play.
10. How can you help a toddler develop a sense of responsibility?

Thinking Critically

1. How might newfound mobility affect a toddler's intellectual growth? What about social growth?
2. Using terms that you have learned in this chapter, explain what is happening when a toddler sees a water tower from the car window and calls it a balloon.
3. Why might a two-year-old have feelings of frustration? What behavior might display this sense of frustration?
4. What choices would you allow children to make concerning what they eat, what they wear, and what activities they pursue?
5. Suggest two rules you might set for toddlers. What reasons for obeying these rules would you give them?

Activities and Applications

1. **Handling Curiosity.** Write five "why" questions two-year-olds might ask and five responses that would satisfy their curiosity.
2. **Understanding Fears.** Imagine you are a two-year-old encountering a

new situation, such as starting day care or meeting a large dog. Write a paragraph describing your fears and anxieties from a child's viewpoint.

3. **Categorizing Toys.** Using a toy catalog or advertisements, make a list of those that would help develop gross motor skills and fine motor skills. If you wish, create a poster for each type.

SCHOOL TO WORK

Your Professional Portfolio

Begin a glossary of terms that you want to learn and remember for use in your work with children. Start with selected vocabulary terms from this unit of the text. Include definitions and examples of how the terms are used. Add to the glossary as your study continues, using terms from the text and from other sources. If possible, keep your work in a computer file that can be regularly updated. Place the glossary in your portfolio.

Observing and Analyzing

Toddlers—An Observation Challenge

Observing busy, energetic toddlers can be a challenge, especially when you are watching a group of them all at once. The challenge is worth taking, however, because the physical activity of toddlers can teach you much about overall development. Try these observation ideas in order to discover more about toddlers:

- **Attention Span.** How long can a toddler stay focused on one activity? In order to observe attention span in toddlers, don't observe the entire group. Instead, choose three toddlers, one who is barely walking, one who has some mastery of walking, and one who is taller and heavier than most of the others. At a designated time when all three are in the same area, record what activity each one has selected and how long each child stays at each activity. Continue to follow the same three toddlers for an hour, if possible. Which activities held their attention for the longest amount of time, and why?

- **Sleep/Awake Comparison.** In a program that includes infants (not yet walking), observe and record the sleep/awake hours of three infants of about the same age. Then do the same for three toddlers. The differences between the two groups will be more obvious if they are least a year apart. Compare the information. What similarities and differences are there between the two groups' sleep/awake patterns?

- **Self-Help Skills.** Mealtime provides an excellent opportunity to observe infants' and toddlers' attempts at self-help skills, however messy. Take notes on their abilities in these areas: eating with fingers, holding utensils, holding a cup, "fingerpainting" with food, and any other self-help skills attempted. How are these early attempts handled by the caregiver? Is the child encouraged to continue or immediately cleaned up? Which is the better solution? What progress do you see from infancy to toddlerhood?

Chapter 6

Understanding Preschoolers

CHAPTER OBJECTIVES

- Identify signs of preschoolers' physical, intellectual, emotional, social, and moral development.

- Describe what children understand in Piaget's preoperational period of intellectual development.

- Explain how caregivers should react when preschoolers stutter or make grammar and pronunciation mistakes.

- Explain the role of accomplishment in developing a preschooler's self-esteem.

Terms to Learn

- centration
- classification
- conscience
- conservation
- cooperative play
- dramatic play
- empathy
- gender identity
- initiative
- one-to-one correspondence
- preschoolers
- rational counting
- rote counting
- seriation
- stereotype

omorrow I go to kindergarten," Zachariah proudly announced to his preschool teacher.

"It won't be long, Zack," Sheri Morrison responded casually, "but not tomorrow. You have to finish preschool first. When summer is over, you can go to kindergarten."

Zack looked concerned. "But it's my birthday tomorrow. I want to go to school with my sister," he said with frustration. "My mother said I could."

Mrs. Morrison looked at Zack for a long moment. She wondered why he was so sure about this. "Zack," she said gently, "why do you think you should go to kindergarten tomorrow?"

"It's my birthday tomorrow," Zack repeated impatiently. "I'll be five. My mother told me I could go to kindergarten when I'm five."

Mrs. Morrison held back the amusement she felt. She placed her hand on Zack's shoulder. "Come over here, Zack. Let's look at the calendar and see if we can find the day when kindergarten begins. I think you will still be five when that day comes. That's going to be a special day, isn't it? What do you think it will be like?"

Distracted from his concerns, Zack followed Mrs. Morrison to the calendar. He did wonder what it would be like. Maybe Mrs. Morrison would tell him.

THE PRESCHOOL AGE

By the time children reach preschool age, they have learned so much, yet the process has only just begun. Much more development is ahead. Anyone who works with preschoolers will tell you that surprises are an everyday occurrence. Preschoolers haven't figured everything out yet, but like Zack, they are trying. This quality alone can make them refreshing, amusing, and exciting to be around.

Children three, four, and five years old are commonly referred to as **preschoolers**. This term tells you something about children of this age. They are getting ready to learn and interact with others in a school setting. The physical, intellectual, emotional, social, and moral development children experience during the preschool years is necessary for success both in and out of the classroom.

PHYSICAL DEVELOPMENT

Physical growth during the preschool years is slow and gradual, which keeps the appetite small. The chart on page 112 shows the average heights and weights of children at different preschool ages. Because preschoolers consume such small amounts, making sure that what they eat is healthful is essential. Adequate vitamins, minerals, and other nutrients are needed.

By their fourth year, preschoolers show obvious physical differences from toddlers. How do these changes in height, weight, proportion, and posture influence physical abilities?

As children of this age grow, their bodies appear less baby-like. Body fat is reduced, and most growth occurs in the muscles and bones. Posture becomes erect. The neck lengthens, the shoulders widen and flatten, and the once protruding stomach flattens as well. Legs become proportionally longer.

Motor Development

Preschoolers grow increasingly active as new physical and motor abilities rapidly emerge. These skills gradually become refined and complex. By age five, preschoolers can run fast and powerfully and can balance when walking on a beam.

Each year, physical skills develop more fully. Three-year-olds ride tricycles. Five-year-olds can usually ride bicycles. At three, children like to move and sway to music. By five, they can learn specific rhythms and dances. A three-year-old can throw a ball. A five-year-old can also catch a ball.

Preschoolers have mastered control of their bodies, so they can move in a variety of

Average Heights and Weights of Preschoolers

AGE	HEIGHT	WEIGHT
Three years	38 in. (96.5 cm)	32 lbs. (14.5 kg)
Four years	41 in. (104 cm)	36 lbs. (16 kg)
Five years	44 in. (112 cm)	41 lbs. (18.6 kg)

What skills are needed for a preschooler to successfully master climbing equipment?

ways. They hop, gallop, and run. They zigzag while running and change directions with increasing ease. Climbing is a favorite activity of preschoolers. The older they become, the more challenging the structures they try to climb.

Perceptual Motor Development

Preschoolers become more skilled in eye-hand coordination and fine motor skills. Three-year-olds learn to use crayons and paintbrushes to create pictures. By five, they can draw and paint letters and shapes too. These are important first steps in learning to read and write. Other activities that develop perceptual motor skills include simple cooking tasks. For example, they can help spread peanut butter on vegetables. An enjoyable woodworking skill for a preschooler is pounding nails.

Preschoolers learn to coordinate what they see with the use of their hands. They see the shape of a puzzle piece, look for the shape on the puzzle, and then move the piece with hands and fingers until it fits into the right place. This is perceptual motor development.

INTELLECTUAL DEVELOPMENT

During the preschool years, children's intellectual abilities also become more refined and complex. Attention span lengthens. Children gradually develop more elaborate thought processes.

The Preoperational Period

Although Piaget's preoperational period began during the toddler years, by the time children are preschoolers, the characteristics of this period are much more evident. With their increasing ability to think symbolically, children readily add new concepts to their understanding.

Classification and Centration

Preschoolers are beginning to learn **classification**. They can *mentally group objects into categories according to similarities.* Thus, they can separate a mixed set of cards with pictures of cats and dogs into two smaller groups of just cats and just dogs.

Preoperational thought, however, limits children to *focusing on only one characteristic at a time,* what Piaget termed **centration**. Younger preschool children, for example, can sort objects by color alone. They can find all the red items in a group of toy cars, trucks, and airplanes. Not until children are almost six can they pick out only the red cars. Considering two characteristics at once is very hard for preschoolers.

Seriation

Around age five, children begin to become capable of **seriation**, *organizing objects according to increasing or decreasing size.* As with classification, their understanding is very limited. If you give a three-year-old ten blocks and say, "Line these up from biggest to smallest," the child may put a large block beside one of the smallest ones. The child will not be able to see the relationship between the sizes of all ten blocks for several more years.

Sorting by only one characteristic, such as color, is typical of preschoolers. Later, around age six, they learn to sort by two qualities.

Numbers and Counting

Children in the preoperational period are just beginning to understand numbers and counting. Often two-year-olds are capable of **rote counting**—*reciting numbers in order without understanding that each number represents a specific amount.* If asked to bring three balls, a child who could only count by rote might bring one ball or ten balls. When counting by rote, preschoolers may count some objects more than once and some not at all.

The understanding that, when counting objects in a group, each item is counted once and only once is called **one-to-one correspondence.** Children must comprehend this mathematical concept before they can count accurately. When one-to-one correspondence is grasped, **rational counting**—*the understanding that the last number counted in a group represents the entire number of objects*—is possible.

Preschool children also have difficulty with the idea of time. While they may have learned the difference between "now" and "later," more detailed concepts are too abstract for their limited understanding.

Conservation

A preschooler's understanding is limited by what is seen, making some concepts difficult to grasp. Note how this is illustrated by the following description of what happened when four-year-old Maya tried to interpret what she saw.

Maya was watching as Chantal poured equal amounts of juice into identical glasses for Maya and her twin brother Angel. Since the children were going to take their drinks outside, Chantal decided to pour the juice into plastic cups. Chantal poured Maya's serving into a shorter, wider cup and Angel's into a taller, skinny one. When Chantal handed the children their juice, Maya looked inside the cups and asked, "Why does Angel get more than I do?"

Although she had seen that their servings were equal before, *now* Angel seemed to be getting more because the juice line was higher in his glass. Even if Chantal had poured the juice back into the original glasses, Maya probably would still not have understood that the amount of juice remained constant regardless of which glasses were used. *The understanding that an object's physical dimensions remain the same even when its appearance changes* was termed **conservation** by Piaget. This concept is beyond children in the preoperational period.

Development of Language

Scientists are not completely sure how language is acquired. Language expert Noam Chomsky believes part of the human brain is specially designed to learn language. Provided the brain has developed properly, children then learn their native language from their environment. They are quickly praised by adults for first making sounds, then words, and finally sentences.

With this encouragement and reinforcement, language blossoms during the preschool years. The average three-year-old has a vocabulary of 300 words. Four-year-olds speak about 1500 different words. By five years of age, an average child speaks 2200 words. As with most age groups, preschool children understand more words than they can speak. Language also becomes more expressive during the preschool years. Children use facial expressions, tone of voice, and more gestures to convey meaning. The language of older preschoolers can be surprisingly similar to that of adults.

Children develop language ability more quickly when provided with good examples. Talking and reading to children daily helps them expand their language use and comprehension. For instance, a three-year-old may simply say, "My ball." An adult can

Preschoolers use facial expressions both unconsciously and on purpose. In both situations, they give clues to what a child is feeling or thinking.

encourage more complex language by responding, "Yes, that is your big, red ball. Show me how you can bounce the ball." Children should be encouraged to ask questions and tell stories or jokes.

Grammar and Pronunciation

Gradually, children learn rules for grammar and pronunciation. This often causes some confusion. When Ashley was three, for example, she tried to form plurals in the best way she could. Since she commonly heard "s" on the ends of words

From the Mouths of Babes

*L*anguage development involves more than learning new words. It is also learning the effect of those words. Children quickly discover that using certain words and phrases produces a desired response in others, especially adults. They don't necessarily understand what they are saying, but they enjoy the attention it brings them.

If adults laugh when children use obscene language, the children interpret the response as approval. They don't recognize the crudeness of their own words. The same principle applies when children say "I hate you!" if someone makes them angry. They don't truly hate, but the forceful-

ness of that word produces a strong reaction. It gets the adult's attention.

In neither instance is the child misbehaving. Both cases are the result of partial development. The child has learned the power of language itself before understanding the specific words.

that were made plural, she used this knowledge to form the plural of the word "foot." She referred to her feet as "foots." Later, as she became more aware of the exceptions to the rules, her "foots" became "feet."

When working with children, be careful how you handle their grammar and pronunciation mistakes. Criticism hurts them. Since children learn by hearing, casually rephrase the child's statement to provide the correct model and continue the conversation. Focusing on content rather than on grammar or speech mechanics encourages children to use language. In turn, language usage promotes development.

Stuttering

During the preschool years, most children learn to speak clearly; however, mispronunciation of some sounds is to be expected. Some preschoolers have problems with stuttering. They may leave long pauses between words or repeat a sound or word many times before continuing a sentence. This is not "true" stuttering. It is the natural result when thinking ability exceeds speaking ability. Once speaking abilities catch up with thinking abilities, this speech pattern usually subsides. By not making an issue of it, caregivers preserve the child's self-esteem. If children stutter past age six or seven, they are usually referred to a speech therapist for evaluation.

EMOTIONAL DEVELOPMENT

Preschoolers experience an increasing range of emotions, including loneliness, disappointment, anticipation, and sympathy. Development of language helps preschoolers identify their many new feelings.

Better control over feelings is a positive achievement that occurs during the preschool years. With increasing language skills, preschoolers are able to identify feelings and vent their emotions appropriately with words, rather than by hitting or pushing. Emotional self-control leads to more cooperative social behavior.

In what ways does reading to young children encourage development?

Friendships help preschoolers become less egocentric. They begin to be able to see things from another person's perspective.

Though often self-centered, preschool children begin to develop **empathy**. *This is the ability to recognize and understand the feelings of others.* Preschool children begin to help others without expecting a reward. This emotional development paves the way for making friends, fostering further social development.

Preschoolers may still have a variety of fears. Most of these will pass with time and more experience.

Development of Self-Esteem

Around the preschool age, feelings of self-esteem become more distinct. Preschoolers' self-esteem comes largely from their pride in the physical and intellectual skills they have worked so hard to achieve. They often ask for attention when climbing, running, or hopping. "Teacher, see what I can do!" is frequently heard in a child care center. Preschoolers also enjoy demonstrating their intellectual skills. They may name the colors they see or recite the alphabet repeatedly.

Tip
F R O M   T H E
Pros

*M*any preschoolers cope with fears and insecurities, by clinging to *items of attachment.* These objects provide a feeling of familiarity and stability. You may want to allow children to bring a favorite toy or a "security blanket" into the child care setting if they want to. By respecting this need, you contribute to their comfort. Most children give up the attachment as they grow more confident and socially skilled.

Building Professional Skills

Patience

WHAT IS PATIENCE?

Patience is the willingness to tolerate a trying situation. Sometimes it is simply the willingness to wait for a desired event. When you are patient, you can put aside your own concerns for the moment in order to do what needs to be done first. A patient person sees that some things are more important even though other options might be more personally satisfying.

Patience in Action

Valeska was ready to bake muffins for the children in her family day care home. It was early in the morning and, so far, only four-year-old Jamie had arrived for the day. Jamie was eager to help bake.

"I can do that!" Jamie exclaimed as Valeska began measuring the flour.

"Okay," Valeska agreed. She held the measuring cup while Jamie slowly, carefully filled it by the scoopful with flour.

"Let me!" Jamie cried when Valeska started to mix the ingredients. Valeska glanced at the clock as she watched Jamie stir the mixture in the bowl with awkward but determined strokes. The other children would start arriving soon. After a few stirs, she gently took the mixing spoon from Jamie. "I think you've about got it," she said.

"What else can I do?" Jamie begged.

Feeling a bit rushed, Valeska reached for the box of colorful, paper baking cups and handed a small stack to Jamie. "Here. You can put these in the pan for me," she said, showing Jamie how to do the first one.

Jamie set to work, carefully separating and placing the cups in the muffin pan. As Valeska watched, she noticed that the little girl was deliberately placing cups of the same color in individual rows. She had a row for each of the pink, blue, and green cups.

"That's very good, Jamie," Valeska told her, smiling. She pulled a silver baking cup from the box. "You're a very helpful assistant. I think we'll let you fill this cup with batter to make a special muffin just for you."

Your Analysis

1. How would you describe Valeska's ability to be patient? Give two examples that show patience.

2. How might an impatient person have reacted to Jamie?

3. What effects would an impatient approach have had on Jamie? How do you think Valeska's approach affected Jamie?

4. Why do you think patience is an important quality in a child care professional?

5. Why is it sometimes difficult for adults to be patient with children?

6. Are you a patient person? How might you go about making any necessary improvements?

Self-esteem also increases as preschoolers develop their self-help skills. They like to take care of themselves and their personal needs. Preschoolers want to "do it myself." Three-year-olds can begin lacing shoes. With practice, five-year-olds can tie them. By four, children are efficient at dressing themselves. Four-year-olds can eat neatly and use proper manners.

As the list of accomplishments grows for preschoolers, they are excited by the feelings of independence and self-worth that result. According to Erikson, these feelings give rise to a sense of **initiative** (ih-NIH-shuh-tiv)—*motivation to accomplish more.* Children feel good about what they learn to do and therefore try to accomplish more in order to increase the good feelings. As a result, preschoolers are very willing to be helpful. They especially like contributing to the group. In the classroom, they can pick up toys, water plants, set the table, feed animals, and help pass out name cards.

SOCIAL DEVELOPMENT

Before the preschool years, most social interactions for children are centered around adults. By three years of age, peers increase in importance.

The Role of Play

Three-year-olds like to play in small groups of two or three. By five, children enjoy playing in groups of five to eight. Through play, preschoolers develop social skills. They learn to get along and trade with each other. They gain the willingness to give in a little in order to reach compromises. They can also negotiate, or bargain, for what they want. Preschoolers become more comfortable joining in activities with others and suggesting their own. They learn to capture other children's interests with their play

Learning self-help skills, such as lacing and tying shoes, boosts a child's self-esteem. What physical and intellectual skills are necessary for lacing and tying?

Conflicts occur frequently among preschoolers. Use good judgment in deciding whether and how to intervene.

ideas. This enables them to engage in **cooperative play**—*playing together and agreeing on play themes and activities.*

When given many opportunities to play, children become skilled in forming relationships. Learning how to form relationships helps children create a support system of friends during all stages of life.

Forming Friendships

By four, children begin to form close friendships with one or two other children, whom they refer to as their "best friends." By five years of age, children form close-knit groups of preferred playmates. They can be cruel in their rejection of anyone who is not in their "group."

Preschoolers often "bribe" other children into friendship. A child might offer to let another child play with a favorite toy on the condition that they become best friends. These friendships are usually temporary. Preschoolers may have a different "best friend" every day of the week. After age six, friendships become more stable.

Dealing with Conflict

When conflicts arise between preschoolers, it is often over toys or personal property. Preschoolers can be very territorial. Children in group care often need to be reminded of which toys are the program's and which belong to individuals. When children are allowed to bring personal items

What are the benefits of dramatic play? How can adults encourage dramatic play activities?

from home, caregivers may ask that they bring only items that are easily shared, such as books and tapes. Individuals who have trouble sharing are often asked to keep personal belongings in their own private storage space so that disagreements don't occur.

Around four or five years of age, some children begin to use name-calling. They often direct silly, crude, or hurtful names at others. Some of this can be ignored by adults. If it becomes too frequent or intense, however, caregivers should firmly tell children that name-calling will not be allowed because it hurts people's feelings. In addition, caregivers themselves must be good role models by never calling children names.

Development of Identity

Around age three, children begin to notice that boys and girls are physically different. This is the beginning of **gender identity**, *the awareness of being male or female.* A person's appreciation for his or her own gender is an important part of good emotional health, including the development of self-esteem.

One way children develop gender identity is through **dramatic play**, *the imitation of real-life situations.* They might play house or play school. During dramatic play, children often pretend to be adults. Through this type of play, children learn about themselves as well as about others. Dramatic play allows them to explore the wide range of roles and careers that grown men and women have. Seeing both women and men in caregiving roles further emphasizes this lesson.

Preschoolers also become aware of differences in racial and ethnic backgrounds. They need to take pride in their own heritage and respect the heritage of others. These attitudes are encouraged when books, posters, music, and foods in the program represent many different cultures. It is also helpful if caregivers are from different cultural backgrounds.

Gender and racial stereotypes do not belong in any early childhood program, or anywhere else, for that matter. A **stereotype** is *a preset idea about a person or group of people based solely on one characteristic, such as gender, nationality, race, or religion.* A stereotype may be true of a few people in the group, but it is not true of all. For example, saying that all blondes are dumb is simply not true. Moreover, such statements can be hurtful. In addition, the statements often affect the thinking and attitudes of people. When stereotyping is not allowed, children can feel proud of who they are and more confident about developing their potential.

MORAL DEVELOPMENT

*C*hildren aged four and under have no real sense of right or wrong. They choose some actions and avoid others based on the understanding of consequences. They drink their juice because it makes a parent happy. They don't hit others because it results in punishment.

By age five, children begin developing a **conscience** (KAHNT-shunts). This means

they start to form *attitudes about right and wrong that guide their behavior.* They continue to base behavior on consequences; however, they also experience feelings of guilt when they believe they have behaved inappropriately or displeased an adult. Preschoolers can be very serious about right and wrong. They eagerly tell an adult whenever they see someone break a rule.

THE NEXT STEP

*G*rowth in the preschool years is dramatic and exciting. As preschoolers become more mobile, as their vocabulary grows, as they learn to play with others, they can no longer be called "babies." They are in fact ready for the next major step in life: the beginning of formal education.

THE MULTICULTURAL CLASSROOM

*A*t the preschool age, children are beginning to recognize similarities and differences and are very curious about things that are new to them. This is the ideal time to integrate activities with a cultural theme into the curriculum. Here are some ideas for ongoing, not just occasional, use:

- **Dress-Up Clothing.** Find sources of clothing, shoes, hats, and accessories that represent different cultures. You might receive donations from religious organizations and cultural centers. Also check thrift shops and catalogs.

- **Housekeeping Corner.** Supply an assortment of ethnic cooking tools. Include ethnic food containers, as long as they are safe for play. Plastic repli-

cas of ethnic foods can be obtained from some school supply companies.

- **Doll Area.** Handmade and store-bought dolls should represent many cultures and have appropriate clothing. Include male and female dolls. Dolls that depict older as well as younger ages add to dramatic play too.

- **Books and Music.** Sources for books and music are the public library, community cultural centers, early childhood organization chapters, and school supply catalogues. A travel agency might be a good resource for some items, including posters and brochures. By circulating the collection between classrooms, a limited budget can be stretched.

Chapter 6 Review

Chapter Summary

- Growth rate is slow and gradual during the preschool years.
- Motor development improves during the preschool years. Perceptual motor skills are also becoming more refined.
- Piaget described preschoolers' intellectual development as the pre-operational period.
- Preschoolers rapidly expand their vocabulary and expressive language skills.
- Preschoolers have better control over their emotions. They may still have a variety of fears.
- Self-help skills and other physical, as well as intellectual, accomplishments enhance preschoolers' self-esteem.
- Play is important to social development.
- Social development includes the ability to make friends, keep friends, and deal with conflicts with peers.
- Preschoolers are developing a sense of gender, racial, and ethnic identity.
- Preschoolers begin to develop a conscience.

Reviewing the Facts

1. Give three examples of how a preschool child's physical abilities develop from age three to five.
2. Describe the characteristics of the preoperational period of intellectual development.
3. How should you handle children's grammar and pronunciation mistakes?
4. Describe the type of stuttering that is common in many preschoolers. What is usually the cause of their stuttering?
5. What is empathy? How does this emotional development affect social development?
6. What is initiative? Why does Erikson believe preschoolers strive to develop initiative?
7. Describe the relationship between children's self-esteem and their physical and intellectual accomplishments.
8. What is cooperative play?
9. What is gender identity? Describe how children often develop gender identity.
10. What is a conscience? At what age does it begin to develop a conscience?

Thinking Critically

1. Why might caregivers tend to discourage preschoolers from learning self-help skills?
2. Should preschoolers be discouraged from bribing other children into friendship? From accepting such an offer? Explain your answer.
3. Do you think preschoolers should be allowed to resolve some conflicts among themselves, without adult intervention? Is so, what types of conflict? If not, why not?
4. What type of environment encourages initiative in preschoolers? What activities are provided? What other traits are promoted? What is the attitude of caregivers?
5. Do you think caregivers might promote stereotypes without realizing? Explain.

Activities and Applications

1. **Friendship.** Question several five-year-olds about friendship. Ask them to define "friend." Have them tell what they

think a good friend is and does. Write a paragraph that summarizes your findings.

2. **Moral Development.** With a partner, write a skit in which a five-year-old must make a moral decision commonly faced by preschoolers. Have the character describe his or her feelings, thoughts, and reasoning as the decision is made about what to do.

SCHOOL TO WORK

Your Professional Portfolio

Begin to accumulate a list of outstanding children's books that you would like to use if you work with children someday. Read and review the books as you add them to your list. Use suggestions from librarians, your instructor, and other sources to get your list started. Keep the list in your portfolio and develop it as you complete this course.

Observing and Analyzing

Observing the Preschool Child

Once children reach the preschool age, observing becomes even more interesting. Language skills have developed to a level that is easily understood by most observers. The following observation ideas will help you focus on some of the preschooler's growth achievements:

- **Dramatic Play.** The area of the center that is used for dramatic play or housekeeping can be an ideal place to get well acquainted with preschoolers. While staying within hearing range but as much out of sight as possible, observe the roles children play. Listen carefully to what they say. How do the youngest play and interact in this area? How is the play of the older children different?
- **Preoperational Stage.** Find an opportunity to observe preschoolers while they are using molding clay. The teacher gives all of the children fairly equal amounts. Do any of the children ask for more in order to have as much as another child? When the children start to roll, pound, and create objects from their clay, listen carefully to their comments about who has the most and the least. What other activities are available for developing the principle of conservation?
- **Perceptual Motor Development.** Look at the drawings done by a group of three- to five-year-olds. Record some of the details you notice, especially of people. Look for facial expressions, fingers, necks, clothing, and body proportions. What details distinguish the drawings of a three-year-old from those of a five-year-old?

Chapter 7

Understanding
School-Age
Children

CHAPTER OBJECTIVES

- Describe the physical and intellectual development of school-age children.

- Explain how improved motor and perceptual motor skills influence school-age children's activities.

- Analyze the impact of puberty, self-esteem, competition, fear, stress, and rules on school-age children.

- Compare and contrast friendship among preschoolers to that of school-age children.

Terms to Learn

- concrete operations period
- depth perception
- diversity
- growth plateau
- hormones
- industry
- inferiority
- puberty
- school-age children
- stress

Approaching Whittier Elementary School for an orientation meeting, Marc Caruso saw that he'd arrived during recess. Next semester he would be a student teacher at the school, and he was about to learn more about his assignment. Even before he could see the playground, he could hear the sound of children.

"Bet I can run faster than you!"

"Oh, Brian, you're such a show-off!"

"Aileen, want to come over after school tonight?"

As he rounded the corner of the building, Marc saw a display of energy and emotion. A group of girls and boys played a boisterous soccer match on a grassy field. Three children went for the ball at once and sprawled in a shrieking, giggling tangle of legs. At the basketball hoop, four children dribbled, passed, and shot the ball, while a fifth "announced" the game into his fist. On the swings, three children sat close together, heads hung in solemn conversation. One girl reached toward the girl in the center and hugged her around the shoulders. The girl in the center began to smile and wipe her eyes.

Marc took a deep breath. As a young teacher-to-be, he was filled with a range of emotions: excitement, enthusiasm, uncertainty, caring. "From the looks of it," he thought to himself, "I'm not the only one."

THE SCHOOL-AGE YEARS

Whether on the playground or anywhere else, school-age children are an interesting mixture of emotions and energy. Working with them presents new challenges.

As with any age group, you need to understand school-age children in order to work well with them. **School-age children** *include a wide range of ages, from six to twelve.* Because children change so much during those years, it helps to break the ages down for discussion. In this text, school-age means children who are six to ten. References to older children means eleven to twelve.

Development Continues

Imagine that you are hiking up a steep and winding trail. Halfway to the end you start to feel winded. You slow your pace for a while to replenish your energy reserves and then push off again with renewed vigor. The school-age years are similar. After a half-dozen years of rapid growth, school-age children ease off the pace. Physically, they level off before the final surge toward maturity. Socially, they strengthen friendships. Intellectually, emotionally, and morally, they begin to feel the expectation to act more like adults than children. Even more than in other stages of life, growth in school-age children points to greater development to come.

PHYSICAL DEVELOPMENT

*Y*ounger school-age children are in a **growth plateau.** They have reached *a period of relatively slow and steady growth.* Children in this age range continue to build muscles and bone and to develop a longer, leaner appearance.

The chart below shows approximate heights and weights for children from ages six to eight. Throughout this period, boys are a little heavier than girls. By age eight, however, girls catch up with boys' weights.

At five or six years of age, children begin losing their baby teeth. Gaps left by missing teeth may temporarily affect speech, causing some children to lisp—"s" and "z" may sound like "th." By ten, these children have many of their adult teeth.

Signs of Puberty

Around age twelve (slightly younger for girls), children undergo a surge of growth. This marks the beginning of a new, even more dramatic kind of physical development, a transition stage of life. Older chil-

Compared with infants and toddlers, school-age children grow more slowly. Individual children of the same age can still vary significantly in size.

Average Heights and Weights of Six- to Eight-Year-Olds

AGE	HEIGHT	WEIGHT
Six Years	46 in. (117 cm)	45 lbs. (20.4 kg)
Seven Years	48 in. (122 cm)	50 lbs. (22.7 kg)
Eight Years	50 in. (127 cm)	55 lbs. (25 kg)

Nutrition and the School-Age Child

Getting proper nutrition can be a challenge for school-age children. Most children who have been taught healthful eating habits continue to follow them. However, a number of factors in their increasingly independent lives begin to present obstacles.

Television viewing can be a problem. Watching television encourages an inactive lifestyle. Also, foods advertised during children's programming tend to be high in sugar, fat, and sodium but low in other nutrients. These factors contribute to childhood obesity. Obesity is defined as being 20 percent or more over a healthful weight. In children, it is linked with heart and respiratory disease, diabetes, and poor self-esteem. The number of obese children in the United States has increased by 50 percent in the last 20 years.

Active children, too, may have poor eating habits. They may become so involved with school, friends, and other interests that they do not make time for nutritious eating and end up "eating on the run." Their food choices then tend to be limited and not always healthful.

A small number of school-age children suffer from eating disorders. These are caused in part by society's emphasis on thinness as a desirable quality and partly by anxieties over growing up.

Children with eating disorders often resort to starving themselves or forcing themselves to vomit after meals in order to lose or avoid gaining weight. Young athletes, especially gymnasts and wrestlers, may be encouraged to diet to stay small or to compete in a particular weight class.

Caregivers have less control over what school-age children eat, but they can still help children make nutritious food choices. They can teach young children healthful eating habits. They can also be careful of the messages they send children about food, eating, and dieting.

---

dren end childhood and begin **puberty**, *a stage when boys and girls undergo a series of physical changes and begin to develop into men and women who are able to reproduce.* Puberty is the result of an increase in **hormones**, *growth-regulating chemicals that are produced by the body and carried in the blood.* Puberty leads to adulthood.

Girls may experience the onset of puberty six months to a year younger than boys. Hormones that cause girls to menstruate begin to be secreted, usually around ages ten to twelve but sometimes as late as age fourteen. Girls begin to weigh more than boys as their body fat increases slightly. This is normal and healthy for girls during puberty. At this time, it is not unusual for girls to pass up boys in height as well.

Once boys are well into puberty, their heights and weights surpass those of girls. Boys develop more muscle tissue, which adds considerable weight. The growth of facial hair is another development. Also as a result of male hormone production, boys experience a change in their voices. Their voices may frequently "crack" or sound squeaky until permanently lowering in pitch.

A Sense of Humor

WHAT IS A SENSE OF HUMOR?

Having a sense of humor lets you see the lighter side of a situation. You still recognize problems, and you know when a serious approach is needed. At the same time, you realize that many problems are less threatening and easier to deal with when you can find a way to laugh about them.

A Sense of Humor in Action

"I hate my nose!"

"I'll never be as tall as the other boys."

"Why can't I be pretty like my sister?"

Every day, Gwen heard self-critical remarks like these from her sixth-graders. She wished she could make them understand that what they were experiencing was only temporary. Eventually their bodies would grow in all the ways they were supposed to. Not everyone would be as tall or as pretty as each would like, but that didn't matter either.

One day Gwen came to class with bright orange hair and a big red nose. Two of her teeth appeared to be missing, and a wart had sprung up on her face overnight. She wore enormous shoes, a green-and-blue plaid skirt, and a purple blouse.

At first the students greeted her with stunned silence; a few began to giggle.

"What are you looking at?" she asked innocently.

"You look . . . funny," said one.

"You look *weird*," corrected another.

"Oh?" Gwen acted surprised. She sat on her desk and raised her oversized feet. "I rather like the way I look."

They started talking then about appearances, and why people look as they do, and what makes some people unhappy with their looks.

"Does it really matter whether I have orange hair—" she pulled off the wig—"or brown? Does it make me a better teacher? Or a better person?" Her eyes met a room full of smiling, understanding faces. She smiled back.

"Whatever they learn this year," she thought, "nothing else could be more important."

Your Analysis

1. How did Gwen show a sense of humor in dealing with this problem?

2. What might have been some consequences if Gwen had tried to discuss the matter seriously? Do you think a serious approach would have been more effective or less? Explain your answer.

3. Might there be negative consequences of looking at a problem humorously? If so, explain what these might be.

4. Describe a time when you faced a problem with humor.

For both boys and girls, the high level of hormone production during puberty can cause intense mood swings. Also, new oils are produced that can lead to acne, oily hair, and body odor. Older school-age children must pay extra attention to hygiene and grooming.

Motor Development

School-age children perfect the skills they need for body control. Large muscles now work in unison, improving coordination. By age ten, all types of gross motor movement, such as galloping and leaping, are possible. School-age children often like to challenge their bodies with daring feats of climbing and risk taking.

Control over small muscles is most often fully achieved by age seven or eight. Their ability to control muscles in the wrists, hands, and fingers enables children to handle writing instruments, a skill they need for school participation. Playing a musical instrument also requires the control of these small muscles.

As both genders experience increased muscle strength and coordination, as well as improved perceptual motor skills, they become more involved in team games and sports. These activities require quick movements, coordination of the body, and **depth perception**, *the ability to judge distance and see objects in perspective.* With perceptual motor development come many new opportunities to challenge the body. Younger school-age children can learn to skate, play T-ball, and snow ski. By ages eight to ten, many can play hockey, dodge ball, and baseball with skill.

Both genders participate in rough and tumble play, but you may notice that more boys choose this type of play. After eight to ten years of age, girls may be as active in sports as boys, but many do not roughhouse as much. Caregivers need to be cautious

Sports both require motor skills and improve them. What motor skills are needed to play baseball?

about pushing children into activities that are traditionally considered "male" or "female." Children will be happier when they are allowed to pursue hobbies and interests that suit their personalities rather than gender stereotypes.

INTELLECTUAL DEVELOPMENT

*T*he ability to create, analyze, and evaluate ideas progresses rapidly during the school-age years. According to Piaget, school-age children are no longer bound to learning through their senses, as were preschool children in the preoperational period of development. They are now in what Piaget termed the **concrete operations period** of development. *This is a period of intellectual development during which children (ages seven to eleven) think logically. In other words, they use valid reasoning to think things through. They relate logic to actual objects and experiences.* With greatly improved thinking processes, children have a better grasp of complex concepts.

Once they have reached the concrete operations period, children can grasp the principle of *conservation*. Remember Maya, who in the last chapter thought the quantity of juice changed after it was poured into a different glass? As a school-age child, Maya understands that the volume, or quantity, of a liquid does not change just because the shape of the glass holding it does. School-age children can also consider several variables at one time. This allows them to classify and order different categories of objects, important skills when studying math and science.

Why is it difficult for many young school-age children to learn basic math skills?

Complex concepts become clearer in the concrete operations period. Children can understand and calculate the passage of time. School-age children can remember the past, consider the present, and anticipate and plan for the future.

Although children in this period are beginning to think logically, they still learn best by direct experience. The younger the child, the more dependent he or she is on handling or seeing material objects in order to solve problems. For example, seven-year-old Dana cannot mentally subtract 3 from 19. When given buttons to use as a visual cue, however, she can count 19 buttons, remove 3, and see that 19 minus 3 leaves 16. As Dana progresses through the concrete operations period, she will need fewer and fewer visual or sensory cues to analyze and solve increasingly complex problems.

Many children use computers for both learning and play. For children with disabilities, such as those that limit movement or speech, computers play an important role in everyday life.

Curiosity about a wide variety of topics is characteristic of school-age children. By ten, they have mastered the basic language skills of speaking, reading, comprehending, and writing. They understand basic mathematical concepts and can apply them to solving problems. These skills enable school-age children to explore new subjects. More detailed explorations of biology, geography, and social studies are possible. Their abilities to create and analyze ideas, as well as to plan, also allow children to try such hobbies as woodworking, crafts, and cooking.

Word Power and Mind Power

Development of language skills in school-age children reflects overall intellectual growth. What signs of intellectual development do you recognize in the progression of language skills below?

SIX TO SEVEN YEARS
- Learns to print capitals and small letters.
- Learns short vowel sounds and common consonant and vowel blends.

- Reads a simple book alone.
- Recognizes common word endings, such as -er and -ing.

EIGHT TO NINE YEARS
- Prints all letters and begins to learn script (handwriting).
- Reads aloud fluently.
- Writes a simple story alone.
- Begins to use a dictionary.

TEN YEARS AND OLDER
- Writes in script automatically.
- Reads for information and writes a simple factual report.
- Begins to use indexes, appendices, and footnotes to find information.
- Learns to use prefixes and suffixes to identify meanings of words.

EMOTIONAL DEVELOPMENT

Although you may not remember much about your own years as a preschooler and younger, you may have memories about your school-age years. What were your emotions like? If you were typical as a young school-age child, you had a wide array of emotions, and you had the ability to express them. Language skills, refined during the preschool years, allow school-age children to express their emotions frequently and more clearly than ever before.

School-age children understand the viewpoints of others better; however, they don't always agree with others. True discussions and debates begin to surface during the school-age years.

School-age children further develop empathy and begin to feel compassion. With empathy improved, they are better able to recognize and understand the feelings of others. As *compassion* is added, they are able to sympathize with another's feelings and difficulties. Their increased empathy and newfound compassion inspire school-age children to become part of a campaign to better the world. They may join causes, perhaps aiming to help animals or preserve the environment.

School-age children can be very sensitive and sentimental. It is not unusual for them to cry over a sad movie or book. Properly channeled, all these traits can lead to the development of good citizens and caring adults.

Development of Self-Esteem

By age six, most children have established a clear identification with their own gender. They have developed strong ties to their family and cultural background. All of this helps them form a stable and secure self-concept.

Self-confidence and pride are reinforced by new physical accomplishments. In addition, the ability to converse on a more mature level often allows school-age children to participate more fully in adult conversations. Increasing attention from adults adds to building the self-esteem of school-age children.

Learning emotional self-control is not easy. What emotions does society tell us are acceptable to show openly? Which are considered unacceptable? Do you agree with these attitudes?

According to Erikson, school-age children strive to develop a sense of **industry**. This is *the desire to perform skills, succeed at tasks, and make social contributions.* School-age children want to put their energy to use. Erikson claimed that if school-age children are not able to feel productive, they will develop a sense of **inferiority,** *a feeling of not having met expected standards.* Feeling inferior greatly damages self-esteem. School-age children need to be provided with many opportunities for success in their interactions with peers—games, sports activities, and group projects, as well as in learning situations—in order to prevent feelings of inferiority from developing.

Many, but not all, children enjoy competitive activities. In some cultures, cooperation is emphasized, not competition. What effects do you think this would have?

Competition

The issue of competition among school-age children has been widely debated. Think back to the competitive activities that you participated in as a child. Your impression of how they affected you will influence your thinking about how much competition you believe is good for children.

School-age children begin to compare themselves to other people. As they progress through the school years, they experience more emphasis on competition in sports and school subjects. Looking at what others can do and comparing that to their own skills is only natural. Trying to measure up can be a challenge, but it can also be a disappointment.

Many people see healthy, reasonable competition as good for children. It motivates them to do their best and helps them assess their individual abilities as compared to the group. Competition can refine skills and talents. Participating in team competition

rewards children for cooperating with others and recognizing their contributions.

Excessive emphasis on competition—the idea that winning is more important than enjoying the activity—can be harmful. Some children may focus more on their weaknesses than their strengths. This also damages self-esteem. Children may avoid participating in activities for fear of failure, thereby hindering their development. To avoid these situations, many teachers emphasize cooperative games over competitive games, especially in the early school-age years. Helping children identify their own strengths and take pride and pleasure in them is better than making comparisons.

Change in Fears

When children reach school age, they usually let go of the more specific fears that they had at the preschool age. They are not as likely to be afraid of things like dogs and storms. Instead, their increased reasoning powers allow for anxieties that are more vague but every bit as troubling.

School-age children are fearful of not belonging to a group. They are afraid of being teased and criticized by children and adults. They often worry that they won't have friends. They sometimes imagine that others are talking about them behind their back. They fear being different, which could result in not being accepted.

Many school-age children fear failure. They hate the thought of disappointing parents, teachers, and other respected adults.

Some school-age children worry about world events that are beyond their control, such as war, earthquakes, famine, and drought. The fact that they are better able to understand other points of view probably contributes to this concern for problems in the world. These children are able to think more abstractly and are less egocentric. Thus, they begin to worry about people other than themselves and family members.

All of these fears are very real to school-age children. Adults should take them seriously and not make fun of children for having them. Giving children opportunities to talk about their fears is helpful. If fears become very exaggerated and irrational, caregivers may wish to consult mental health professionals.

Increased Stress

You've probably heard people long for "the good old days," a time when life seemed more simple and enjoyable. Increasingly, this is true for school-age children.

Stress is present at every stage of life. **Stress** is *mental and physical tension and strain caused by problems, pressures, fears, or unsettling changes.* School-age children have always had their own particular sources of stress. They must devote hours of energy toward developing new intellectual and physical skills. They must concentrate for long periods of time during the school day. They may face the added stress of fears or excessive emphasis on competition.

School-age children these days may also have less relaxation time at home. A typical schedule is group care from 6:00 a.m. to 9:00 a.m., school until 3:00 p.m., and group care again until 6:00 p.m. Many have organized activities that take up some of their evening

The fear of being excluded is very real during the school years. Dressing and acting like everyone else are often keys to popularity. How could the experience of being excluded by others be harmful? Could it be helpful?

time. The leisure hours left for family and friends are often limited.

Family and personal problems can also greatly increase stress. Illness or injury, the addition of a sibling, and the divorce of parents can all make children tense and strained.

Children show stress in many ways. They may develop fatigue, apathy, and even depression. Some children become easily angered, aggressive, and disobedient. Such signs as biting their nails and pulling out their eyelashes also point to stress. Teachers and caregivers should watch for these signals and consult with parents and mental health professionals when necessary.

Approaching Puberty

Older school-age children have additional emotional challenges. Developmental transitions are hard at any age, but especially so for school-age children

> ## Tip
> ### FROM THE
> ## Pros
>
> *T*o better understand school-age children, try to find schoolwork, letters, a diary, and other mementos from your own childhood. These can give you insights into their attitudes and behavior.

approaching puberty. It's not uncommon for older school-age children to behave differently from day to day. One day they are struggling to be an adult; the next day they are clinging to the security of childhood. Their increased desire for privacy can add to their moodiness. At these times, children need patience and respect. They need plenty of chances to talk about their new feelings, as well as reassurance that what they are experiencing is not unusual.

SOCIAL DEVELOPMENT

*F*rom preschool to school age, the way friendships are handled changes. During the school-age years, friendships become more lasting and meaningful. They are formed because children sincerely appreciate the characteristics of another person rather than because of convenience or personal gain. Feelings and values are shared during the school years. This "bonding" results in friendships. Younger school-age children have many friends of both genders. By seven or eight years of age, children prefer friends of the same gender.

School-age friendships remain fairly stable despite periodic conflicts. Squabbling seems to be just another part of being friends. Socially competent school-age children know how to be close and nurture friendships.

Think about a special friend you had while growing up. How did that relationship make a difference in your life?

When school-age children make friends, it is sometimes at the expense of other children. An "us versus them" attitude sometimes exists. School-age children do have the capacity for great sensitivity. Their growing concern for acceptance by peers, however, can lead them to be cruel toward those who are not considered "friends." They can engage in unmerciful teasing and sometimes even hurt other children physically.

If teasing or physical conflict occurs, caregivers should firmly communicate that it is not acceptable. Child care programs should be a haven where children are protected from verbal and physical abuse.

Recognition of Diversity

Diversity is *the term often used today when talking about all the qualities people have that make them different from one another.* By the time children reach the school-age years, they are aware of differences. They see variations in gender, race, culture, and physical and mental abilities. They observe the way other people react to differences and easily adopt similar attitudes.

You are probably aware of what can happen when differences are the basis for dislike. Racial problems, gang violence, and simple rejection from a social group are all examples. These situations hurt individuals—as well as society.

Children need to grow up with positive attitudes toward differences. Differences should be discussed openly and honestly. A child care program that integrates children from many different economic levels and social and cultural backgrounds helps school-age children accept and enjoy diversity. An environment that not only acknowledges, but also celebrates, differences helps school-age children become compassionate, tolerant, and accepting.

MORAL DEVELOPMENT

With intellectual and social development comes moral growth. Younger school-age children are very concerned about rules. They continue to obey them to earn rewards and avoid punishment. They also begin to see that rules are needed for people to live together peacefully. They may not always follow the rules, but they do know that they are necessary. With development of

In life children will meet and work with people of many different backgrounds. Help them to see people as individuals, not stereotypes.

THE MULTICULTURAL CLASSROOM

Preadolescent children are often embarrassed to draw attention to themselves. They may prefer to blend in or even be anonymous. Promoting acceptance and understanding of all ethnic backgrounds means taking a sensitive approach with children of this age. Here are some ideas for creating an atmosphere of sharing and caring:

- **Mapping Origins.** Put a large world map on the bulletin board. Use map tacks to indicate the birthplace of each child and possibly parents or grandparents. This is also a great tool for teaching about world news.

- **Star of the Week.** Set up a list for use in featuring one child each week on a special bulletin board. Include a current photo and a "star questionnaire" that has information filled in about the child's favorite television show, book, hobbies, sports, foods, etc. Other photos of family, pets, and home may be added when possible. Cover the entire bulletin board with a sheet of acrylic or plastic to protect photos.

- **Sharing Thoughts.** During group time, an occasional survey allows the children to understand each other better and discover ways that they are similar. Some suggested topics include fears, likes and dislikes, ideas for room improvements, and group decisions, such as plans for a field trip. Decision-making is also a hands-on lesson in democracy.

conscience, children like to make sure everybody else obeys the rules as well.

Awareness of rules and their purpose allows children to develop and participate in group games. The games may focus on intellectual skills and have rules that must be obeyed. Children might play card games or such physical games as hopscotch and soccer. Playing fairly takes on great importance to school-age children.

As children become older and develop stronger personal relationships, they are more likely to feel outside pressure when deciding between right and wrong. They are highly influenced by the expectations of family, peers, teachers, and other influential groups. The ideas children have about right and wrong may vary according to whatever group is most important to them.

Limited though it is, this developing sense of morality makes school-age children different from younger children. They are slowly discovering their ability to make their own decisions and control their actions.

APPROACHING ADULTHOOD

You might think of the school-age years as the last act in the stage drama of childhood. Much has to be learned and resolved before the curtain falls. When it rises again, the main characters will be as close to adulthood as to childhood. They need a firm foundation to fulfill this most challenging of roles. When children get what they need from skillful, concerned caregivers, they can approach and eventually manage adulthood with confidence and competence.

Chapter 7 Review

Chapter Summary

- Younger school-age children (six to ten years old) are in a growth plateau. Older school-age children (ages eleven to twelve) are approaching, or experiencing, a growth spurt and the beginning of puberty.
- Motor and perceptual skills develop rapidly during the school-age years.
- School-age children are in the concrete operations period of intellectual development.
- Self-esteem can suffer if children do not experience successes.
- Competition, fears, stress, and puberty affect emotional development.
- School-age children form deep and meaningful friendships.
- Social rules are important for school-age children.
- The developing sense of morality in a school-age child is used to help the child make decisions and control actions.

Reviewing the Facts

1. Define puberty. Describe the physical changes that take place during puberty for males and females.
2. Briefly describe the motor development of school-age children and how this development affects the activities they enjoy.
3. Discuss some of the abilities displayed in the concrete operations period of intellectual development.
4. Explain Erikson's beliefs about the relationship between industry and inferiority concerning school-age children.
5. Describe both the positive and negative effects of competition on emotional development. How is competition best handled?
6. How and why do school-age children's fears differ from preschooler's? Give examples.
7. What is stress? What stresses are common in the life of a school-age child?
8. How does puberty affect school-age children's emotional development?
9. What is the basis for friendship in the school-age years?
10. How do attitudes about rules change in the preschool years? How does this affect game-playing?

Thinking Critically

1. How might the physical changes associated with the approach of puberty make school-age children feel different from their peers? What effect might this have on self-esteem?
2. Do you think school-age children today are pushed into becoming adults before they are ready? If so, what evidence of this do you see? What might be some causes? How can the problem be combated?
3. Why do you think some school-age children tease or exclude others? What can be done to prevent this?
4. What kinds of situations do you think help build a school-age child's self-esteem? Do they have to be ones that involve other children? What happens that allows self-esteem to grow?

Activities and Applications

1. **Motor Skills.** With a partner, compile a list of activities that would help school-age children develop gross motor skills, fine

motor skills, and depth perception. Make a separate list for each type of development.

2. **Stress.** In newspapers and magazines, find articles and advertisements related to the stress and pressure school-age children face today. Discuss which types of stress are inevitable and which can be avoided.

SCHOOL TO WORK

Your Professional Portfolio

Begin a collection of ideas for cooperative games. Talk to others and consult references that include such games. (You might record these on index cards.) Then create a cooperative game of your own to include in the collection. As you write descriptions of the games, explain them as accurately as possible, so that you can use them easily if you work with children someday. Keep the file in your portfolio.

Observing and Analyzing

Gaining Insight on the School-Age Child

If you were in charge of guiding the activities for school-age children, what might be one of your most challenging tasks? It could be planning activities that hold their interest as well as assist their development.

School-age children cover a wide range of ages. The six-year-old just out of kindergarten won't have the same interests or abilities that the twelve-year-old has. Knowing what works at each age level is a skill you can build through study and observation.

Whenever you are around children in this age range, pay attention to what abilities they have. Take note of the activities that they enjoy and how they benefit from them. If possible, visit a school-age program. As you observe, use these questions to guide your thinking:

1. What ages are grouped together?
2. Which activities are intellectually challenging?
3. Which activities are physically challenging?
4. What kinds of projects and activities enhance the child's self-esteem?
5. What are the most and least popular activities?
6. What options do children have when they do not wish to participate in the planned activities?
7. Describe the attention span of the children you observed. How did it affect their activity?
8. What, if anything, caused interference in any of the activities?
9. What contributed to the effectiveness of activities?
10. What changes would you recommend to improve this program?

Career Profile

Meet James Lee, a pre-kindergarten teacher in a public school. James helps children at risk of academic failure improve their readiness for kindergarten. James teaches morning and afternoon sessions of twelve four-year-old children. He is assisted by one aide and one parent volunteer.

Why did you choose this career?

"I began working with children as an aide in a Head Start program. While working there I earned my CDA credential and was placed in charge of my own classroom. That experience got me interested in being a teacher. I learned about pre-kindergarten teaching jobs at a conference of the NAEYC. Although I loved Head Start, I thought it would be exciting to work in other areas of early childhood education."

What education and skills do you need?

"For this job, the public school system requires a bachelor's degree in early childhood education. Part of my coursework in college helped me learn how to teach children with special needs. That training has been very useful, since many of the children in the program have learning problems or other difficulties. I also attend several conferences each year.

"To be an effective pre-kindergarten teacher, it's important to know typical child development. I must be able to observe and document development that is different or unusual in each child.

"Curriculum planning is a big part of my job. I'm responsible for coming up with creative activities to stimulate intellectual, emotional, social, and physical development.

"Communication skills are important, too. I talk frequently with parents about how their children are progressing. Outside of class I conduct parent conferences, home visits, and write a weekly newsletter.

"To encourage parents to read to their children at home, I organized and manage a lending library. Like many aspects of my job, this requires close attention to detail."

What is a typical day on the job like?

"As all good teachers do, I arrive about half an hour early to review plans and prepare for the day. At 8:00 a.m. I meet the first group of children as they arrive on the bus. Throughout the morning the children play in learning centers and participate in planned activities, such as baking mini-pizzas or playing with magnets. I move from one small group to another guiding children's learning. I also spend individual time with children when needed.

"Some days a speech therapist comes into the classroom. Many of my children have language delays, so the speech therapist and I work together to stimulate language development.

"After the morning session ends at 11:30, I have a quick lunch and catch up on paperwork. Some days I use this time to telephone parents, make field trip arrangements, and record information about children's development for their file. At 1:00 p.m. the process starts all over again. My afternoon class leaves at 4:30. I use the last hour of each day to develop lesson plans and attend to other program details."

What is most challenging about your job?

"Some children need more help than I can give them. For instance, one child was very aggressive toward the other children. Nothing I did could stop the behavior. I tried to convince the parents to go for family counseling, but they were too embarrassed to seek help."

What is your favorite part of being a pre-kindergarten teacher?

"I love seeing children bloom after attending our program! After just a few short months, children who barely spoke begin to speak in complete sentences. Children who were quiet and afraid to play with others often end up being leaders by the end of the year. By helping children develop in the early years I believe I'm helping prevent possible school failure. That makes me feel really proud of my job!"

SHARE YOUR THOUGHTS

1. What would be the benefits of having only twelve children per classroom?
2. What information would be important for teachers to include in parent newsletters?
3. What part of being a pre-kindergarten teacher sounds most interesting to you? What part would you like least?

143

Unit 3

THE CHILD CARE CENTER

Reflections

"I guess you could say it was a dream come true for me. When I first saw this old building, I just knew I could turn it into the preschool I had always wanted to have. The structure was sound, and the layout of the building was just right. All it needed was a little work. Well, I was right about the 'work' and wrong about the 'little.' Some friends helped me get started. We planned, scrubbed, sanded, pounded, and painted. It took a lot of effort. It also took getting over some financing and licensing hurdles, but it was worth it. The Morning Glory Preschool is a great place for children to spend time. It's lively, loving, and interesting—and for me, it's finally a reality."

—Miriam

Chapter 8

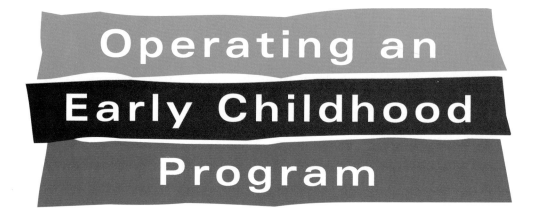

Operating an Early Childhood Program

CHAPTER OBJECTIVES

- Give examples of program philosophy statements and goals.

- Describe different types of early childhood programs.

- Assess the impact of licensing laws and other regulations.

- Explain the roles of director, staff, advisory board, and parents.

Terms to Learn

- advisory board
- liability insurance
- licensing laws
- philosophy
- policy
- program goals
- self-correcting
- staff-to-child ratio

That's my favorite part of the classroom," Lilly Brazelton said as she pointed to the art center. "There's just something about art activities that allows us to put so much of the program philosophy into action."

Lilly was doing something that she really enjoyed—showing off her early childhood program to an inquiring parent. As the director, Lilly was proud of what they accomplished, and she loved introducing new children and their parents to the program.

"Watch Mr. Gasparini work with the children, and you'll see what I mean," Lilly went on. "These little ones don't worry about whether they have artistic talent or not. They just want to try things. They have to learn to listen to Mr. Gasparini first. We believe communication is important. Then they practice all kinds of other skills—everything from fine motor skills, to sharing, to creativity. Mr. G makes sure they feel good about what they do. If that isn't a self-esteem booster, I don't know what is. When the children help clean up, they learn responsibility. I could go on and on, but you can see why I like art activities so much."

Mrs. Alvarez smiled in response to Lilly's enthusiasm. She was quickly getting good vibrations about this place. The program philosophy was becoming clear to her as she listened to Lilly speak, and she liked what she was hearing. "I could feel comfortable leaving Conrad here," she thought to herself. She was well on the way toward making a decision.

PROGRAM PHILOSOPHY

*I*f there is one element that can be called the core of any early childhood program, it is the philosophy of that program. The **philosophy** of an early childhood program *describes general beliefs, concepts, and attitudes the program has about how children learn and how the program should serve and educate young children.* A sample program philosophy is shown on page 149. Principles like these are what guide the operation of a program. They are what parents look for in hopes of finding a program that fits with their own thinking.

Lilly Brazelton and her staff have a clear idea about the philosophy of their program. Because they do, their actions reflect that philosophy in the activities they plan and the way they handle the children. When Lilly introduces people to her program, she talks freely about what goes on, showing the link between philosophical principles and the activity in the center. In any well-managed early childhood program, you might hear a director like Lilly describe a program by saying something like, "We believe that . . ." You know then that you are learning about their philosophy.

PROGRAM GOALS

*P*rogram goals are an outgrowth of philosophy. Once the general philosophy is established, program goals that support the philosophy can be set up. **Program goals** *identify basic skills, concepts, and attitudes to be developed and encouraged in children.* They are usually more specific than philosophical statements. While philosophical statements talk about beliefs that the program holds, the program goals spell out what children should gain because of these beliefs. For example, a program might expect children to:

- Gain high self-esteem and a positive attitude.
- Learn self-help skills that lead to independence and responsibility.
- Develop positive social skills, such as cooperation and sharing.
- Learn problem-solving skills.
- Develop gross and fine motor skills.
- Improve communication skills, including listening, speaking, reading, and writing.
- Develop curiosity about the world.
- Improve creative thinking and playing abilities.
- Gain respect, acceptance, and understanding of the rights and feelings of others.
- Learn how to handle and store play materials properly.

Writing down program goals helps make sure they are achieved. How might these children's teacher follow up on their curiosity about caterpillars?

*A*s a child care professional, you can do a better job when you have a clear idea of the program philosophy. Ask about philosophy before you take a job. Then you will know whether you agree with the principles and can support them in your work. Knowing the philosophy improves your communication on the job too. When you understand why the program operates as it does, you are better able to discuss qualities of the program with parents and other staff members.

A Sample Program Philosophy

*B*elow are some of the beliefs that guide program development in one specific child care center:

- Children need many sensory, concrete, hands-on learning experiences.

- Different children have different learning styles, rates of learning, and developmental levels.

- The classroom should be designed to nurture curiosity, exploration, and investigation.

- Children need time for independent activity as well as cooperative effort.

- The curriculum should evolve from the interests and needs of children enrolled in the classroom.

- Activities should address the development of the whole child, including physical, intellectual, social, emotional, and moral development.

- The classroom and teacher-child interactions should encourage problem-solving and creativity.

- Children learn best when allowed to explore and arrive at answers and understand concepts through their own process of thinking. Trial and error is an acceptable means of trying to make sense of the world.

- Parent involvement is desirable and, in fact, necessary in order to enhance the overall development of the young child.

- Because a child's self-esteem is very precious, teachers are employed who like, respect, and enjoy children, and who delight in the milestones of development that take place in the early years of life.

EARLY CHILDHOOD PROGRAMS

*W*hen you examine early childhood programs, you will notice both similarities and differences. That's to be expected. Each program aims at providing a safe environment in which children can develop and learn. However, their sponsors and the reasons why they were created are not the same. Moreover, the philosophies behind them are different.

Some of the early childhood programs you were introduced to in Chapter 1 are described more fully in the text that follows. As you read, think about what philosophies guide each one.

Child Care Centers

You may sometimes hear the term "child care center" used in a general sense to describe almost any type of child care facility. However, the term also has a more specific meaning. In this more specific sense, child care centers (also called *day care centers*) have as their primary purpose the care of children whose parents must work or attend school during the day. Many child care centers also provide learning activities for children, even though education is not generally the main goal.

Child care centers are typically open from 6:00 a.m. to 6:00 p.m. to accommodate parents' schedules. This means that they serve breakfast, lunch, and two snacks each day. Because days are long, nap time is part of the schedule.

Some child care centers serve only two- to six-year-olds. Increasingly, however, centers take children from six weeks to twelve years of age. Centers vary in size, with enrollments ranging as high as 200 children.

One quality that sets child care centers apart from each other is their sponsorship. Sponsors of child care centers include religious organizations and social service agencies. Originally, these organizations set up centers primarily to serve children from low-income families. Today families of all economic levels use the centers these organizations maintain. The federal government provides money to centers that serve low-income families. This is called Block Grant funding.

When different organizations put programs in motion, each center takes on its own unique qualities in structure and program. Often principles that the organization operates under are reflected in the center's philosophy and goals.

Corporate Centers

One specific type of child care center that you have read about is provided by some corporations, either on or close to the parents' workplace. A corporation may operate the center itself or contract with someone else to manage it.

As with any issue, the need for on-site child care is accompanied by a mixture of opinions. Corporations want to keep employees happy, loyal, and productive. Providing on-site care has been shown to contribute to all of these, making work and family life easier to manage for employees in many companies. The cost of providing on-site care, however, is high. Not all companies can afford the expense, and when they do, they want to be sure it is worthwhile. When companies provide benefits, they tend to look for those that are useful to many employees.

Not all employed parents favor on-site care. They may prefer another center, one that has a different program or is closer to home. Some couples find that using on-site care puts the burden of transportation and attention on only one of them—the person who works at the site.

Serving nutritious meals and snacks is a responsibility child care programs must take seriously. What might happen if children are routinely fed inadequate or poor quality food?

It is often difficult for parents who work at night or on weekends to find quality care for their children. This hospital operates an on-site child care program that accommodates its employees' work schedules.

Despite the negatives, many reports about on-site care are favorable. The experience of Myra Abraham typifies what people like about on-site care. Since Myra's company provides care, she didn't have to spend time hunting for a program for her child. Her schedule runs smoothly, since she just brings Grant to work with her and doesn't have to rush to pick him up. Having him close by for regular contact and in case of illness eases her mind. For reasons like these, the interest in on-site child care is likely to continue.

As an alternative to on-site care, some companies offer vouchers to employees. These coupons are worth a certain amount of money toward child care services selected by the family.

Laboratory Schools

Some universities, colleges, and high schools provide child care for students and employees. These centers usually serve as laboratory schools to help students who are studying child development or early childhood education learn more about children. Many of the students who work and study in lab schools go on to find careers in the child care field.

Because lab schools are the training ground for future child care professionals, many are at the forefront of what is going on in the field. Children often receive care, education, and guidance based on the latest research and methods. While the atmosphere may be different from those centers in the "real" world, they make an excellent learning environment for children and students.

Profit and Nonprofit

Child care centers sponsored by religious organizations, corporations, and many schools and universities are usually *nonprofit* (also called not-for-profit) operations. This means that there are no stockholders who receive money from income earned by the child care center. Money earned by a nonprofit child care center goes back into the center budget or into savings for future use. Staff members receive salaries in nonprofit centers just as they do in others.

Some centers are created for the purpose of earning a profit. *For-profit* child care centers may be privately owned by individuals or by large child care corporations. Profit-earning centers provide income for the own-

What might be the advantages and disadvantages of a for-profit child care center?

ers. The largest chain of child care centers in the United States is Kinder-Care™. They have over 1,000 child care centers. Surplus money earned goes into the child care budget but also to stockholders and other investors.

Preschools

Preschools are set up for the main purpose of providing educational services to children from three to five years of age. Preschools are often used by families to give children extra stimulation and experiences prior to formal education. Children also have a chance to learn social skills as they spend time with other children.

Preschool is usually scheduled for 2 1/2 hours in the morning or afternoon. Children generally attend two or three days per week. With the short preschool schedule, employed parents may find enrolling a child in preschool inconvenient unless they can work out transportation as well as child care for the rest of the day.

Different organizations sponsor preschools. Sometimes religious organizations manage them or provide space for them. Preschools may also be owned by private individuals. Thus, there are both for-profit and nonprofit preschools.

In a preschool setting, children ages three to five learn as they play. This type of program is often chosen by families who do not need an all-day child care provider.

Parent Cooperatives

As you may recall, some parents join together to form and run their own preschools, called parent cooperatives. They usually follow a schedule similar to other preschools.

In a cooperative, the parents hire a teacher, determine the goals, and set the rules and procedures to be followed in the preschool. Since parents are in charge, the philosophy behind the program reflects their ideas and attitudes. Child care professionals who work in the preschool conform to this philosophy. Although disagreements can occur, often a bond forms as teachers and parents work closely together toward the same goals.

Cooperatives typically require parents to work in the preschool a few hours every month. They may assist the teacher and do administrative work. This helps keep the costs lower and gives the teacher more time to spend working with the children.

Head Start

As part of President Johnson's *War on Poverty*, Head Start was created in the mid-1960s. The philosophy behind this program was clear and remains so today. Because children who live in low-income environments often have limited opportunities, many enter school not as well prepared as other youngsters. Catching up is difficult and, in fact, may never happen. To counteract this situation, Head Start aims to do just what the name suggests—give children a "head start." When young, disadvantaged children are given experiences they might otherwise miss, these children have a better chance of succeeding educationally and ultimately breaking the poverty cycle.

Serving primarily four-year-olds, Head Start is designed to foster intellectual as well as emotional, social, and physical growth. Besides educational programming, Head Start coordinates such services as health and dental care. Specialists plan meals and snacks that provide children with a healthful diet. Those in charge of the program know that only when children feel good and are alert and healthy can they focus on intellectual tasks.

Head Start also requires parents to get actively involved in their child's education. For children under four years of age, Head Start employs home visitors to teach parents

Participating in a Head Start program may help these children succeed in school and in life.

how to educate and care for children in the home. By getting involved, parents have a better chance at fulfilling their role as the primary teacher in a child's life.

Head Start programs may operate for a half or full day. Because the program is federally funded, no fees are charged to children and families who are accepted into the program.

Head Start has been subject to many evaluations over the years. Most reports show positive outcomes. Higher IQs and greater school achievements have been demonstrated when children in the program were compared to those who were not but had similar backgrounds. The economic benefits to society have also been studied. In general, for the children involved, Head Start reduces the need for remedial education, welfare, and the justice system. For all of these reasons, Head Start has become a significant contributor to early childhood education.

Pre-Kindergarten Programs

Head Start is not the only program designed specifically to prepare children for school. Some children who are not economically disadvantaged can also be at risk of academic failure when they enter school. Factors other than low income that are associated with poor performance include slow development, lack of language skills, and premature birth.

Public and private schools offer pre-kindergarten programs that are designed to prevent school failure by remedying problems early. Three- to five-year-olds are served by these programs. Pre-kindergarten programs differ from Head Start in that they are open to all children, not just those who are economically disadvantaged.

Pre-kindergarten classes are usually half-day and free of charge in public schools. Most pre-kindergartens operate only during the school year. Parent involvement, including home visits, is heavily stressed.

Montessori Programs

From Chapter 1, you know that Montessori programs originated with the philosophy and teachings of Dr. Maria Montessori. She lived in Italy from 1870 to 1952. Montessori's philosophy has influenced all of early childhood education. Maria Montessori was one of the early pioneers in the study of how children learn. She theorized

In Montessori programs, real-life experiences are used as learning experiences.

that children learn best by being active and by doing. She believed in self-education and that children should "learn how to learn." Preschools that follow the Montessori philosophy encourage independent learning and stress learning by doing and learning through the senses.

Montessori developed many of her own educational materials. Each of these materials is designed to teach a specific lesson, and each must be used only in the prescribed manner. Children are shown by the teacher how to use the materials and are then left to practice and master the lesson independently. Materials for lessons are **self-correcting**. This means *the child gets immediate feedback after correctly (or incorrectly) finishing the task.* Materials are organized from simple to complex, so children progress to increasingly challenging tasks.

The role of the teacher in a Montessori preschool is much less active than in a traditional classroom. The teacher observes children to determine their needs, chooses proper educational materials, and then quietly demonstrates to each child how to use the new materials. There is little talk from the teacher. Montessori felt that children should be motivated by the inward satisfaction that is gained when a job is well done.

Montessori schools usually serve three- to six-year-olds, but a few enroll children from infancy through eight years. Teachers receive one year of Montessori instruction before they can teach. Montessori schools may be for-profit or nonprofit.

Programs for Children with Special Needs

Finding child care for children who have special needs—physical, intellectual, emotional, or social disabilities—can be a challenge for parents. Some centers lack personnel with specialized training to care for special needs children. They may also lack needed equipment and space in the building.

By age four, (and sometimes earlier) children with special needs are served, by law, in public schools. Finding private child care for special needs children younger than this can be a challenge. Private centers are not required to enroll these children, but must prove why they can't. Building renovation and specialized staffing costs may be the deciding factors.

Children with physical, intellectual, or emotional disabilities can benefit from inclusion in an early childhood program. Their peers benefit, too.

When a special needs child is enrolled, teachers work closely with parents to make sure all goes well. Social service agencies, such as the Easter Seals Society, can be helpful resources when integrating a child with special needs.

Remember that children with special needs are children first. They have most of the same needs, wants, and feelings as children without disabilities. Their presence brings an opportunity for all children to learn more about diversity and develop qualities of compassion and empathy.

KEYS TO OPERATING SMOOTHLY

By this time, you are well aware that early childhood programs come in all shapes and sizes. Regardless of format, however, no early childhood program can run well without paying attention to certain key components.

Suppose that a plan for setting up a program is in place. The sponsors know what type of program they want and have developed the philosophy to guide it. What else must be done to insure that the program operates smoothly?

Licensing

In most situations, an early childhood program cannot operate until it is licensed by the state. State **licensing laws** outline *rules and regulations that programs must follow*. These rules set minimum standards that protect children's safety and well-being. As part of the licensing process, facilities are inspected to make sure they meet all building, fire, and health codes.

Licensing laws cover hundreds of issues. For example, they specify minimum space requirements and the number of staff members needed for the children at the center. It is generally accepted that there should be a minimum of 35 square feet (3.3 square meters) of indoor space and 75 square feet (7 square meters) of outdoor space for each child. Exceptions may exist depending on the ages of children. Licensing laws also cover such things as the number of required emergency exits, the number of toilets, the types of outdoor fencing, and the minimum qualifications of program personnel.

Licensing laws vary widely from state to state. To find out what the licensing standards are in your state, call the Chamber of Commerce. Ask for the name, address, and telephone number of the appropriate licensing agency.

Before a program is set up, a careful look at licensing can help determine whether a plan is realistic. Modifications to a building can be costly. People who establish programs look at potential expenses carefully before moving ahead.

One of the controversial aspects of licensing is the question of how far requirements should go in regulating child care programs. For the protection of children, careful regulation is critical. On the other hand, unnecessary requirements that place a heavy financial burden on providers can cause them to end, or never begin, operation. A sensible balance is needed in order to keep quality programs going.

A program director has many responsibilities, ranging from recruitment to licensing. What key skills or qualities would be most important for this position?

Leadership

A successful program relies on good leadership. Child care programs employ directors to serve this function. Directors are administrators and managers. They are usually responsible to a board of directors or an owner. Some directors own their own programs. In small programs, directors may teach part-time in a classroom. Programs that enroll more than 85 children usually have an assistant director in addition to one who is full-time.

As the director of a program, Bill Thorndike finds that the most time-consuming part of his job is supervision of all personnel. He recruits, interviews, and hires employees. He must also make sure new personnel are trained. For good communication, he generally holds weekly staff meetings. This allows time to assess and cope with issues before they become big problems. An additional part of his responsibilities includes formally evaluating staff members at least once per year.

Directors work with teachers to plan, implement, and evaluate learning programs and other activities based on the program's goals and philosophy. In addition, they are responsible for financial management—preparing yearly budgets and reviewing them frequently. Organized bookkeeping is necessary in order to keep track of incoming money, such as parent fees, and outgoing expenses, such as ordering supplies

and equipment. The director also makes sure the facility, the physical building that houses the program, meets all licensing laws and other regulations.

Directors talk frequently with parents as they bring their children to the center and pick them up. In addition, they use newsletters, notes on the parent bulletin board, and parent handbooks to communicate center policies and procedures to parents.

Staffing

Besides the director, how many people do you think it might take to staff an early childhood program? At first glance, you might think only of the teachers. Depending on program type and size, however, the staff could be much larger.

There are a variety of job opportunities in early childhood programs. Each staff member is a key to a program's success.

Cooperation

WHAT IS COOPERATION?

Cooperation is the willingness and ability to work with others to achieve goals. It means accepting the knowledge, authority, and assistance of others, as well as contributing your own skills to make the effort a successful one.

Cooperation in Action

"I'll start the water boiling," Walter said as he placed the large kettle on the range. "They'll be happy today."

Casey Alexander, the head cook, smiled. She said, "They always are when it's spaghetti and meatball day." Walter was Casey's assistant in the kitchen of a large preschool program. Together they had prepared the meatball mixture earlier in the day. Then Casey had started the sauce while Walter rolled the meatballs. While Casey cooked the meatballs, Walter cleaned the counter, utensils, and cookware they had used.

"Smells good," Virginia said as she entered the kitchen. Virginia was a parent volunteer in the preschool. She was ready to set the tables for lunch.

"It looks like we need some more napkins. Do you have another package?" she asked.

Casey opened the door to the storage area. "Here you go," she responded, handing Virginia a package of napkins.

The door opened again as Fran Daniels, the program director, walked in. "Will you still have time to go over next month's menu this afternoon?" she asked Casey. "I'd like to finalize it with you and Darlene today if possible. Then you can call in your food orders."

Casey nodded. She liked working with Darlene. As a dietitian, Darlene had taught Casey a lot about nutrition. Good nutrition at a reasonable price was their aim in the preschool.

"I'll be back to help with cleanup after lunch," Virginia said as she went out the door.

"Good! Then I'll just go home," Casey joked. She had a way of making people laugh. She reached out to stir the spaghetti sauce, returning to the business at hand. They had a meal to get on the table.

Your Analysis

1. Identify the individuals who cooperate in the meal program. What skills and knowledge does each bring to the process?

2. What might be some consequences if Casey tried to do all the work herself?

3. What personal traits or attitudes make it easier to cooperate with others?

Staff members are needed in the classrooms. In addition to teachers, teacher's aides may also be employed to work with children.

Food service requires a full- or part-time cook. Larger programs, such as Head Start, employ a dietitian to plan menus with a cook. A *dietitian* is a person who has been specially trained to educate people about healthful foods. Kitchen aides may be hired to assist cooks.

Other personnel positions that may be needed include a bus driver, a bus monitor, a nurse, a custodian, a social worker, a parent education coordinator, an educational program director, a home visitor, and a speech therapist. All personnel are responsible to the director.

Educational qualifications and experience needed for positions vary from state to state. Of course, programs have the right to set staff qualifications higher then licensing laws require. Individual programs create job descriptions for all personnel.

What are some specific ways a low staff-to-child ratio benefits the children? How would it benefit the staff?

Staff-to-Child Ratios

A **staff-to-child ratio** is *the number of personnel in relation to the number of children in a classroom.* For example, a 1-to-5 ratio means there is one caregiver for every five children. States establish minimum staff-to-child ratios to make sure there are enough adults available to evacuate children safely in case of an emergency, such as a fire. Low staff-to-child ratios also help insure that children are well supervised and getting the attention and care they need. Some programs employ more staff members than state licensing laws require.

As you read in an earlier chapter, the necessary number of caregivers to children is higher when younger children are enrolled. Infants require much more individual attention than preschoolers or school-age children. Infant rooms usually have at least one caregiver to every three or four infants. One caregiver might be assigned to a group of three to five toddlers. In contrast, it is not unusual for a group of five-year-olds to have two teachers for 20 children.

When staff members are highly qualified, they may be able to manage larger groups of children. The smallest group size possible, however, is always the best choice.

Legal Responsibilities

No parent would want to place a child in a program that did not have the health, safety, and well-being of children as its top priority. Before beginning operation, a program must meet all local, state, and federal laws and regulations. This is the director's responsi-

bility. For example, the director must make sure that fire alarms are in working order and that evacuation procedures are established.

Directors also advise staff members of their legal responsibilities to young children. For instance, many states require child care personnel to report suspected child abuse to state authorities. Therefore, the director must arrange for the education of all personnel about the procedures to follow when reporting this information.

Centers should have **liability insurance** that covers employees, enrolled children, visitors, and people on or around the site. This means that *if the program is found responsible for an injury or damages that occur at the center or in connection with center activity, insurance will cover costs involved in any resulting lawsuit. Medical costs for injury can be included in this insurance.* Insurance to cover the cost of theft or damage to the facility as the result of storms or fire should also be purchased.

Liability insurance policies are difficult to read and understand. Individuals who are in charge of a program need to ask an insurance agent about coverage for certain situations. They must think about field trips, food-related illnesses, damage to property owned by a landlord, transportation of children, and kidnapping of a child by a parent who doesn't have legal custody of the child.

Advisory Board

Smooth operation relies on expert input and willing workers. Many early childhood programs, especially nonprofit programs, find this kind of help in an advisory board. An **advisory board** *is a group of people, often parents, community members, or people in early childhood careers, who help directors develop and implement center policies.* Advisory boards usually consist of seven to twelve members. A **policy** *is a statement of rules or guidelines that guide the actions and decision making of an organization.*

Parental Involvement

Involving parents is beneficial for a program. Confident child care professionals welcome their input and assistance. A good staff has nothing to hide from parents and appreciates the fact that parents can help make a good program even better. How might this happen?

For one thing, many parents are often eager to provide materials and supplies. They can also be a financial resource. For example, some might be willing to help with a fund-raiser that helps the program cut costs.

An advisory board can bring additional expertise, as well as parental viewpoints, to a program. What kinds of people do you think would make positive contributions to an advisory board?

THE MULTICULTURAL CLASSROOM

In the multicultural classroom, making everyone feel comfortable may take an extra effort. What can you do to make all families feel welcome? Since language is the first barrier that can separate families of different cultures, that's a good place to start.

Most early childhood programs have flyers, brochures, and building signs available to the public. To serve families that are not primarily English speaking, post bilingual signs and circulate bilingual flyers. This is the best welcome mat you could offer.

Some programs provide enrollment forms that have been translated. A phone call to a community cultural or religious center may help you locate assistance in translating vital documents. They may also provide contact with people who can translate at future meetings. If the school offers parent meetings to discuss important topics, such as child abuse, home safety, and community problems, all families should have the opportunity to participate. The effort you put forth can make the difference in preventing people from feeling alienated by a lack of communication.

Extra hands can make operating a program much easier. Involving parents as volunteers lessens the load on staff members and makes parents feel needed. Parents enjoy volunteering when they have time to give. Among the tasks they can do are: assist with children's activities, organize family events, make repairs to toys and equipment, create a newsletter, handle paperwork, share hobbies and knowledge with children, and help with setup and cleanup in the center. Like everyone else, parents are busy people. Giving them an opportunity to choose from different levels of commitment may make them more willing to volunteer.

Before parents can do a job, they need information and perhaps training. Planning a special meeting to welcome and inform them is a good idea. Showing appreciation for their efforts makes them more willing to help again.

Getting involved is beneficial not just to the program but to parents as well. Parents who are involved tend to feel more committed and supportive of a program. They have a better understanding of what goes on, including any limitations and problems experienced by the program.

MANY DETAILS AHEAD

As this chapter comes to an end, you might think that the subject of operating an early childhood program is closed. In truth, it has just begun. Being in charge of children is a huge responsibility. The other chapters in this unit offer much more that you need to know about how programs are set up and managed so that children are well cared for. The rest of this text includes information that applies to many different kinds of programs for children from birth to school-age. However, the main focus is on programs that provide both care and educational experiences for children ages three to five.

Chapter 8 Review

Chapter Summary

- At the core of any early childhood program is its philosophy. Program goals are an outgrowth of that philosophy.
- There are many kinds of early childhood programs. Their characteristics vary because of who sponsors them, why they were created, and the philosophies.
- Some early childhood programs make money for the owners as well as serve children and their families.
- Early childhood programs must meet state licensing laws. These laws vary from state to state.
- In order to operate smoothly, early childhood programs need a director for leadership and a skilled staff.
- Parents can contribute much to the operation of an early childhood program.

Reviewing the Facts

1. What purpose does the philosophy of an early childhood education program serve?
2. What is the function of program goals? Give five examples.
3. For what purpose were child care centers created? How does this affect their operation?
4. What reasons do corporations have for providing and not providing on-site child care?
5. Explain the difference between a profit and non-profit organization.
6. How are preschools different from child care centers?
7. What services do Head Start programs provide? Describe the children served in Head Start.
8. Who sponsors pre-kindergarten programs? Describe the children served in these programs.
9. Briefly describe the characteristics of a Montessori program.
10. What are licensing laws?
11. Summarize the responsibilities a director has in an early childhood program.
12. List six staff positions other than director that an early childhood program might have.
13. Describe three ways a parent could be beneficially involved in an early childhood program.

Thinking Critically

1. Why is it important to understand the philosophy of an early childhood program before becoming an employee?
2. Explore points of view on the following issues:

   a. A large company announces that the child care center it provides on site will be closing. Describe possible points of view of the company, a parent with a child currently enrolled, and an employee who has no children.

   b. A child care center is barely staying in business when new licensing rules require the center to make costly improvements to the facility. Describe possible points of view of the licensing agency, the center owners, and the parents of children in the center.

Activities and Applications

1. **Math Practice.** Suppose you are setting up a child care program that will enroll 75 children. The ratio of teachers to children will be 1 to 5. How

many teachers will you need to hire? How many teachers will you need if you decide that 15 of the 75 children will be infants, requiring a ratio of 1 to 3?

2. **Licensing.** Obtain licensing information for child care programs in your state. With a group of classmates, evaluate the regulations. What is the reasoning behind specific regulations? What would you add or eliminate? Why?

SCHOOL TO WORK

Your Professional Portfolio

Professionals sometimes develop their own philosophy about their career: why the work is valuable; their attitudes and beliefs about the work; and what they feel their approach to the job should be. Putting your philosophy into words compels you to think about the significance of your chosen career and your role in it. Assuming that you will work in child care, write your own personal philosophy on working with children.

Observing and Analyzing

Observing How Programs Operate

First-hand observation is the best way to see how early childhood programs operate. If you are able to visit several different programs, so much the better. Use the ideas below to discover the scope of child care in your community:

- **Comparing Programs.** Observe two different programs that provide child care, such as Head Start, corporate child care, a parent cooperative, pre-kindergarten, or a Montessori program. Make a chart to compare the following characteristics: age range, number of children, fees, staff salaries (not always revealed), profit or nonprofit status, hours of operation, staff-to-child ratio, provision for special needs children, and minimum educational requirements for teachers and aides. Also inquire about the philosophy of each of these programs. Create a bulletin board by combining the information in your chart with that of your classmates. Compare results. Include philosophy statements in the bulletin board display and analyze their similarities.

- **What Agencies Provide.** If possible, spend a morning or an afternoon at a resource and referral agency or a child care licensing office. Observe the tasks of the staff. What knowledge about child care programs do the people who staff these agencies need in order to serve their clients? Ask for brochures, current legislation, and any other pertinent information to share in class.

Chapter 9

Providing an Appropriate Environment

CHAPTER OBJECTIVES

■ Identify principles to use in planning early childhood environments.

■ List and describe the kinds of learning centers.

■ Explain the purpose of learning centers.

■ Describe how learning centers are set up in the classroom.

■ Explain how to choose equipment, materials, and toys wisely.

■ Be able to evaluate an early childhood environment.

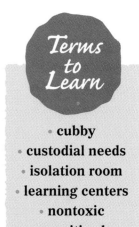

Terms to Learn

- cubby
- custodial needs
- isolation room
- learning centers
- nontoxic
- sanitized
- toxic
- traffic pattern

Now this is what I like to see," Irene Sullivan thought to herself as she gazed around the room. The preschool was buzzing with activity, but it was the kind of noise she always enjoyed hearing.

"Teacher, teacher, look! Our tower's getting tall!" Michelle called out to Irene. The cardboard block tower certainly was growing. Irene could see that it was about to tumble, but that was half the fun—watching the blocks fall to the carpet.

Not surprisingly, the tower came down, accompanied by squeals of delight. Two children in another corner of the room turned to look. One was wearing a large, floppy hat that nearly covered her face. Her dress hung in folds on the floor, and her oversized high-heeled shoes barely showed. A long feathery scarf completed Erika's outfit. After watching the excitement over the block tower, Erika folded her arms across her chest in the most adult manner she could put together and shook her head. "Those children are just too-oo noisy," she said to the little girl beside her.

As Irene continued to walk around the room, she stopped to admire a painting that Rob was hanging on the clothesline to dry. "What pretty, bright colors you used, Rob," she said. "Are they your favorites?"

"No," Rob replied. "I didn't paint with my favorite colors because I didn't want to use them all up."

Irene chuckled to herself as she began to get ready for a science activity. "There's never a dull moment," she thought.

INSIDE THE CENTER

Imagine for a moment that you are walking into a child care center or preschool. What do you think you will see? If the classroom has been carefully planned and equipped, you could come upon a scene similar to the one just described. You might notice that the children are participating in different activities. Because the atmosphere is inviting, a sense of warmth and enjoyment is present. Behavior problems are minimal. None of this comes about by chance. It comes with careful planning.

PLANNING THE ENVIRONMENT

Because child care facilities come in many shapes and sizes, what you discover inside isn't always the same. The physical space, whether several rooms or one large one, must be arranged so that similar functions can be carried out. When planning how to use space for a child care program, think about these principles:

- Does the plan meet program goals?
- Will the needs of all the children be served?
- Will the staff's needs be met?
- Does the plan encourage parental involvement?

When children work and play in interesting environments, they are more likely to behave well. Activity is constructive, not destructive. Children are less likely to be bored and frustrated, both of which can lead to inappropriate behavior.

Meeting Program Goals

The environment created in a child care facility has a strong impact on the staff's ability to meet program goals. With goals in mind, you can plan effective use of space.

Independence is one example of a goal that a program might promote. The aim is to create an environment that helps children become independent. In one center, after the children finish painting, the teacher hangs the smocks in a storage room. In another center, the children hang up their own smocks on hooks that have been placed within easy reach. Which technique do you think promotes independence? The children who hang up their own smocks are actually learning more about doing for themselves. Planning the environment with independence in mind helps make the goal achievable. The information below gives more ideas for linking the environment to program goals.

Meeting Program Goals

*H*ere are some ideas for promoting program goals in the early childhood classroom. Can you add other goals and techniques to the list?

STRONG SELF-ESTEEM
Display children's work. Provide toys and equipment that match the children's age and developmental level. Enable children to make choices.

SOCIAL SKILLS
Provide toys and activities that encourage children to play and work together.

PROBLEM-SOLVING ABILITY
Supply toys and materials that can be used in many creative ways. Blocks are an example.

LANGUAGE SKILLS
Place an interesting assortment of books at children's eye level. Label toys, equipment, and storage locations.

LARGE MUSCLE DEVELOPMENT
Include space for active play, making sure it is separate from quiet areas. Provide equipment and activities that require the use of the whole body.

SMALL MUSCLE COORDINATION
Provide toys and activities that encourage children to use their fingers and hands to practice small motor skills.

Planning for Development

Physical Development. All developmental areas are addressed when a child care environment is planned. Often one activity promotes different kinds of development. When Kevin paints, he develops his fine motor skills, which is part of his physical development.

Emotional Development. Painting also contributes to emotional development. Kevin uses his artwork to express emotions. He feels good about what he can do, especially when a caregiver recognizes his efforts.

Intellectual Development. Kevin's intellectual development progresses as he acquires new information. He learns the names of colors and begins to recognize different shapes. His creative abilities are tapped as he expresses himself artistically.

Social Development. Painting might also be part of Kevin's social development. This could happen in several ways—talking to a caregiver about his artwork, showing his painting to other children, and displaying his art during open house.

Meeting the Needs of Children

Everything you have learned about how children develop can be useful when planning space for a child care program. What a preschooler needs is quite different from a school-age child's needs. A preschooler will be frustrated if activities and toys are not age-appropriate. A school-age child won't be comfortable in a preschool setting. Understanding what a child is like at each stage of development enables you to provide a program that is

not only satisfying and safe for children but also provides opportunities for growth.

Remember to plan for all areas of development. As you can see from the illustration above, even one activity can be handled so that several types of development are addressed.

Custodial Care

In planning space for children, physical needs are high priority. These **custodial needs** include *toileting, hand washing, eating, napping, and resting.*

Toileting and hand-washing areas have child-size toilets and

> **Tip**
> **FROM THE**
> **Pros**
>
> **W**hen arranging classroom space, bend down to a child's level. How does everything look from a child's viewpoint? Is it inviting? You may not know for sure until you try this.

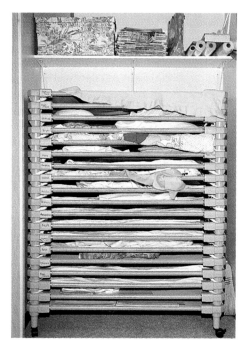

These cots are conveniently stored. The storage space used is minimal, which is often a concern in a child care setting.

sinks mounted low enough for children to reach. If necessary, a small stool can be stored close by. Mirrors are best placed at children's eye level.

Meal service is provided on low tables that can be used for play activities throughout the rest of the day. Chairs should be a comfortable size for children. Hard-surfaced flooring, such as tile or wood, under eating tables makes cleanup easier.

Full-day programs provide cot space for napping. By moving classroom equipment from the middle of the classroom, you can make space to set up cots. Equipment mounted on casters simplifies this job. When not in use, stack cots away from play space so children do not climb on them.

Children who become ill need a place to wait for their parents. A separate **isolation room** provides the child with *a cozy, comfortable place to rest when sick.* Children can be away from the curious eyes of other children, and illnesses are less easily spread. An adult must always be present with a child in an isolation room.

FOCUS ON INFANT/TODDLER PROGRAMS

The environment for infant and toddler programs differs somewhat from preschool programs. Because of diaper changing, proper ventilation and easy access to diaper disposal areas are necessary. Changing tables should be the proper height to limit caregiver back injuries. Hand-washing sinks should be close by in order to limit the spread of organisms that cause diseases. Low windows allow toddlers to see the outside world. A warm room adds to the children's comfort.

Specialized equipment is needed for infant/toddler classrooms. Also, infants and toddlers need more toys than just baby rattles. Think how much pleasure and discovery these youngsters can get from other types of toys. A few possibilities are mobiles; cradle gyms; toys that squeeze, pull, push, stack, and snap; nesting barrels; and sorter boxes.

Insuring Safety

When electrical appliances are present in the child care facility, caution is the byword. Such devices can be a hazard. Improperly placed cords are easy for children and adults to trip over. A small child might grab a dangling cord, pulling an appliance from a shelf or counter. Try taping cords to the wall so that they are out of reach. Electrical shock is possible when an appliance is kept near water. Place appliances in safe locations. Also, put protective covers over electrical outlets that are within the reach of children. Always take the safe approach, making sure cords and appliances are correctly handled.

Storage

Children arrive each day with an assortment of belongings and treasures. They may bring coats, hats, extra sets of clothing (for use in case of spills and toileting accidents), and special items for "show and tell." Many programs provide a cubby for each child. A **cubby** is *a small space for storage of personal items.* Often cubbies resemble small lockers without doors. Placing them near an entrance makes them convenient to use.

Cubbies can be identified by printing each child's name in bold letters over or under the cubby. Children who can't read their names need a snapshot of themselves posted beside each cubby. In some centers parents tape a family photo inside the cubby, both for identification purposes and so the child can see it when feeling lonely.

Children with Special Needs

Early childhood programs must be willing and able to serve children with special needs. An environment that is planned with foresight is more easily adapted when a special needs child enrolls. Wider classroom pathways accommodate wheelchairs and devices that aid walking. Ramps provide access to classrooms. Depending on a child's disability, some modifications may need to be made in restrooms and eating areas. Many other adaptations are possible, depending on the particular disability. By working closely with families, caregivers can meet the needs of all children, including those with special needs.

Meeting Staff Needs

To perform their duties effectively and efficiently, staff members also have certain needs. When space is planned with staff members in mind, their jobs are easier and more enjoyable. A good working environment helps keep staff morale high. In turn, their attitude toward the children is more likely to be positive.

Directors need a private office for conducting confidential business. Important files and records are kept here. The director's office is usually placed near the entrance so the director can monitor who comes and goes in the center.

Teachers need storage space for classroom materials, such as art supplies. A quiet location where they can take breaks is helpful. They also need space for storing personal belongings and teaching materials.

The kitchen staff needs space and equipment for food preparation and storage. Custodians keep cleaning equipment and supplies in a locked closet, since many cleaning supplies can be **toxic** (*poisonous*).

Meeting the Needs of Parents and Visitors

In a child care facility, an entrance that is inviting and convenient for parents as well as children helps get every day off to a better start. Parents sign the children in and out at a check-in table. A bulletin board at the entrance is useful for posting items of interest. You might see articles on parenting, newsletters, and menus for the week or month.

Many programs have an observation window. On the classroom side, this looks like a mirror. From the other side, however, parents and child development students can observe the children without being seen.

Some early childhood programs have a parents' room. This provides space for relaxation and often includes a lending library of parenting books. Parent support groups may meet here.

THE CLASSROOM

Large or small, every child care program has space for the activities that keep children constructively busy throughout their stay. This is the area, often called the classroom or playroom, where children spend most of their time. The size of the classroom space dictates how many children the program can serve.

People who plan child care facilities pay special attention to the classroom space. What would you do to make such areas pleasing, safe, and easy to use for children

Staff members function best when they have proper facilities. This kitchen enables employees to prepare tasty, nutritious meals in an efficient manner.

A learning center should entice children to participate. It should also enable children to see exactly where to return the toys and materials they use. This is one way to promote organization skills. Books displayed openly at eye level create interest. Children can clearly see where they should be stored when done.

and staff? Wall colors that are warm and bright and area rugs contribute to a pleasant atmosphere. Windows also add brightness. What matters even more is how space is arranged and what is contained within.

Learning Centers

The classroom area of a well-planned child care program is divided into learning centers. **Learning centers** are *areas clearly defined for specific types of play.* Each learning center is organized around a theme or curriculum topic, such as blocks, art, or science. Each is suited to the age of the children who will use it.

Tip
FROM THE
Pros

*B*attery-operated toys often perform *for* children rather than encourage active involvement. In addition, batteries need to be replaced frequently, making the toys expensive. Batteries may also leak chemicals. Look for better alternatives to these toys.

Learning centers provide an organized way to arrange space and manage the activity in a center. Specifically, they:

- Direct children to activities and focus their attention.
- Allow children to learn by doing, while working at their own pace.
- Provide opportunities for independent and small group play.
- Distribute children throughout the classroom, minimizing conflicts and noise in any one area.

A child care program may not be able to offer every type of learning center that is possible. Budget and space can be limiting. Most programs, however, do try to include certain learning centers as a core. These are centers for art, language arts, dramatic play, social studies, music, science, math, blocks, and active play. Other learning centers, such as woodworking and computers, can be added to the program as space and resources allow. The size and scope of each learning center also depends on space and resources.

Many preschoolers are becoming familiar with computers. A touch screen makes this educational game easy to use.

Arranging Learning Centers

A typical child care classroom is a large rectangular room. Deciding how to arrange the learning centers within the room can be a challenge. You want each area to be distinct from the others, yet for safety reasons, they all need to be visible to supervising teachers. When space is limited, combining or rotating learning centers works well. An example of how the learning centers are arranged in one preschool is shown on pages 174-175. You will learn much more about the contents and use of these centers later in the text.

When learning centers are well marked, children understand the limits for play. Most areas need at least three boundaries. For instance, a block center can be placed in a corner of the room. The two walls make automatic boundaries. A block storage unit can serve as a third "wall." Colored tape on the floor can also divide play spaces. A piano might separate the music area from the art center.

Learning centers can be arranged so that children have a degree of privacy when

Focus on School-Age Program

After a long day at school, the school-age child may be ready for either action or a little time to rest and recover. A well-equipped play yard scaled to the children's size and abilities helps release pent-up energy after sitting all day. A quiet corner with a bean bag chair and books is good for relaxing. When children have homework to do, they need a place to complete it.

Even though they are gone much of the day, school-age children still need a storage place for their belongings. Jackets and coats, as well as school books and supplies, can be stored in lockers or another handy location.

needed. Lofts (platforms raised a few feet off the ground) allow children to get away from more boisterous activities and be "alone." Books, puppets, and puzzles are used in this area. Large wooden crates (checked for splinters and protruding nails) can provide a small enclosure that is comforting to children. If you drape a colorful bedsheet over a table, children can cuddle up underneath. Add floor pillows and this space becomes cozy and inviting to young children. Although areas like these are aimed at giving children a chance for privacy, adults must still be sure that children are supervised at all times.

When arranging space, consider *the direction of movement that children take as they go from one part of the classroom to another*. This is called the **traffic pattern.**

Well-planned traffic patterns limit congestion from the time children enter until they leave the center.

Outdoor Play

Although an indoor area is included for some active play, an outdoor area extends this learning center. Play yards may be equipped with climbers, low slides, and soft-seated swings. Children enjoy sand and water activities as well as gardening. They need accessories that challenge them to develop their large motor skills. Many programs provide balls, hoops, tricycles, wagons, balance beams, and scooters. A boundary, such as a fence, surrounds the outdoor play area to keep children from wandering away.

Even a few steps up into a loft can give a child a sense of privacy. Note that these children can still be observed by caregivers as they read.

The Learning Center Plan

Blocks

The block center is rich with learning opportunities. For a classroom of 20 children, 400 blocks are recommended. Placing the block center on a carpeted area helps reduce noise. Toy vehicles and plastic zoo and farm animals add to the enjoyment.

Science

The science center encourages children to investigate the world through their senses. A low table displays science collections. Magnifying glasses, balance scales, and magnets aid children's investigations.

Math

Math concepts, such as matching, sorting, comparing, counting, and classifying, are explored in the math center. Concepts related to color, size, and shape are also developed.

Music

As expected, musical instruments are part of this center. Tambourines, finger cymbals, triangles, and drums are all possibilities. Compact disks, records, and audio tapes are also located in the music center.

Art

The art center allows for creativity and imagination. The center should be uncarpeted and near a water source. Children may draw, paint, and paste. They might work with dough, clay, fabric, wallpaper scraps, and cardboard.

Active Play

Here children exercise their large muscles and develop coordination. Children might play with bean bags or streamers. Well-supervised areas for climbing, tumbling, and sliding are desirable.

Language Arts

This center, which includes social studies, lures children into the love of speaking, listening, reading, and writing. A quiet area with good lighting, it might contain a rocking chair, large pillows, and bean bag chairs for comfort.

Dramatic Play

In the dramatic play center, children use child-size furnishings, dress-up clothes, dolls, and stuffed animals to act out the world as they see it. Props are changed to reflect changing themes.

CHOOSING TOYS AND MATERIALS

*O*nce you have the space arranged for learning centers, you need the right toys and materials to put in them. Use good judgment, knowledge of children, and creativity when deciding. Good choices promote learning. Poor choices can create safety hazards and increase behavior prob-

lems. Some questions to ask when selecting toys and equipment are listed below. The following guidelines will also be helpful when making choices:

- ***Toys and materials should be appropriate for children's ages and abilities.*** Four-year-olds can use blunt scissors with supervision. The same scissors, however, would be unsafe for a two-year-old.

Selecting Equipment and Toys

*C*areful thought pays when choosing equipment and toys. You are likely to be more satisfied with your selections when you ask questions like these before choosing:

- Is the item safe? Metal, wood, and plastic edges should be rounded rather than sharp. Paint should be nontoxic. **Nontoxic** means *not poisonous.* Some paints and other finishes contain ingredients that are toxic, especially to young children who may chew on them.

- Will the item withstand heavy or rough use by a group of up to 20 children? Is it durable?

- Will the toy be easy to clean? Can it be **sanitized**, or *cleaned in a way that will kill the organisms that can cause illness?*

- Can children of different ages use the toy?

- Does the toy encourage cooperative play rather than aggressive, or even violent, play?

- Can more than one child use the item at a time?

- Does your classroom have storage space for the item?

- Can the item be used in more than one way? Will it generate creativity?

- Does the item encourage children's active involvement rather than passive observation? Will it hold a child's interest?

- Will children learn basic concepts while playing with the toy? Will it support program goals? Will it reinforce curriculum themes and objectives?

- Will the toy allow for sensory learning?

- Would both girls and boys enjoy the toy? Is the toy free of racial, cultural, and gender stereotypes?

- Are children likely to have fun with the toy?

THE MULTICULTURAL CLASSROOM

Sensitivity is a good guide when choosing multicultural toys and other items for the early childhood classroom. Will just anything work? The answer is "no." Some books, posters, puppets, and dolls may be insulting. They may show stereotypes of different cultures. They may focus only on historical images, rather than today. They may be inaccurate representations. Before you include an item in the classroom, examine how it depicts the culture. Would you feel good about having the item in the classroom if the culture were yours? If the item passes your inspection, include it along with others. Make multiculturalism ongoing, with many items visible and usable every day. A single doll or poster that appears only on certain holidays teaches children that multiculturalism is here today and gone tomorrow. That's not reality.

Safety is a high priority when choosing toys and materials. What evidence do you see that safety is a concern in this activity?

- ***Provide a variety of materials.*** Children need variety and novelty to keep their interest. They become bored if offered the same learning materials every day. Rotate items regularly, maintaining a balance between familiar items and new ones.

- ***Include materials that children can look at, touch, listen to, smell, and sometimes taste.*** Such materials enable children to use all their senses for learning.

- ***Materials should include different cultures.*** Children's books, puppets, dolls, and posters can reflect many ethnic groups. Activities using foods, customs, and music of multiple cultures make learning interesting and exciting.

- ***Provide enough materials so children can comfortably share.*** Having too few materials frustrates children and sets the stage for fights. The younger the children, the more important it is to have duplicate toys.

PLANNING FOR QUALITY

Wherever you work in child care, there are likely to be improvements you want to make. Sometimes resources are limited. Even small spaces, however, can be carefully arranged to make the most of them. With knowledge and a little ingenuity, you can make the environment work well for you and the children in your care.

Toys should be suitable for the children's age. Has that guideline been taken into consideration in this setting?

Building Professional Skills

Management

WHAT IS MANAGEMENT?

On many jobs, the ability to be a good manager is vital. What does it mean to be a good manager? The person who knows how to use resources to accomplish goals is likely to manage well. This skill is useful in many situations.

Management in Action

Ted Hargrove sighed with discouragement. After only two weeks on the job at the Sunshine Child Care Center, he was running out of materials. He was responsible for the art and woodworking centers, and his budget was limited. "It's time to do something," he thought to himself.

With determination, he started to make a list. "What do I need and where can I get it?" were the two questions that guided his list making. When the list was complete, he was ready for action.

It wasn't long before the art and woodworking centers were in good shape again. Ted had placed an article in the center newsletter, asking parents for donations of computer paper, scraps of wallpaper, leftover fabric, cardboard, and any other materials that might be useful for art projects. The response had been terrific. A trip to the lumber yard had yielded free scrap lumber. He was able to get assorted nails and screws as a donation from a hardware store. "That was easy on the budget," Ted thought. "Now what else can I find?"

Your Analysis

1. What was Ted's goal?

2. What resources did Ted use to meet his goal?

3. What might have happened if Ted had not used his management skills?

4. How might management skills help in the situations below?

   - Many of the toys in a preschool need repairs.

   - Children enter a center from two doors, causing confusion as the center opens.

   - Several child care workers seem to be unhappy on the job.

Chapter 9 Review

Chapter Summary

- Basic principles guide the planning for how space is used in a child care facility.
- Program goals should be addressed through use of space in the classroom.
- Classrooms should be planned to allow for the space and equipment needed to meet children's custodial needs.
- Space should be designed according to children's ages and stages of development. Children with physical disabilities or limitations may have special space needs.
- The handling of space must also take into consideration the requirements of staff, parents, and visitors.
- Classrooms contain learning centers that are suited to the age of the children. They provide an organized way to arrange space and manage activities.
- Boundaries define the areas of learning centers.
- Outdoor as well as indoor play can address the need for children to be active.
- Toys and materials must be carefully chosen.

Reviewing the Facts

1. What four principles guide the planning of space in a child care program?
2. What helps make goals achievable in a child care program?
3. What are custodial needs?
4. Why does a child care facility need an isolation room?
5. For what is a cubby used?
6. Why is a good working environment needed for staff members?
7. Of what use is an observation window in a child care program?
8. What is a learning center?
9. List nine typical learning centers.
10. List five guidelines for choosing toys and materials.
11. What special features are needed in an infant/toddler program? In a school-age program?

Thinking Critically

1. What signs would indicate to you that the environment in a preschool was poorly planned?
2. In what ways might the arrangement of a child care center teach the children organization skills?
3. Why is behavior likely to be better in a well-planned child care environment?
4. Do you agree or disagree with this statement: a good learning center is expensive to equip. Explain your answer.
5. What would you do if a parent donated splintered blocks and plastic building bricks that were cracked to the program?

Activities and Applications

1. **Evaluation Checklist.** Imagine that you are the parent of a preschool child who is going into a child care program. Develop a checklist that you would use to determine the quality of a program's environment.

2. **Entry Design.** Using words and drawings, design an entry area for a child care program. Include the traffic pattern, furnishings, and equipment.

3. **Choosing Supplies and Equipment.** Review at least two catalogs of early childhood equipment and supplies. Make a list of the items you would purchase to equip one learning center. Calculate the total cost.

SCHOOL TO WORK

Your Professional Portfolio

How would you design a child care classroom? Try your hand at becoming a designer by drawing your own layout for the learning centers in a preschool program. Include labels to show the centers and the contents that you would include. Also indicate the main traffic patterns. Place the completed design in your portfolio.

Observing and Analyzing

Evaluating Environments in Early Childhood Programs

Observing child care environments can tell you much about a program's effectiveness. More than one visit may be needed. First, examine the facility to see how space is used. Find out about the program goals and look at how state licensing requirements are met. Finally, examine the effectiveness of learning centers.

To observe environments, choose one or more of the locations listed below. Be sure to telephone ahead to schedule your visit. Ask for printed information about the program.

After observing, write a one- to two-page summary of what you saw. If you visit more than one location, describe the similarities and differences in the programs. Then share results with other students in your class. How do your observations compare and contrast?

- **Observing Preschools.** Observe a preschool classroom both before the children arrive and while children are there. Notice what kinds and sizes of furniture are in the room. Is the furniture appropriate for children in this age group? Where and how is it arranged? Does the classroom have learning centers? If so, what are they and how are they arranged? How is the traffic flow between centers? Can the children move freely? Describe the kinds of equipment you find in the learning centers. What large muscle equipment is available for children for indoor and outdoor use? What health and safety measures do you see?

- **Observing Child Care Centers.** Observe at a child care center both before the children arrive and while children are there. Look for the same information described above for preschools.

- **Observing Family Day Care Homes.** Observe at a licensed family day care home, realizing, of course, that this type of child care program will differ from a larger program. Spend some time talking with the child care provider when children are not present. What licensing requirements are necessary? What amount of space is required for the number of children served? How are children's needs met for active and quiet play and for large motor and small motor play? How is the space arranged for children? What equipment is available? How are health and safety requirements met?

Chapter 10

Keeping Children Safe

CHAPTER OBJECTIVES

■ Explain who has responsibility for children's safety.

■ Develop an effective safety policy.

■ Describe the safety forms used in an early childhood program.

■ Identify and explain how to eliminate safety hazards.

■ Explain how to promote safety with children.

■ Describe what should be done during medical, fire, and weather-related emergencies.

■ Assemble a first aid kit.

Terms to Learn

- accident log
- accident report form
- cardiopulmonary resuscitation (CPR)
- emergency treatment waiver form
- Heimlich maneuver
- liable for negligence
- prevention
- safety hazards
- safety policy
- syrup of ipecac

s far as I'm concerned," Nick Turner said, smiling at Melinda, "every child in here is an accident waiting to happen." Nick chuckled as he gave his newest employee the introductory tour of the child care center. "You know how children are. They love to explore. They don't think about danger. They're energetic but not well coordinated. And they just don't have the knowledge and experience that adults have. That's why we do everything we can to keep them safe."

As Melinda followed Nick around, she noticed some of the signs of safety in the center. Fire extinguishers and smoke detectors were on the walls of every room. "That's the medicine cabinet," Nick said as he pointed to a cupboard in the nurse's office. "There's a first aid kit and medications in it, but it's always locked. I'll show you where the key is."

A few minutes later Nick and Melinda were in the play yard, where six preschoolers were having fun. The yard was surrounded by a sturdy fence with a gate and lock. "This looks like a nice, safe play area," Melinda commented.

At that moment, one child ran across the grass and bumped another one, sending her into tears. "I guess that's one thing we can't completely control," Nick said to Melinda, shrugging his shoulders as he gave the child a hug. "Even though we do our best, we can't always protect them from each other."

SAFETY—WHOSE RESPONSIBILITY?

Proper safety in an early childhood program is everyone's business—the director, teachers, teacher's aides, cooks, bus drivers, and custodians. A safe environment comes about with careful planning and continuous attention.

The very nature of children makes them prone to injury. They are excitable and impulsive; they act first and think later. Their curiosity and enthusiasm urge them to explore and investigate. Unfortunately, however, they are not able to anticipate threats to their safety.

As an example, at one preschool, three-year-old Angelo caught a glimpse of a butterfly floating by a window. He was just about to climb onto the windowsill to get a better look when his teacher gently redirected his attention to a poster with butterflies on it in the science center.

Child care employees have a legal as well as a moral obligation to watch for children's safety. No one can care for children without taking this responsibility seriously.

Individual state governments establish minimum safety standards in their child care licensing laws. This is the government's contribution to insuring children's safety in child care situations.

Everyone who works in a program must know and follow the program's safety policy. An effective policy not only includes all major areas of safety, but also identifies specific procedures to insure safety.

Additional regulations affecting child care include fire marshal codes, building safety codes, and health department codes. These regulations represent the community's role in protecting young children.

Safety is of supreme importance in child care programs. If child care professionals do not prevent or handle accidents to the best of their ability, they could be held **liable for negligence.** This means they could be *held accountable in a court of law for neglecting to prevent an accident or to handle an emergency in a responsible manner.* Early childhood programs should carry liability insurance to cover costs if sued for injuries. Some staff members choose to carry personal professional liability insurance when they are not covered by the employer's insurance.

DEVELOPING A SAFETY POLICY

To make their commitment to safety clear to everyone, program directors develop a **safety policy**. *This policy states the rules and procedures to follow to insure children's physical and emotional well-being.* A safety policy must address many areas of concern, including:

- Maintaining a safe facility.
- Toy safety.
- Rules for children's conduct.
- Positive methods of discipline to prevent questions of child abuse.
- Transportation safety.
- Safety inspections.
- Emergency procedures.
- Evacuation procedures.

Staff training manuals should include the written safety policy. This should be reviewed with employees when they begin work. Some programs provide in-service (on-the-job) training on the rules and procedures to follow. Employees may be asked to sign a paper stating that they have read and understand the safety policy.

Safety policies should also be clearly identified in parent information materials. This helps reassure parents that their children will be carefully and responsibly looked after at all times. It also informs parents of their role in complying with safety rules.

SAFETY FORMS

In following safety policy, staff members need to be familiar with the forms that they have to fill out as they work with children. These forms apply to:

- *Injuries.* All incidents involving injury, no matter how minor, must be recorded on an accident report form and an accident log immediately after a child is treated. The **accident report form** is *used to record specific information about any accident involving a child.* It should include the child's name, injury date, and time of injury; names of witnesses to the injury; the classroom location of the injury; equipment or products involved; the cause of the injury; the type of injury; who gave the first aid and what they did; and any action taken by a doctor or dentist. This form is placed in the child's file. An **accident log** *is used to keep a written record of all injuries as they happen.* Logs may be used to record other types of information as well. Explanations are written in the log (perhaps a notebook or clipboard) on a day-to-day basis. This documentation can be referenced later if questions or problems arise.

- **Suspected Abuse.** Any suspected cases of child abuse or neglect must be documented and reported. Chapter 11 includes more about this subject.

- **Releasing Children.** Children may leave the program *only* with their parents, unless parents have signed a waiver that gives their permission for someone else to pick up the child. In addition, many programs request a picture of any other person that the parents authorize for pickup. Before the child can be released, the person who picks up the child must show a form of identification that indicates his or her name.

- **Emergency Treatment.** An **emergency treatment waiver form** must be filled out for each child. *This statement, signed by a parent or legal guardian, gives the program permission to secure emergency medical treatment for a sick or injured child.* It usually states that no emergency treatment will be given to a child without parent/guardian consent except in a life-threatening situation. Also included on the form are: telephone numbers of parents or guardians at home and at work; times when they can be reached at these numbers; additional people to contact when the parent or guardian is unavailable, including telephone numbers and relationship to the child; and the name and telephone number of the child's medical care provider.

Give two reasons for documenting accidents in writing.

THE MULTICULTURAL CLASSROOM

Educating staff and parents about safety and emergency procedures can be especially difficult when working with people of diverse backgrounds. They may have been taught standards and procedures that are different from the policies in your program or community. Home remedies and cures for such things as burns, headaches, insect bites, hiccups, and upset stomachs are not the same everywhere. To build understanding, one solution is to invite specialists or a panel of experts to discuss these topics, handle the questions and answers, and make suggestions in a nonjudgmental way. You might include the information in a parent orientation meeting.

Children need to learn safety rules and the reasons behind them. Frequent reminders will be needed.

PREVENTING ACCIDENTS AND INJURIES

By definition, **prevention** means *taking action to keep something from happening*. Of course, no child care program is completely free of accidents. With prevention, however, the number and severity of incidents can be limited.

Possibly the single most important precaution regarding safety is to *supervise children at all times*. Never leave a child unattended.

Another way to prevent accidents is to anticipate problem situations. By understanding child development and children's behavior, caregivers can reduce the risk of mishaps. Knowledge makes them aware that what is perfectly safe for a four-year-old may be hazardous for a one-year-old. Teachers should never assume children will use toys and equipment in appropriate ways. They should ask themselves, "How else might some children use this item?"

Keen observation is also important for accident prevention. Always be on the lookout for **safety hazards**. These are *items, conditions, and situations that could put*

Building Professional Skills

Common Sense

WHAT IS COMMON SENSE?

Common sense is a combination of experience, observation, and reasoning skills. It allows you to see actions and aspects of a situation that might cause problems and to take steps to avoid them. It also helps you deal with a problem in a logical, rational manner. Common sense is the practical use of your thinking skills.

Common Sense in Action

"We'll have an 'outside' day when we can really enjoy it," Javier told the children. He was as disappointed as anyone by the unexpectedly cold and cloudy weather. He had promised his preschoolers that they could work on their art projects and eat lunch outside that day. True, most of them had jackets, but he felt the sudden change in the weather would be especially uncomfortable when they weren't used to it.

Although disappointed, the children accepted his decision and began to work on their art projects. After a while, however, one girl began to complain of a headache. Javier sent her to the school nurse, who called the girl's father. After lunch, two boys also said they had headaches, and stomachaches as well. They, too, were sent home.

Javier was starting to worry. "What could be making the children sick?" he wondered to himself. "The graham crackers I gave them as a snack were from the same box I used yesterday. Their art supplies are all nontoxic and haven't caused problems before. And the two boys brought their lunches from home, so they ate different things. What's going on?"

An idea came to mind. "Is this the first time the furnace has been on since last winter?" he asked the school custodian.

"Yes, it is," the custodian replied, "but I wish the weather had held off. I haven't had a chance to clean the furnace yet."

Javier took his suspicions to the school director, who immediately called the utility company. Tests of the air showed that the furnace was giv-ing off unusually high levels of some fumes—not dangerous, but enough to make some younger children sick. Immediate steps were taken to correct the situation. "We're all grateful for your alertness, Javier," the director said to him. "You just might have prevented something worse from happening."

Your Analysis

1. What was Javier's first common sense decision?

2. How did knowledge of children's health help Javier discover the cause of their illness?

3. What might have happened if Javier had not pursued his concerns?

4. What can people do to improve their common sense?

A safe outdoor play area gives children an opportunity to develop new skills. How could you minimize the possibility of injury from a swing set?

children in physical or emotional danger. Hazards can be found in indoor and outdoor play areas, on field trips, and even on short walks. In fact, wherever you find children, there is a potential for mishaps.

Environmental Safety Precautions

Indoor and outdoor play areas and learning centers should be inspected daily for safety hazards, as suggested in the information below and on page 189. Toys, equipment, and facilities should be checked for wear and damage. Such hazards as torn carpeting and exposed wiring should be reported for immediate repair. Keep children away from these until repairs are made. Litter, especially glass, should be disposed of quickly. Full safety inspections, using a checklist, should be conducted frequently.

Outdoor Safety Precautions to Take

- Surround play yards with at least four-foot tall (1.25 m) fencing with a locked gate.
- Choose climbing equipment that is the right size for children's height and abilities.
- Check equipment frequently for splinters, jagged edges, and rusted metal.

- Place padding underneath and around climbing and swinging equipment to cushion falls.
- Locate swing sets away from the traffic pattern so children running by aren't injured.
- Make sure shrubs, bushes, and trees do not have leaves and berries that could be poisonous if eaten.

- Provide safety goggles and nonelectric tools in the woodworking area.
- Supervise wading pools constantly. Surround pools with a locked fence.
- Choose soft, grassy areas for play space; provide cement or asphalt for wheeled toys.

Indoor Safety Precautions to Take

- Use only nontoxic materials in art projects and in the science center. Remember that some plant leaves and berries can be poisonous if eaten.

- Provide only round-tipped scissors.

- Take special care with electricity, particularly when cooking with electric appliances and playing with electric and battery-operated toys. Make sure wires are not frayed and batteries are not leaking. Cover all unused electric outlets.

- Provide appropriate padding under climbing equipment.

- Provide handrails on stairways.

- Use nonslip rugs on hard floors.

- Lock the staff's personal belongings in a closet or cabinet. This applies especially to purses, which may contain such hazards as fingernail files, scissors, pocket knives, and matches.

- Label potential poisons and lock them out of children's reach. This includes cleaning preparations, aerosol sprays, drain cleaners, and even medicine. (Some children like the taste of flavored medicines, which may result in overdose.)

- Place decals at children's eye level on low windows and sliding glass doors. This helps children be aware of the glass and keeps them from running into or even through it.

- Bolt tall toy shelves to the wall to prevent them from toppling onto a child.

- Make sure water temperature in bathrooms is warm, not hot, to prevent burns.

- Do not allow children in kitchen and garage areas.

Toy Safety

Suppose you were buying a stuffed animal for an infant nursery. Would you choose one with sewn-on button eyes or one with embroidered eyes? This is the kind of safety decision you make routinely when stocking a center with toys. The button-eyed animal is a poor choice because the eyes could come off and be swallowed by an infant. Here are some tips that will help when choosing toys:

- Select toys that are appropriate for the ages of children you care for.
- Read labels and catalog descriptions for age recommendations before purchasing toys.

- Check all toys for sharp edges by running your fingers carefully over the edges of the toys. By law, new toys that are to be used by children under eight should be free of sharp glass, sharp points, and metal edges.

- Examine labels to be sure that plastic toys are shatterproof and nonflammable.

- Make certain that painted toys and art supplies are labeled nontoxic.

- Check to be sure that toys, and any removable parts from toys, are not small enough to swallow or inhale. For children under the age of three, these items should be no smaller than the approximate size of a child's fist.

| Children need to learn new skills but in a safe way. Safety scissors, for example, minimize the possibility of injury.

• Avoid toys with long cords or strings for use by infants and toddlers. If a cord becomes wrapped around the neck, the child may strangle.

When programs have children of different ages, older and younger children should play with their toys in separate areas. Teach the older ones to keep their toys away from younger children. Storage areas for these toys should also be out of the range of young children.

To manage toy safety, a program might assign the responsibility to one employee. For example, as part of her morning routine before the children arrive, Fala examines the toys stored on shelves and in crates. She removes anything broken, making note of the repairs to be made. Fala rarely finds broken toys anymore, since the teachers have encouraged the children to bring broken toys immediately to them. This makes Fala's job easier, and the center is a safer place.

FOCUS ON INFANT/TODDLER PROGRAMS

Infants and toddlers are especially vulnerable to safety hazards and emergencies. Because they cannot communicate their difficulties or get themselves away from danger quickly, adults are needed for good supervision.

Fires require especially quick action when infants are involved, because they must be transported away from the danger. For speed, caregivers often put several infants in one crib with wheels and rapidly move them to safety. This is much quicker than carrying two infants out at a time.

Infants and toddlers put everything in their mouths. Therefore, rattles and shaker toys must be sturdy so small beads inside do not fall out.

Movable pieces of equipment used around infants and toddlers must have locking wheels so they stay in place. Doors on low cabinets should be equipped with childproof locks to prevent injury and poisoning.

Transportation Safety Precautions

Child care facilities sometimes provide transportation for field trips and to and from home or school. Many precautions must be taken to make sure that children are protected. These include:

- Conducting safety inspections on vehicles.
- Making sure all drivers are legally licensed to drive a large vehicle.
- Equipping vehicles with seat belts and carseats.
- Providing an adult bus supervisor.
- Having a first aid kit in each vehicle.
- Making sure all vehicles are equipped with a working two-way radio, flashlight, fire extinguisher, and city map with the location of hospitals clearly identified.

Tip FROM THE Pros

Keeping track of children can be a challenge on a field trip. Try using safety pins to fasten the name tags to the backs of children's shirts. When name tags are on the children's backs, they are less likely to be torn off and lost.

Field Trip Safety Precautions

Since field trips may take you to places not specifically designed for children, they offer added safety concerns. You can plan for these. For example, when Dominic was arranging a field trip to a fire station, he toured the station beforehand and talked with the fire chief to identify any safety hazards they might encounter. Prior to the field trip, he told the children (and also the staff and parent supervisors) about these hazards and the rules they would follow to prevent possible accidents. Dominic also made sure that he collected the permission forms signed by the children's parents or legal guardians before the trip. In addition, he took all emergency treatment waiver forms with him.

At any field trip site, vehicles should be parked in a safe, off-street area as children

Field trips can provide wonderful opportunities for learning, but they require careful planning and extra supervision to insure safety. An alternative is bringing the community to the children. These preschoolers have been eagerly awaiting the policeman's visit.

enter and exit them. Each child should wear a name tag identifying the child care facility's name and telephone number. Inviting parents or other adults on the field trip increases supervision and can add to the enjoyment.

PROMOTING SAFETY WITH CHILDREN

*C*hildren can learn about safety in many ways. As with other behavior, role modeling by adults is one of the best teachers. Children also learn safety concepts in the classroom. They can create posters on safety practices and listen to stories about safety. Field trips can reinforce safety practices too. Visits to the fire station, hospital, and doctor's office emphasize the importance of being careful. Children also learn about safety when taking part in safety inspections with teachers.

When talking to children about safety, speak in positive terms. Stress good safety habits, rather than listing all of the "don'ts." Here are some simple safety rules children should be taught to follow:

- Walk indoors. Running is for outside.

- Play with toys carefully. Give broken toys to a teacher.
- Stack hard blocks only to (the child's) shoulder height. (Higher buildings might topple on children.)
- Settle conflicts with words, not by hitting, biting, pushing, or throwing toys.
- Tables and shelves are for games and toys, not for climbing.
- Stay with the teacher when on walks or a field trip.
- Ask permission before going to the play yard.
- Obey safety rules when using art supplies, cooking utensils, and woodworking tools.
- Be careful when playing on riding toys. Try not to bump into other children or into their toys.
- Tell a teacher right away if a stranger comes into the classroom or play yard.
- Tell a parent, teacher, or good friend who is an adult if anyone touches you on a private area of your body.

Learning what to do in an emergency situation gives children confidence. This is one of a series of activities to help these children learn and remember fire safety rules.

FOCUS ON SCHOOL-AGE PROGRAMS

School-age children enjoy rough-and-tumble play, which means they are likely to get scrapes, bumps, and bruises. With this age group, plan games that allow children to use their physical energy without getting hurt. Some games school-age children want to participate in, such as tackle football, can be dangerous to muscles and bones. Program rules should not allow these sports. Such games as touch football, dodgeball, catch, and relay races tend to result in fewer injuries.

Although rare, some school-age children experiment with drugs, alcohol, and cigarette smoking. Changes in behavior may indicate a child's involvement. You might notice withdrawal from friends or a change in friends, a change in grades or attitude toward school, or outbursts of violent or destructive behavior. A teacher should keep a watchful eye for behavior signals and report them to parents.

EMERGENCY PROCEDURES

How do you react in an emergency? Not everyone responds in the same way. Emergencies can cause pain and confusion, especially when people are not prepared for them. Establishing, reviewing, and practicing emergency procedures can help staff and children remain calm and respond quickly to any emergency.

Emergency procedures should be outlined in staff training manuals and reviewed regularly during staff meetings. The child care staff should take part in ongoing safety training to instruct them on emergency techniques.

Children should also be prepared for emergencies. Such information as fire escape routes should be prominently posted in halls and classrooms. The telephone numbers for the fire, police, and weather stations; hospital; ambulance service; child abuse hotline; and poison control center should be listed next to every telephone. In many areas, 911 can be dialed to summon emergency medical technicians and other emergency help. Children as well as staff members should practice emergency procedures regularly.

In an emergency, children look to adults for guidance and comfort. The calmness that comes from being prepared and knowing what to do can literally be a lifesaver.

Handling Medical Emergencies

Even when prevention is practiced conscientiously, accidents and injuries do occur. A confident, appropriate response is much more likely when you have thought ahead of time about what to do and you know the basic procedure to follow.

In any medical emergency, the first rule is to stay calm. Determine how severe the injury is. Decide what kind of on-site care is appropriate and whether professional treatment is needed.

When Injuries Are Minor

Often injuries are minor and can be quickly treated. For bumps and bruises an ice pack minimizes swelling; a scraped knee may require thorough cleaning with soap and water, a mild antiseptic, and a bandage. First aid training gives employees the knowledge to treat simple injuries.

Certain supplies are needed to handle minor injuries. Blankets and towels should be available. Each classroom should also have a first aid kit that is easily accessible to teachers yet out of the reach of children. In addition, a kit should be available outdoors and taken along on field trips. First aid kits contain these items: a first aid book, bandages, gauze pads and strips, adhesive tape, thermometers, flashlight, tongue depressors, cotton balls, blunt scissors, liquid soap, dis-

posable latex gloves, tweezers, and syrup of ipecac (IH-pih-kak).

Syrup of ipecac is *a substance that, when swallowed, causes vomiting*. Remember that syrup of ipecac is recommended only in some cases of poisoning. Call the poison control center before you give syrup of ipecac to a child. Some poisons may cause more damage to a child's esophagus and mouth when vomiting forces the substance back up.

When Injuries Are Serious

If a child requires professional medical treatment, the teacher should stay with the child and administer any appropriate first aid while someone else calls an ambulance or other emergency assistance. The child's parents should then be called, and the medical treatment waiver should be obtained from the child's file. If parents do not arrive in time, a teacher should go to the hospital with the child.

Occasionally an injury is life threatening, requiring immediate attention. Staff members should be certified in infant/child **cardiopulmonary resuscitation (CPR)** (CAR-dee-oh-PULL-muh-NAIR-ee ree-SUH-suh-TAY-shun). This is *a life-saving technique used when the heartbeat and/or breathing has*

Bumps, bruises, and scrapes are common injuries for young children. Supplying sympathy and comfort is as important as giving first aid.

The Heimlich maneuver is used when a child over age one (or an adult) is choking. Only use it if the child is conscious but cannot speak or cough. Stand behind the child and make a fist with one hand. Press the thumb against the child's abdomen just beneath the rib cage. Grasp your fist with your hand. Give quick, upward thrusts until the object is dislodged.

stopped. Gentle puffs of air are given to the person while forcing the heart to pump blood by applying gentle pressure to the chest. CPR can be used for suffocation, electrical shock, choking, drowning, and heart failure. CPR, which should only be administered by trained people, can keep the person alive until professional help arrives. The American Red Cross, along with many hospitals, provides excellent first aid and CPR training.

Choking

An important technique to remedy choking in adults and children over one year of age is the **Heimlich maneuver** (HIME-lick muh-NOO-vur). *With this technique, pressure on the body is used to dislodge an object that is blocking air through the windpipe or throat.* A diagram that shows and explains how to use the Heimlich maneuver should be posted in the eating area, and staff members should be trained to use the procedure. This maneuver should not be used on infants because of the possibility of internal injury. With infants, trained caregivers use a first aid procedure called *back blows.*

Poisoning

Poisoning is a very serious medical emergency and one of the greatest hazards to children. The chart on page 196 contains a list of some poisonous subtances. Signs that may indicate poisoning are:

- Burns around or in the mouth and throat.
- Vomiting from swallowing poisons or chemicals.
- Burns or rash on the skin from direct contact with poisons or chemicals.
- Burning or irritation of the eyes or blindness caused by poisons or chemicals coming in contact with the eyes.
- Choking, coughing, headache, nausea, or dizziness from inhaling fumes, sprays, or poisonous gases.

Examples of Poisonous Substances

PLANTS
English ivy

Daffodil bulbs

Rhubarb leaves

Holly berries

Poison ivy and oak

Contact: swallowing and skin

MEDICINE
Aspirin

Sleeping pills

Tranquilizers

Vitamins

Cold and allergy preparations

Contact: swallowing

CLEANING PRODUCTS
Ammonia

Laundry detergent

Bleach

Drain and toilet bowl cleaners

Disinfectants

Furniture polish

Contact: swallowing, skin, eyes, and inhaling

PERSONAL CARE PRODUCTS
Shampoo

Soap

Nail polish and nail polish remover

Perfumes and aftershave lotions

Mouthwash

Rubbing alcohol

Sunscreens and lotions

Contact: swallowing, eyes, and inhaling

MISCELLANEOUS PRODUCTS
Insecticides

Insect repellant

Paint thinner

Paint

Mouse poison

Contact: swallowing, skin, eyes, and inhaling

If poisoning is suspected, quickly try to determine the cause. Remember that emergency procedures described on product labels are not always correct. Instead of using them, immediately call a poison control center and follow their directions. Be prepared to give the following information when you call:

• Symptoms the child is displaying.
• Child's age and weight.
• Substance that poisoned the child, if you know.
• When and how much poison was ingested, if it was swallowed.

• The list of ingredients on the product container, if possible.

Handling Fire Emergencies

Fire extinguishers should be located in each classroom and in the kitchen and laundry area. All staff members should be trained in using them. In the event of a fire, sound the alarm at the first sight of smoke or flames.

Fire evacuation diagrams should be posted in each classroom. The diagram should include arrows showing the directions to take to reach exits. By making sure there are clear pathways to exits, evacuation time can be kept to a minimum. Fire drills should be held monthly, often along with the assistance of the fire department. Staff and children will react more calmly, quickly, and correctly if the drill has been practiced repeatedly and children are familiar with the sound of the alarm. Record the time of each drill and identify any problems that need to be solved. Take attendance sheets outside during the drill and make sure all children arrive at the planned destination. Always use the same destination.

Handling Weather Emergencies

Weather emergencies include electrical storms, tornadoes, hurricanes, blizzards, and floods, depending on geographic location. Some teachers also have to plan earthquake procedures.

Safety procedures vary according to the emergency. The fire department or weather station can give you recommended responses to specific types of severe weather. Here are some general rules that apply to weather emergencies:

- Keep battery-operated radios and flashlights readily accessible.
- Post directions to rooms designated as shelter areas.
- Take shelter at the first sound of an alarm and remain there until the all-clear signal is given.
- Take attendance immediately after reaching shelter and try to locate missing children as quickly as possible.

YOUR RESPONSIBILITY

*W*hen a parent places a child in a child care program, there is trust. The parent believes that you will do everything in your power to keep the child safe and to respond correctly if a problem arises. As a child care professional, you owe that kind of dedication to every child. There may be no better way to take responsibility for the safety and well-being of children than thinking of each child as your very own.

As a teacher, would you know how to react if a tornado warning sounded? Regular drills help children and teachers practice what to do.

Chapter 10 Review

Chapter Summary

- One of the most important responsibilities of any child care program and of its staff is to keep children safe.
- Child care facilities have safety policies stating rules and procedures to follow to insure safety.
- Prevention is the key to safety.
- Hazards to children's safety are everywhere. Children should be supervised at all times.
- The child care staff is responsible for identifying safety hazards and preventing accidents.
- Children learn about safety through adults' examples, classroom lessons, field trips, and taking part in safety inspections.
- First aid training is helpful in handling many medical emergencies. First aid kits should be readily accessible.
- Staff members should be thoroughly trained in procedures to follow during fire and weather emergencies, as well as a wide variety of medical emergencies. Training and practice should be ongoing.

Reviewing the Facts

1. What does "liable for negligence" mean?
2. What areas of concern are included in a safety policy?
3. Briefly describe three safety forms that are used in child care programs.
4. What is the link between prevention and safety hazards?
5. List four indoor and four outdoor safety precautions.
6. Give four tips for choosing safe toys.
7. Cite four safety precautions for field trips.
8. List five safety rules that children should learn.
9. What is the first rule to follow in a medical emergency?
10. List eight items that should be included in a first aid kit.
11. When and by whom is CPR administered?
12. What information must be given when calling a poison control center in the event of poisoning?
13. Why are fire drills necessary?

Thinking Critically

1. One of the children at your lunch table becomes very quiet. His eyes are wide and watery. His face is turning blue. He keeps grabbing his throat. Describe what you would do.
2. What specific things could you do to keep children calm in an emergency situation?
3. Predict the consequences of failing to pay regular attention to safety details in the early childhood classroom. How might this affect the children, the program, and the staff?
4. Do you think it is possible to make children overly concerned about their own safety and well-being? How would you instill a healthy awareness of safety without making children afraid?

Activities and Applications

1. **Investigating Equipment.** Investigate types of padding available to use with outdoor climbing equipment. List the pros and cons of each.

2. **Demonstrating Fire Extinguisher Usage.** Prepare a demonstration on how to use fire extinguishers.

3. **First Aid Kit.** Compare the costs of commercially prepared first aid kits to the cost of putting together a first aid kit on your own. Do commercially prepared kits supply all the items necessary for an early childhood classroom?

4. **Safety Pledge.** With a partner, write a pledge that every child care professional could make as a commitment to the safety of children in a child care setting.

SCHOOL TO WORK

Your Professional Portfolio

Prepare a checklist that could be used to evaluate the safety conditions in an early childhood classroom. Include environmental safety, medical safety, transportation safety, etc. Place the completed checklist in your portfolio.

Observing and Analyzing

Checking for Safety

The numerous inspections that are required to license child care programs are usually safety-based. In other words, safety is the most significant factor in licensing a facility, and the inspector's name attesting to this fact should be in plain view on the posted license. To discover more about how child care programs manage safety, observe some programs and analyze what you discover.

- **Licensing.** Visit a child care program to examine licensing requirements. Where is the license posted? Is it within view of visitors? Count the number of children in the building. Is this number less than, or more than, what is shown on the license? Is the license current? Is all of the other information on the license accurate? What are some of the repercussions if the license is not correct or has expired? Should the families be told? Why or why not?

- **Safety Preparedness.** While visiting an early childhood program, observe the classroom(s) for safety preparedness. Look for the method used to cover electrical outlets, the way appliance cords are kept safely out of the way, how cleaning supplies are stored, safety measures in the play yard, and the locations of smoke alarms. Do you see other signs of preparedness? Keep looking. Can you find an emergency evacuation plan posted on a wall in each classroom? What about emergency phone numbers, including the poison control center? Do you see an emergency drill schedule? These are all signs that the child care setting is a safe one.

Chapter 11

Promoting
Good Health

CHAPTER OBJECTIVES

- Describe how to maintain a healthful environment in a child care setting.

- Explain practices used to monitor illnesses.

- Describe concerns that arise when children have special health conditions.

- Discuss health problems associated with weather, abuse, neglect, and emotion.

- Assess the health procedures used in a child care program.

Terms to Learn

- antibodies
- child abuse
- child neglect
- communicable diseases
- grand mal seizure
- immune system
- immunization
- infectious diseases
- noncommunicable diseases
- pathogens
- petit mal seizures
- vaccine

But it hurts," Alex complained, holding his arms over his stomach. He had a look of pain on his face.

Ms. Jasper, the new teacher's aide, watched as Mr. Morgan knelt to talk to Alex.

"Stomachaches aren't fun, are they?" Mr. Morgan asked him. Then he put his arm around Alex's shoulders and gave him a little hug. "Did I tell you how much I like your shirt? What kind of horse is that on the front?"

Alex looked down at his shirt and started to explain what kind of horse he thought it was.

"You know, Alex, I think we have a book about all kinds of horses. Some horses have patches of black and white. They're called pintos. Have you ever seen one?"

Alex seemed to have forgotten his pain. In a short time he was totally absorbed in the pictures of horses in the book Mr. Morgan found for him.

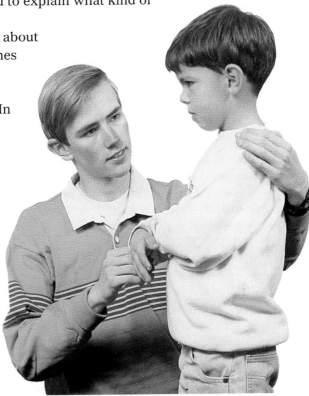

"He wasn't really sick, was he?" Ms. Jasper asked.

"No," Mr. Morgan replied. "I've learned to tell when Alex just needs a little attention. Sometimes that's his way of getting it. We have to be careful though. When you're responsible for children, it pays to take things seriously. I watch all the children closely. We have some who think they're sick when they're not and some who don't tell you they're sick when they are. Getting to know all of them well helps."

TAKING HEALTH SERIOUSLY

Safety is not the only part of children's care that deserves close attention. Health does too. As anyone who works with children knows, physical illnesses are common, and emotional problems can also cause concern.

Child care professionals take their responsibilities toward children's health seriously. Not only do they aim to provide a healthful environment, but they also keep accurate records on the health of children. They establish practices and procedures designed to prevent illness and limit its spread. These are covered in staff training workshops, staff manuals, parent handbooks, and newsletters. Above all, child care professionals become knowledgeable about the care that children need so they can take the right steps when physical, as well as emotional, health problems arise.

CHILDREN AND DISEASE

Children are subject to many **infectious diseases.** *These illnesses are caused by organisms that enter the body and damage tissue.* The *disease-causing organisms* are called **pathogens** but are more commonly known as germs. Bacteria and viruses are two kinds of pathogens.

Some infectious diseases are *passed from person to person.* Called **communicable diseases**, they include colds and the flu. Chicken pox and strep throat are other examples.

Communicable diseases spread easily, especially among children in group settings. Many pathogens are present in fluids from the nose, mouth, lungs, and eyes. Thus, coughing, sneezing, and simple contact enable certain illnesses to pass from one child to another. Everything touched—toys, drinking glasses, infant teething rings, bedding, food, books, and other people—becomes a possible source of illness. Some disease-causing organisms are found in feces and urine as well as blood. In these cases, too, contact with the sources can result in the spread of disease. Changing diapers and caring for injuries, for example, pose a risk when not handled properly.

Other infectious diseases do not pass from person to person. These are **noncommunicable diseases**. Some are transmitted by way of food, animals, and insects. Such conditions as ear infections and diaper rash are also noncommunicable.

The Immune System

Have you ever wondered why children get sick so easily? One reason is that a child's **immune system** is not as well developed as an adult's. *This bodily system produces antibodies that resist disease. When released into the blood,* **antibodies** *help destroy pathogens.* Until immune systems develop and children learn how to protect themselves better against illness, caregivers have to do all they can to keep children healthy.

HEALTH PRECAUTIONS

As you can see, putting children together in groups is an invitation to illness. Only by paying particular attention to what goes on within the environment can limits be put on the spread of disease.

Healthful Air

Although they aren't visible, the organisms that cause diseases are often in the air. Breathing puts them in the air, and a cough or a sneeze propels them through the air.

One way to limit the spread of communicable diseases in a child care program is to teach the children good health habits.

Knowing this, many child care professionals take some basic precautions. Kristin, for example, spoke to the custodian in her center about proper air circulation and ventilation. She wanted the air to be as clear of pathogens as possible. As long as weather permitted and pollution was not a problem, she let the children play outside for a while each day. Indoors, she kept the children spread out in small groups. She even spaced cots a few feet apart during nap time. She also made sure the children covered their mouths when they sneezed or coughed and washed their hands afterwards.

Cleanliness

Cleanliness not only makes the environment look better and feel more comfortable, but it also helps reduce the presence of disease-causing organisms. Classrooms should be cleaned nightly by a custodian. Special attention must be given to bathrooms and diapering areas, drinking fountains, and kitchen and meal service areas. Classroom walls and floors should also be cleaned on a regular basis.

Doing laundry is part of the cleanliness routine. Cot covers, blankets, sheets, pillowcases, and pillows should be washed weekly or whenever they become soiled due to toileting accidents or illness. To limit the exchange of illnesses, children should each be assigned a crib or cot complete with personal bedding. Cots should be labeled with children's names. Kitchen towels, cloths, and aprons should be laundered daily. Children's dress-up clothes, puppets, stuffed animals, and lounging pillows require regular cleaning.

Standards of cleanliness apply outdoors too. Make sure sandboxes are covered nightly to prevent animals from depositing their waste there. Climbing equipment and swinging tires must have drainage holes to prevent standing water. Mosquitoes, which can carry harmful diseases, breed in standing water. Part of your job as a child care professional is to insure that all cleanliness tasks are performed as needed.

Sanitizing

Sanitizing is essential. Toys and equipment need regular sanitizing. The health department has information on how to sanitize items. Eating tables should be washed with a sanitizing solution before and after each meal. Diapering surfaces must be sanitized before and after each use. A common sanitizing solution is one part bleach mixed with four parts water. Clearly label sanitizing solutions and keep them out of children's reach.

Tables where children eat need to be sanitized before and after meals and snacks. What are some other situations that might call for sanitizing surfaces during the day?

Hand Washing

The most important step in keeping children and staff free of communicable diseases is frequent and thorough hand washing. Children and staff should wash hands upon arrival, before and after preparing or eating meals and snacks, and after coughing, sneezing, and toileting. Staff members must also wash their hands before and after diapering. Everyone should wash after such play activities as sand or water play, finger painting, and using clays and doughs. The information below shows the proper method for thoroughly washing hands.

Washing areas should be easily accessible. Ideally, washing areas are provided in the classroom, in restrooms, in kitchens and staff lounges, and outdoors . All washing facilities should have *liquid* soap and *disposable* paper towels. Bar soap and cloth towels can spread illnesses.

You can teach children good health practices, such as hand washing, through classroom activities and daily routines. Monitor them as they wash so that you can guide their technique. Posters, signs, and bulletin boards educate and remind everyone. Most importantly, be a good role model by following the hand washing rules yourself.

Universal Precautions

All of the precautions you have just read are essential for limiting the spread of disease. A few additional ones, sometimes called universal precautions, should be taken during specific procedures. Because some disease-causing organisms are present in blood, urine, and feces, the universal precautions should be taken whenever you might come in contact with these. Whenever you change diapers, help with toileting, or treat an injury, always wear a fresh pair of

Steps for Proper Hand Washing

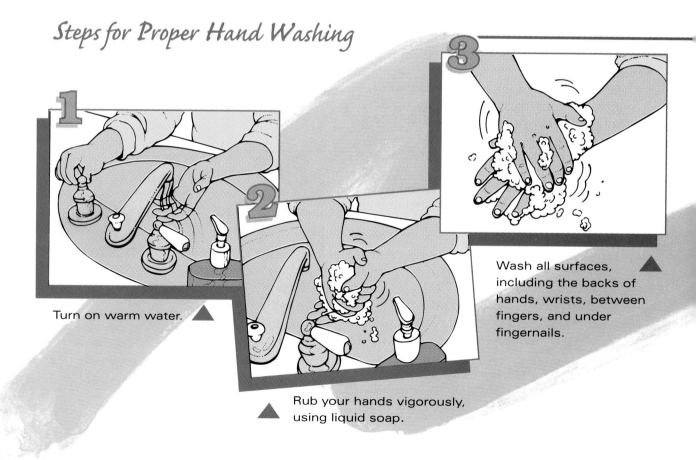

Turn on warm water. ▲

Rub your hands vigorously, using liquid soap.

Wash all surfaces, ▲ including the backs of hands, wrists, between fingers, and under fingernails.

FOCUS ON INFANT/TODDLER PROGRAMS

Infants and toddlers are especially vulnerable to illness. They have had little time to build a strong immune system. To decrease the risk of illness, infants should consistently have the same caregivers. Frequent rotation of caregivers increases exposure to disease-causing organisms.

Infants are especially vulnerable to illnesses involving diarrhea. Severe diarrhea can cause dehydration, which can be fatal for infants.

Giardia (jee-ar-DEE-uh) is a common disease in infants that results in diarrhea. It is spread through poor sanitary practices. It can be passed from child to child when caregivers do not clean children's or their own hands after diapering, as well as through toys an infected person has touched. Proper diapering and hand washing are the best ways to prevent the spread of giardia and other disease-causing organisms.

Since infants and toddlers constantly put toys in their mouths, daily toy sanitation is another important means of avoiding illness. Some programs put toys in a large mesh bag and put this in the dishwasher for sanitizing. Others hand wash toys in a bleach solution at the end of each day.

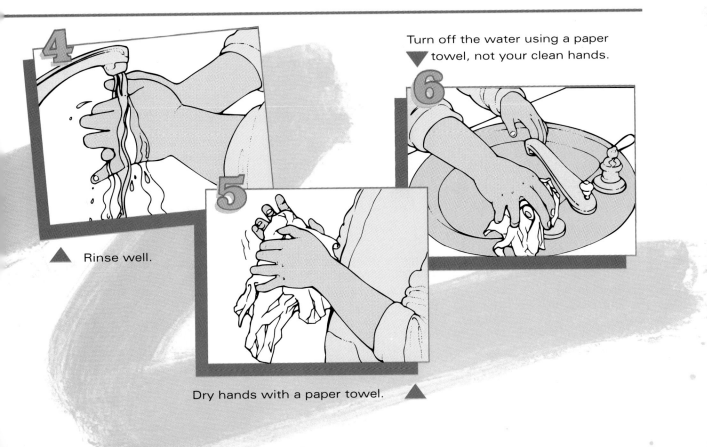

Rinse well.

Turn off the water using a paper towel, not your clean hands.

Dry hands with a paper towel.

Thoroughness

WHAT IS THOROUGHNESS?

Thoroughness means doing a job well and completely. When you are thorough, you pay attention to details; you believe that "little things mean a lot." You don't assume that someone else will finish your work or hope your lack of attention won't be noticed. Diligence and commitment are part of thoroughness.

Thoroughness in Action

"You must have too much time on your hands," Rene said to her friend Joanna. "Every time I come over here it seems like you're cleaning something."

Joanna laughed. "Not really," she replied. "It's just part of my work. I have to make sure the children that come to my home are protected. If I don't spend some time each day getting things done, I'll have a problem— and so will the little ones."

It was true. Joanna did spend some time every day on cleanup in the rooms used for her family day care home. Every evening she dry-mopped floors and vacuumed carpets. She checked under furniture for potentially dangerous objects. She made sure the windows were securely locked and none of the panes were cracked. She also cleaned the restroom. Every other day she dusted the blinds and window sills and wiped down the chalk ledges along the blackboard. She even cut off the loose strands on the edges of an area rug.

"This is a place for children to grow and learn and be happy," Joanna added as she stopped to look at Rene. "If health and safety aren't high priority, then my home won't be right for them, and that's important to me. Give me ten more minutes to finish cleaning this hamster cage, and we'll head for the movie. You see, I don't spend *all* my time cleaning."

Your Analysis

1. Identify the actions that demonstrate Joanna's thoroughness. Explain why each task is important and tell what might happen if she neglected to do it.

2. How is respect for yourself and your work related to thoroughness?

3. Think of an activity you enjoy or a service you use regularly. How often do you think about the individuals whose work makes the activity or service available? What might this say about their thoroughness on the job?

disposable latex gloves. The materials used to clean up body fluids should be disposable too. Paper towels, tissues, and diaper wipes are possibilities. Once used, place these in a plastic bag and then in a plastic-lined, covered trash container.

Many centers have special procedures for handling materials that contain blood. Check on these and follow them closely. Often such materials are labeled as medical waste and disposed of separately. The container must be kept out of children's reach.

Next, clean any surfaces—walls, floors, diapering areas—with soap and water and sanitize with a disinfectant. Then remove gloves by pulling them off inside out. Place the gloves in a plastic bag, tie it closed, and dispose of it properly. Gloves should only be used once. To complete the process, thoroughly wash your hands with liquid disinfectant soap under running water for at least ten seconds.

MONITORING ILLNESS

*E*ven in the best of environments, illnesses still occur. Child care professionals monitor illness for several reasons. They need to protect children from each other's illnesses and to care for sick children appropriately. They also need to keep track of health information

in order to comply with health codes and licensing requirements. In addition, careful monitoring enables caregivers to make accurate reports to parents.

Health Checks and Screenings

Health checks are routine procedures used to spot health problems. Usually they are conducted by the staff each morning as children arrive. This practice allows symptoms to be discovered in the early stages, when an illness is most treatable and can be kept from spreading.

Most programs conduct informal health checks. Caregivers take note of children's appearance, attitudes, and behavior. They check for physical signs of ill health. A rash, blisters, watery eyes, harsh coughing, inflamed throat, fever, or discharge from the nose or mouth could sig-

A child who shows possible signs of illness during a health check may need additional evaluation. Johnathon did not have a temperature and stayed for the day's activities.

FOCUS **O**N SCHOOL-AGE PROGRAMS

School-age children may experience less sickness than younger children. With more exposure to different illnesses, they have better developed immune systems.

School-age children often resist going to the doctor, even when very sick. With these children and their parents, emphasize the importance of regular medical checkups.

During the early school years, vision and hearing problems become more apparent. Signs of vision problems include holding a book very close to the face or avoiding reading entirely. Hearing problems may be indicated if a child often seems to ignore directions. If children exhibit these behaviors, a vision and hearing screening should be recommended.

nal illness. Unusual behavior, such as tiredness, crankiness, and whining, may too. All signs that concern teachers should be discussed immediately with the parent and recorded in the child's file. Some programs employ a part-time nurse to conduct daily health checks.

Screenings are examinations usually given to a group of children to look for one specific health problem. Those children who have the problem can then be referred for special treatment.

Screenings for vision and hearing problems are usually started at age three—earlier if problems are suspected. Some children are checked for diseases they might have inherited, such as blood diseases. Lead poisoning, which can cause serious illness and brain damage, is another condition that can be detected with screening.

As a rule, early childhood programs do not provide health screenings, but they do educate parents about how to locate this service in their community. Screenings may be conducted by a physician or the health department.

Restricting Attendance

A child or staff member who has a communicable illness may have to be absent temporarily. Restricting attendance helps protect others from becoming ill. Most programs establish specific guidelines, often with the help of the health department, so that parents and staff understand when attendance is not acceptable. A child who shows symptoms specified in these guidelines should rest in the isolation room until taken home by a parent or guardian. The guidelines also specify when a person who has been ill may return. For example, one guideline might be: "Children and staff must be fever-free for a 24-hour period before resuming attendance."

Notifying Parents

When such communicable diseases as measles and chicken pox occur, all parents of children in the program should be notified. Alert them by sending letters that identify:

- The illness or condition.
- Associated symptoms.
- Time that elapses before symptoms become apparent.
- Typical length of the illness.
- Suggested treatment.
- Point when a child can safely return to the classroom.

Certain communicable diseases should be reported to the health department for tracking of possible epidemics. Measles, mumps, and chicken pox are typical outbreaks that require reporting.

Maintaining Health Records

Health records are a protection for everyone involved in a child's care. Child care professionals need them to become informed about a child's health status. Parents use them to provide important information about their child's health. These records include:

- **Physician's Reports.** Most states require a physician's exam stating that a child is free of any serious communicable diseases upon entering a program. Proof that the child has had a negative tuberculosis test may also be required. In addition, immunization records should be included. Through **immunization**, children are *given a vaccine that protects them from particular diseases.* A **vaccine** is *a small amount of a disease that is introduced into the body, usually by injection, so the body can build a resistance to it.* A sample immunization schedule is on page 210. The physician's report is kept in the children's files. Similar health records for staff members are also kept on file.

THE MULTICULTURAL CLASSROOM

If you can't read a child's health record, it won't do you much good. Moreover, if parents can't read health bulletins sent out by your program, that won't do them much good either. Any time language barriers may get in the way of important communication, translation is needed.

Health forms need to be completed by someone who can write in the primary language used by the program professionals. Often this will be English. Before sending letters home regarding head lice,

chicken pox, Halloween candy warnings, and other precautionary topics, be sure those who need the message will receive it. Making arrangements with someone who can do translations for you on a regular basis is a good idea.

Communication is difficult enough when people speak the same language. A little foresight can eliminate some of the problems when people speak different ones.

How can requiring a physical exam before a child enters child care benefit both the child and the child care program?

• **Health Histories.** Health histories are provided by parents and guardians. They give information about the child's developmental growth. Any allergies, medications needed, and medical problems or injuries experienced before, during, or after birth are also listed. This information is confidential and should be shared only with a child's direct-care staff. Some programs employ a nurse to collect and interpret health histories.

Recommended Immunizations

RECOMMENDED AGE	IMMUNIZATIONS	COMMENTS
Birth	Hep B	Timing for certain immunizations may vary according to doctor's advice. Some are given within a recommended age range. Certain follow-up immunizations are affected by the time at which earlier ones are administered.
One month	Hep B	
Two months	DTP, IPV or OPV, Hib	
Four months	DTP, IPV or OPV, Hib	
Six months	Hep B, DTP, OPV, Hib	
Twelve months	DTP, Hib, MMR, Var	
Four to six years	DTP, OPV, MMR	

Hep B=Hepatitis B
DTP=Diphtheria, tetanus, pertussis
   (whooping cough)
IPV or OPV=Inactivated polio vaccine or
   Oral polio vaccine

Hib-Meningitis, pneumonia, infections
   (Hemophilus influenza type b)
MMR=Measles, mumps, rubella
Var=Chicken pox (varicella zoster virus)

- ***Emergency Forms.*** These forms are kept in file for every child and staff member. They list the telephone numbers and addresses of people to be contacted in case of emergency. The physician and preferred hospital are also noted. For those who have special health conditions, emergency treatment procedures are needed. Duplicate forms may be kept in the classroom for quick teacher reference.

- ***Medication Forms.*** The licensing laws in some states put restrictions on administering medicine in child care settings. Programs that do administer medication set up a system to insure that children receive the correct dosage. Parents complete and sign a medication permission form that indicates the exact time, amount, and method of dosage, as well as any side effects the medication may have on the child. When staff members give the medicine, they indicate that on a log and sign their entry.

MILD ILLNESSES

Simple illnesses are common in any child care setting. For example, a mild cold without fever may not keep a child at home. Special arrangements may need to be made for some children, especially if medication is to be administered. Mildly ill children may need a restricted diet, extra rest, or restricted activity. Teachers, teacher's aides, and cooks need this information.

Some children with asthma use an inhaler to deliver medication directly to the respiratory system. As with all medications, strict guidelines must be followed to protect both the child and caregiver.

SPECIAL HEALTH CONDITIONS

Unfortunately, not all illnesses are simple ones. Some children have conditions that require special attention. Information about care and medication should be noted on enrollment applications and discussed with parents.

When caring for children with special problems, child care professionals look for signs of a child's needs. They must be sensitive to the child's feelings and find ways to avoid setting the child apart as "different."

Every special health situation has its own set of concerns. A few of the ones you might encounter are described here. The more knowledge you have about these and other conditions, the better able you will be to handle children competently.

Asthma

Asthma (AZ-muh) is a respiratory condition characterized by recurring attacks of

shortness of breath. Coughing, wheezing, and whistling breathing are other common symptoms. Asthma attacks may last for a few hours or for weeks. What brings on an attack is not the same for everyone. Dust, weather changes, strenuous exercise, smoke, or pets can be the problem. Parents can tell you about specific triggers that their children have. To help treat asthma, keep children with asthma away from what causes attacks. Sometimes medication is needed.

Allergies

An allergy is an unusual reaction to a substance that most people can tolerate. The substances cause a reaction when eaten, breathed in, or touched. Allergic reactions include nasal congestion, coughing, wheezing, asthma, frequent sneezing, a rash, eye irritation, upset stomach, and diarrhea. Hundreds of substances may trigger allergic reactions, including foods, animal fur, insect stings, dust, pollen, and mold. Some allergic reactions are treated with medication. You can help prevent allergic reactions by keeping children from trigger substances and by maintaining cleanliness standards for the program. Follow parents' directions for treatment of allergic reactions. If an allergic reaction is severe, call the child's physician right away.

Head Lice

Head lice are very small insects that live close to the scalp on human hair. Lice are usually identified when lice eggs, called *nits*, are found. Nits are typically spotted at the back of the neck, behind the ears, and on the top of the head. Signs of lice include itching at the roots of the hair and small red bite marks on the scalp.

Children and adults get lice by using the personal items of someone who is already infected. Sharing a comb or hat might result in transmittal. Acquiring lice has nothing to do with cleanliness, race, gender, or income level.

While very inconvenient and uncomfortable, head lice are easily treated. You as a child care worker should alert parents and other staff members as soon as an outbreak of head lice is discovered. Doctors can provide advice on treating them. Public health departments also provide written materials that outline methods for containing the spread of head lice throughout the child care program.

Epilepsy

Epilepsy is a disorder in which the electrical rhythms of the central nervous system are disturbed, resulting in seizures. There are two major types of seizures—petit mal and grand mal. With **petit mal seizures** (puh-TEE mahl), the person has only *a few seconds during which consciousness is clouded and possibly a few muscles twitch.* A child who is having a petit mal seizure may stop in the middle of an activity, "freeze" in position, and stare blankly; his or her eyelids may flutter. A **grand mal seizure** is *a complete loss of consciousness with stiffening, jerking, or thrashing of the body.*

If a child in your care has a seizure, follow the guidelines on the next page. Afterward, the child will not remember what happened. Sleep is common after a grand mal seizure.

Medication is often prescribed for epilepsy. When caring for children with epilepsy, observe and record any changes in behavior. Report changes to parents as they occur.

Tip FROM THE *Pros*

As a reminder to staff members about which children have food allergies, place a large chart with that information in the meal service area. Be sure to identify the names of children and their specific food allergies on the chart.

Handling Seizures

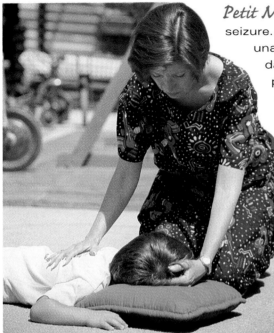

Petit Mal Seizure. Be alert for signs of this type of seizure. The child may simply stop and stare blankly, unaware of what is happening. If the child is in a dangerous location—crossing the street, for example—gently guide him or her to safety. Otherwise, you need not do anything. The seizure lasts only a few seconds.

Grand Mal Seizure. If a child falls to the ground, stiffens, and jerks uncontrollably, remain calm. Guide the child to a safe position on the floor, if possible. Clear the area to allow room for thrashing. Place a pillow beneath the child's head, and turn the head to one side to allow saliva to drain out. *Do not put anything in the child's mouth.* This can cause injury or fatal choking. If a seizure lasts for more than five minutes or the child goes from one seizure to another, contact the child's physician

Diabetes

Diabetes (dy-uh-BEET-eez) is a condition in which the body does not produce enough of a chemical called insulin. Insulin helps the body store and use foods (especially starches and sugars) for energy. Diabetes is usually controlled by medication plus a special diet.

Diabetics need to eat at regular intervals, with snacks and meals at the same time every day. This helps keep insulin and blood sugar at the proper levels. A poor or late meal or excessive exercise may cause an

What steps would you take to insure that a child with diabetes eats snacks and meals when needed?

insulin reaction. For example, after a busy morning of outdoor play, the snack at one preschool was served late. Erica, a four-year-old diabetic in the program, became weak, pale, and sweaty. She started trembling and complained of dizziness and headache. Her teacher gave her a glass of orange juice and some crackers to help counteract this reaction. If her teacher hadn't responded to Erica, the child might have lost consciousness and gone into convulsions.

If you are caring for a diabetic child, keep in close contact with parents regarding treatment. Keep juice and crackers on hand and make sure that meals are served regularly. Exercise should not be excessive.

Sickle-Cell Anemia

Sickle-cell anemia is an inherited blood disorder accompanied by attacks of pain in the arms, hands, feet, legs, and abdomen. Infection or injury can make these attacks more likely to occur. Organ damage can result.

Because children with sickle-cell anemia are very vulnerable to infections, only those with a mild case of the disorder should be in group care. Upon enrollment, you should discuss with parents any specialized care that may be required.

Drug-Exposed Children

Serious effects have come to children from their mothers' drug use. Such drugs as cocaine, crack (a highly purified form of cocaine), and heroin enter a baby's blood stream through the umbilical cord and through breast milk. The number of affected children has become very high in this country, making it very likely that you, as a child care professional, will encounter them in your work.

Drug-exposed children have many problems, some that are lasting. Drugs alter their development. Resulting difficulties are phys-

ical as well as emotional. To care for these children, you need a special combination of skills, knowledge, and compassion. Training can help you meet the challenge. Contact the health department in your area for resources.

HIV and AIDS

Human Immunodeficiency Virus (HIV) is a virus that attacks and gradually weakens the body's immune system. Over time the affected person has frequent illnesses from exposure to disease-causing organisms that a healthy immune system would easily fight off. This cycle of repeated illness from infectious disease is called Acquired Immune-Deficiency Syndrome (AIDS). People with AIDS die from diseases that others usually survive, such as pneumonia and influenza. At this time, there is no known cure for AIDS.

The topic of AIDS is a sensitive one. Misinformation and emotions have fueled the fires of controversy for many people. If you become knowledgeable and think logically, you can take what precautions are necessary and manage without undue concern.

Acquiring HIV

First, you need to understand that HIV is not transmitted through the casual contact that is common with children in a group setting. Touching, hugging, and sitting on a lap do not result in the transmittal of HIV. This has been proven. The virus cannot be caught by touching an infected person's tears, perspiration, or saliva.

Then how is the virus acquired? HIV is a delicate virus than can live only in certain body fluids. It is transmitted through blood, semen, vaginal secretions, and breast milk. No evidence exists that it is transmitted through any other body fluids. HIV is acquired when infected body fluid enters jobs, follow all the precautions described earlier, including the universal ones, in order to reduce risk and help put minds at ease.

Enrollment of Children

Because of the limited risk of a child passing on HIV in group care, the Americans with Disabilities Act of 1990 protects children who have the virus. This law makes it illegal to deny enrollment in a program to children because they are infected with HIV.

At this time, parents are not required by law to reveal a child's HIV-infected condition. You may not know whether a child in your program has the disease. Because the virus is not always actively attacking the immune system, HIV-infected children may not have any noticeable symptoms.

When you do know that a child has HIV, confidentiality is critical. Telling others about such cases can result in discrimination against a child and his or her family. Information about HIV-infected children is generally limited to the main caregiver and the director of the program. Written permission must be obtained from the parents if a child care employee wants to discuss the case with the child's medical doctor.

HIV-infected children benefit from early childhood care and education just as other children do. However, parents of children with AIDS should be cautioned about the risks of group care. Group care exposes children to typical childhood communicable diseases. Because HIV-infected children have very weak immune systems, these illnesses may be quite serious for them. HIV-infected children should not attend group care when there is an outbreak of communicable disease at the child care facility.

By using universal precautions in situations that call for them, you are safeguarding yourself and the children in your care.

directly into the body and reaches the blood of an uninfected person. Sexual activity is the most common method of transmission. Entry through a break in the skin is also possible.

A child may acquire HIV in any of the following ways:

- From an HIV-infected mother during pregnancy or delivery.
- Through contact with infected blood by transfusion or through an open wound or sore.
- During breastfeeding with an HIV-infected mother.
- Through sexual abuse by an HIV-infected abuser.

As you can see, the chances of transmittal are extremely small. Because AIDS is a deadly disease, however, people realize that taking precautions against even the smallest risk is necessary. Thus, those who work in child care programs, and in many other

Keeping Up-to-Date

What you have just read about HIV and AIDS reflects current knowledge about the disease. Research is ongoing, so new developments are always possible. You need to stay informed so that you know if additional information suggests different approaches to take. The health department in your area can keep you up-to-date on this subject.

Hepatitis B

Hepatitis B (hep-uh-TY-tuhs) is an infection of the liver. Its symptoms include jaundice (a yellowing of the skin and whites of the eyes), nausea, fever, and loss of appetite. Hepatitis B can be transmitted from one person to another through blood, bodily fluids containing blood, genital fluids, and saliva. It cannot be transmitted through casual body contact. Health practices for preventing the spread of Hepatitis B include the universal precautions. In addition, health professionals recommend caregivers be immunized against Hepatitis B.

WEATHER-RELATED HEALTH PROBLEMS

Diseases are not the only threat to health. Sometimes weather is the cause. Playing outside can be good for children, but very cold or very hot weather can pose a threat to their health.

Hypothermia, a serious condition in which the body's temperature gets dangerously low, can occur if children are out in very cold weather for extended periods of time. *Frostbite*, the freezing of body tissue, can occur if parts of the body—especially feet, hands, face, and ears—are not well protected from the cold. Even if dressed in warm and waterproof clothing, children may still become frostbitten if allowed outside for long periods in severely cold weather. Signs of frostbite include numbness and white or grayish-yellow skin.

In hot weather, *heat exhaustion* becomes a concern. Heat exhaustion is dizziness and fatigue caused by the loss of fluid and salt due to intense per-

Children playing outdoors in hot weather need extra water. What other precautions might you need to take?

Insuring Safety

Moderate amounts of sunlight are not harmful to children; however, they should wear sunscreen on exposed skin to prevent burning. A sunscreen with at least an SPF number of 15 is needed for the best protection. Children with very fair complexions may also need to wear a hat or cap to protect the scalp and face from sunburn.

spiration. Children who show symptoms of heat exhaustion should be given fluids and allowed to rest in a cool place. You can prevent heat exhaustion by not allowing children to play outdoors for extended periods during very hot weather. Play areas should be as shaded as possible. Encourage children to drink water frequently to replace water lost through perspiring.

Sunburn can be a problem during any season of the year. When playing outdoors, children should wear a sunscreen. Talk to parents about any skin sensitivities that their children may have. You might want to ask each child's parent to supply an appropriate sunscreen.

If any of these conditions arise, refer to a first aid manual for treatment. Medical clinics and health departments can also provide assistance.

CHILD ABUSE AND NEGLECT

*I*t's sad but true that many people in society do harm to children, sometimes their own. Called child abuse and neglect, these conditions are too common in society. They demand the attention of all people who work in the interest of children. Child abuse and neglect happen in all neighborhoods and to children of all races and economic backgrounds.

Child Abuse

Child abuse occurs when *nonaccidental injury is inflicted on a child. The injury may be physical, sexual, or emotional in nature.* As a child care professional, you need to know the signs of child abuse, as listed on page 218. Any signs noted should be documented in the child's records.

Physical abuse often results in visible injury to the child's body. You might notice bumps, bruises, burns, welts, cuts, or unexplained sensitivity. Since children frequently injure themselves through their own activity, how can you tell the difference between abuse and a routine injury? Watch for severe injury, repeated injuries, and indications from the child that something out of the ordinary may have occurred.

Sexual abuse occurs when a person older than the child uses the child to fulfill his or her own sexual desires. Sexual abuse is not limited to sexual intercourse. Genital exposure, touching personal body parts, and other inappropriate sexual acts with young children are also sexual abuse. Often comments young children make are clues to what has happened.

Emotional abuse is generally committed when an adult chronically says things that hurt a child. The hurtful language may be foul, vulgar, or demeaning. Children who experience ridicule, tormenting, and inhumane teasing by a parent or caregiver are considered to be emotionally abused. Emotional abuse may also include placing unreasonable demands on a child to perform beyond his or her capabilities or failing to provide a child with affection and emotional support. Encouraging children to engage in illegal behavior, such as stealing, using drugs, and prostitution, is also considered emotional abuse. Emotional abuse is evidenced by a child's behavior. Emotional abuse can severely lower self-esteem so that a person has difficulty functioning throughout life.

Child Neglect

Child neglect is *the failure to provide a child with the basic necessities of life, including food, clothing, shelter, and medical care.* Because young children cannot care for themselves, they need reliable attention from adults. A child who is neglected may be left without adult supervision for hours, days, or weeks at a time. Neglect puts a child's health and safety at risk. If you notice habitual lack of adequate cleanliness, nutrition, sanitary shelter, clothing, medical care, or dental care, you may be seeing signs of neglect.

Reporting Abuse and Neglect

States have laws that require those who work with children to report circumstances that might involve abuse or neglect. You are required to make a report whether it involves a parent or a fellow staff member. It is your professional responsibility to act in good faith and report only those conditions that cause you to have genuine fear for a child's health or welfare.

Reporting usually means calling a child abuse hotline or notifying the child welfare agency. You will want to obtain the correct telephone number and post it next to classroom telephones and on the parent bulletin board. The number should be handy for you, other staff members, and parents.

All states have agencies that investigate suspected child abuse and neglect. They protect children and provide help to the family.

Prevention

Recognizing and reporting cases of suspected child abuse can help put an end to existing abuse. Other efforts may help prevent it from happening in the first place.

Signs of Possible Child Abuse

*T*he following signs in children may indicate child abuse:

- Unexplained injuries.
- Evidence of malnutrition or dehydration.
- Evidence of repeated skin injuries or bone fractures.
- Unusual sexual knowledge for the age of the child.
- Evidence of being given inappropriate food, beverages, or drugs.
- Appearance of unusual fear.
- Differences in emotional makeup from other children—low self-esteem.

By learning normal developmental patterns and really getting to know the children in your care, you can more easily recognize the signs that a child is experiencing problems.

Although there are no excuses, certain factors seem to be associated with abuse. Parents and others who abuse or neglect children often suffer from low self-esteem. Many have poor coping skills. They may lack knowledge about parenting and appropriate care, causing them to put unrealistic expectations on children.

Some child care programs offer evening workshops for adults to deal with these issues. The programs address such topics as parenting, human growth and development, alternative forms of discipline, and ways to cope with stress. Support groups are also helpful. In your role as a child care professional, you may also refer people to community resources, including such groups as Parents Anonymous.

Staff Protection

Regrettably, incidents of child abuse have occurred in low-quality child care programs. Children need to be protected from this rare occurrence, and staff members need to be protected from false accusation. To eliminate any questions about conduct with children, make sure you always supervise them with another adult present. This is especially important during nap time, toileting, outdoor play, and bus runs. Also remove locks from bathroom doors and install observation windows in all classrooms. You are safe from possible accusations of physical, verbal, or sexual abuse when another employee is with you and can verify that your behavior was appropriate.

CHILDREN'S EMOTIONAL HEALTH

Life isn't always easy for children in today's world. Some have divorced or alcoholic parents. Some have experienced the deaths or illnesses of family members. Sadly, children also know violence—in their homes and their neighborhoods. Any of these can lead to stress, even in young children. To recognize when children are having difficult times, look for the signs listed below. Although some of these may signal other problems, these are often associated with stress:

- Unusual aggression or laziness.
- Complaints of a pounding heart. This may be caused by elevated blood pressure. If this is the case, suggest that parents have their child's blood pressure checked by a doctor.
- Unusual anxiety or fear.
- Nervous tics or habits, such as twisting hair.
- Stuttering or other speech difficulties that have not been present earlier.
- Trouble falling asleep or staying asleep.
- Changes in appetite or regular complaints of an upset stomach.
- Unwillingness to try new things.
- Withdrawing from activities and other children.
- Displaying a sense of hopelessness.

When you discover that a child has problems, what can you do to help? The first step is to listen. Listening to children's thoughts, fears, and feelings is a good way to help children with their emotional needs.

Secondly, talk to them. Remind them of their own past successes in coping with certain stressful situations. Children relate well to their own personal experiences. To build their confidence, praise children when they successfully cope with a stressful situation. Life events often make children feel powerless and out of control. These feelings undermine coping ability. Children need reinforcement from you. Give them as much decision-making power and control over their daytime experiences as is developmentally possible.

Another technique is to provide books and tapes on problems that children face. Reading about going to the hospital, divorce, and moving gives children ideas for coping and makes them feel that they are not alone in the experience.

In addition, provide children with a predictable and consistent routine. This helps them gain a sense of stability and security.

Finally, work closely with parents in helping children through stressful situations. Parents may not realize what children are feeling unless you document and share the signs with them. If necessary, professionals can be consulted. In some cases, you may need the help of doctors, psychologists, law enforcement workers, or social workers.

Reading appropriate stories is just one way to help a child cope with a stressful situation. What are some others?

IN YOUR HANDS

*M*anaging the health concerns of a group of children is a serious responsibility. As you have seen, it is much more than simply wiping a nose now and then. In the child care setting, each child has health needs that are common to all, yet each one also has unique needs to be attended. Without the support of adults, children cannot achieve good physical and emotional health. As a child care professional, children are, indeed, in your hands.

Helping Children Cope with Death

*C*hildren experience death in many ways. A friend or family member may die. A pet may die. Children even see death through violence in neighborhoods and on the news. How would you help a child cope with death? Unless you think ahead, you may not be prepared.

Age affects how children perceive death. Under the age of three, they tend to have little or no understanding of the idea of death. They may grieve for the loss, but they don't realize what has happened. At four, children have some vague notions about death. They see the connection with sadness. A five-year-old may think that death is reversible. At this age, they don't accept the idea that death happens to everyone. Some, however, are just beginning to recognize the finality of death. This recognition becomes clearer by age six or seven. Not until about age nine or ten do children recognize that death is inevitable. Sometime during the preteen years, children are ready to deal with the reality of death.

Regardless of their level of understanding, children do experience grief. They recognize loss and they sense sorrow. If a relationship was close, the death has greater impact. A child's personality and emotional needs affect how the child responds to the loss and copes with it.

As a caregiver, you can give support to children who are grieving. Remember that they may not have the language skills to tell you how they feel. Play with them and notice what they express through play. You could ask a child to draw a self-portrait. Then say, "Tell me about the boy (or girl) in the picture." Puppets and storytelling may also give clues to what is going on in a child's mind. Through play, the child releases stress and finds ways to deal with emotions.

A grieving child needs attention and love. Talk with the child, giving truthful responses to any questions. Remember that phrases like "passed away" and "fallen asleep" are inaccurate and confusing for children. Consider the child's age as you talk and listen. A child who doesn't seem to care may simply lack understanding. Watch for fears that might develop. For example, a child may fear the death of another loved one after a death has occurred. Reassurances can help. You might also look for quality books that help children understand and cope with death. These, along with your sensitive but matter-of-fact approach, can help the child see that life goes on—even after death.

Chapter 11 Review

Chapter Summary

- Staff, children, and parents must all know and practice procedures that contribute to the good health of children.
- Providing a healthful environment helps limit the spread of disease.
- Health checks should be conducted each morning when children arrive.
- Parents should be notified about outbreaks of communicable diseases.
- Before enrolling, children should be examined by a physician and should be up-to-date on all immunizations.
- Programs should plan strategies for caring for mildly ill children.
- Knowledge about special health conditions helps the child care professional handle children with these conditions correctly.
- Child care professionals are required by law to report cases of suspected child abuse.
- Helping children cope with special emotional situations is part of the child care professional's responsibilities.

Reviewing the Facts

1. What is a communicable disease?
2. Why do children, in general, get sick more easily than adults do?
3. Why is proper circulation and ventilation of air necessary in an early childhood classroom?
4. Why do cleanliness habits and routines need to be practiced?
5. What are two ways to teach children about hand washing?
6. Describe the universal precautions to take when taking care of children.
7. Briefly describe three types of health records collected when children are in group care.
8. What are allergies?
9. What precautions can a child care professional take to help prevent insulin reactions?
10. How is HIV transmitted?
11. Identify two weather-related health problems and tell how each can be prevented.
12. Describe the three different kinds of child abuse.
13. Explain three techniques for helping children handle problems that affect their emotional health.

Thinking Critically

1. Why do child care professionals take their responsibilities regarding children's health very seriously?
2. How would you help a child who has an ongoing health problem feel like he or she is no different from other children in the group?
3. Some children are brought to child care when they are too ill to be there. Why do you think this happens? What approach should child care professionals take?
4. Which do you think would be easier to identify and prove, emotional or physical abuse ? Explain your answer.

Activities and Applications

1. **Health Article.** Write a short article on a children's health issue for a parent newsletter.
2. **Inspection Chart.** Assume you are a child care worker. Put together a cleanliness inspection chart for the child care center. Develop a rating system for determining whether

a cleanliness routine was performed effectively.

3. **Job Shadow.** Contact a social worker or law enforcement worker who specifically handles cases involving children. Make arrangements to "shadow" the person for a day and observe the work. What qualifications must they have to do what they do? What personal characteristics make these individuals effective?

SCHOOL TO WORK

Your Professional Portfolio

Young children often need to be reminded about procedures that are routine to adults. Prepare a bulletin board that shows the steps for effective hand washing. Use simple pictures that young children can easily understand. Laminate the pictures so the board may be saved for future use. After writing directions for placing the pictures on the bulletin board, place the pictures and directions in your portfolio.

Observing and Analyzing

Making Health Observations

Young children pick up the organisms that cause illness so easily. Your understanding and appreciation for this fact will increase when you make some simple observations.

- **Placing Objects in the Mouth.** Observe one or more children age one or two informally in a public setting or in a center. For one hour count how many objects are placed in or on the mouth. Also record what happens to the objects during play and when the child loses interest or is redirected.
- **Touching the Face.** Watch three- to five-year-olds in a public setting or center. Record the number of times their hands go to their mouths and noses within a one-hour period.

- **Staff Habits.** Visit a preschool classroom and observe the hygiene habits of the staff. Do they wash hands after wiping noses, before preparing snacks, after fixing hair, and in any other situations that might require it?

What conclusions do you reach from these observations? What suggestions do you have for improving health management in the settings you observed?

Chapter 12

Handling Schedules and Routines

CHAPTER OBJECTIVES

- Explain what a schedule is and describe some considerations when developing one.

- Describe why and how certain common routines are incorporated in the daily schedule.

- Explain why and how transitions are used.

- Assess schedules, routines, and transitions observed in child care settings.

Terms to Learn

- choice time
- job board
- job jar
- personal hygiene
- routine
- schedule
- self-directed
- sphincter muscles
- teacher-directed
- transition

The melody was certainly "Here We Go 'Round the Mulberry Bush," but the words were different. As Emile approached the four-year-olds' room at the child care center, he heard the children singing. Quietly entering the room, he saw a group of children picking up blocks and stacking them neatly on a toy shelf. "This is the way we pick up the blocks, pick up the blocks, pick up the blocks . . . ," they sang as they worked. The children were cheerful and cooperative. They worked independently.

Emile sat in a chair in the corner of the room to wait for direction from one of the teachers. He was a new volunteer in the center. Seeing him, Mrs. Patterson walked over and sat beside him.

As the blocks were put away, the children began to flow in groups of two and three to a large rug. They sat in a circle, gazing expectantly at their teacher Miss Osterlund, who sat at one side of the circle with a storybook. She watched the children finish their task but gave no directions.

While waiting patiently for all the children to arrive, Miss Osterlund began to sing "The Itsy Bitsy Spider," using hand motions with the words. The children on the rug sang with her and mimicked the motions. When everyone was present, Miss Osterlund held the book so the cover could be seen. The face of a large, cartoon spider smiled cheerfully at the children.

"She makes it look so easy," Emile whispered to Mrs. Patterson. "Are they always this well behaved?"

"It doesn't happen by accident," she replied with a smile and a shake of her head. "In time, you'll see what I mean. I've got so much to tell you about what makes it work."

IT'S NO ACCIDENT

Mrs. Patterson was right. When the activity in an early childhood program is calm and orderly, it's no accident. Skillful child care professionals use knowledge and effort to make things go smoothly. What do they know that helps them? How could you achieve the same results if you were a child care professional? The answer begins with a well-planned schedule.

SCHEDULES

Imagine what life would be like without schedules. A **schedule** is *a plan for how time will be used; it places events in the order they will occur and indicates how long each event will last*. Transportation systems run with schedules so that people can easily get where they need to go. Businesses have schedules that enable employees to create products and provide services. You have schedules that tell you when and where you have to be.

Schedules bring order to life. In an early childhood program, the schedule accounts for how the hours will be spent from the time children arrive until they leave. A schedule includes the basics, not details. In other words, time for science might be shown on the schedule, but the specific procedure to follow for an activity is not. A sample schedule that might be used with preschoolers is shown on page 227.

Schedules keep things running smoothly for several reasons. For one thing, there's no need to spend time deciding what to do next. With a schedule in place, such decisions have already been made. In addition, children feel more comfortable with a schedule that has a similar pattern each day, giving them something familiar to rely on. A schedule also contributes to better behavior. Children who already know what comes next are less likely to get sidetracked by their own ideas. Fewer questions arise, and confusion is less likely. A schedule makes children feel independent. As *they respond on their own without having to be told what to do*, they become **self-directed**.

Creating a Schedule

No single schedule works for every child care program. Although some patterns may be similar, each schedule is planned according to the program's characteristics. All of the following affect schedules:

- ***Philosophy and Objectives of the Program.*** For example, if a program emphasizes intellectual development, ample time is allowed in the schedule for activities that promote this type of development.

In this center, children take turns being the "helper" for various parts of the schedule, such as snack time and circle time. They identify their responsibilities by finding their pictures.

- ***Length of the Program.*** Obviously, more activities can be included in a longer schedule than in a shorter one. Setting priorities is necessary.
- ***Children's Ages.*** Older children have longer attention spans and less need for rest, yet younger children need more assistance. These affect the amount of time needed for activities.
- ***Size of the Program.*** A large program requires grouping of children. The schedule must allow for rotation of activities and locations. The more children a teacher must help, the more time will be needed for each activity in the schedule.
- ***The Facility.*** A small center may have multipurpose rooms that require careful scheduling for efficient use.

A workable schedule doesn't just happen. It takes forethought to avoid pitfalls. For example, if you schedule outdoor activity early in the morning during the summer,

Sample Schedule

TIME	ACTIVITY
7:30 to 9:30 a.m.	Families greeted. Self-chosen play—indoor and outdoor learning centers.
9:30 to 9:50 a.m.	Snack. Children wash hands and eat nutritious foods.
9:50 to 11:40 a.m.	Morning Meeting/Project Work/Activity Time. Children and teachers discuss ideas for activities for the day. Children explore activity areas within the indoor or outdoor classroom. Activities may include: art, sciencing, math, dramatic play, language arts, creative movement, water/sand play, woodworking, block play, and table games.
11:40 a.m. to 12:00 p.m.	Music time. Transition to washing hands for lunch.
12:00 to 12:40 p.m.	Lunch time. Children eat in small groups to promote conversation about the day's experiences.
12:40 to 1:00 p.m.	Transition to rest time. Toileting, hand washing, and toothbrushing. Story, play, or movie prior to rest time.
1:00 to 2:30 p.m.	Rest time with calming music. Early risers play quietly.
2:30 to 5:00 p.m.	Gradual wake up, toileting and hand washing, snack, self-chosen play within indoor and outdoor areas. Children help clean up the center by sorting toys and straightening areas at the end of the day.

what happens several months later in a climate that has cold, snowy winters? During this season, the weather may be too cold for children to be outdoors in the early morning hours. Here's another question. What will you plan for children who arrive at different times during the first half hour of the day? Some activities are not easy to join once they have already begun. Also, what do you do when the weather forces a change in plans? Unless an alternative schedule is familiar to all, confusion takes hold. Answering questions like these as you plan a schedule is much easier than dealing with problems when they arise.

Energy Levels

Another consideration in scheduling is managing the energy levels of children.

FOCUS ON INFANT/TODDLER PROGRAMS

All infants operate according to their own sleep, diapering, and feeding schedules, which vary greatly from child to child. As new parents will tell you, attempts at getting infants to follow any schedule other than their own are usually unsuccessful. Instead, caregivers must identify the schedule that best meets the infant's needs.

They can do this by learning to interpret the moods and body language of the child. For example, you might notice that an infant squirms or cries just before needing a diaper change. Rubbing the eyes may indicate the need for a nap. Although infants cannot talk, they offer many signals as clues.

Outdoor play gives children a release for their energy. What alternative activities might be planned for days when the weather prevents outdoor play?

Children need a balance between quiet and active play. Time for activities like running and jumping is just as important as time for putting together a puzzle or creating a work of art. Tired children don't cooperate. Restless children won't settle down. Balancing restful times with energetic ones helps control behavior problems.

Compare planning the daily schedule to riding a bicycle over a hill. As you start out, riding is smooth and leisurely. The further you ride up the hill, the more energy you expend until you reach the peak. After you reach the crest of the hill, your activity level decreases until you reach the bottom of the hill, where a leisurely pace resumes.

This pattern should be reflected in the morning and again in the afternoon when planning children's activities. For example, the schedule for a full day at one child care center starts out slowly and calmly with breakfast. The activity level gradually increases toward the middle of the morning, when the most active play occurs. After active play, children switch to quieter activities while preparations are made for the midday meal. Children need to relax and become more calm as they get ready for their meal. The early afternoon is reserved

for nap time. After napping, the activity level gradually increases toward midafternoon. As the time nears for children to go home, the activity level decreases again. Children play quietly in learning centers until someone arrives to take them home.

ROUTINES

Although important, schedules only set the stage for what goes on each day in an early childhood program. Something else is needed to put the schedule into action. Clear and predictable routines do just that. A **routine** is a *regular, expected procedure that is followed in order to accomplish something*. For example, the schedule includes times for arrival, toileting, naps, dressing for outdoor play, meals, and departure. Each of these needs a routine that is familiar and consistent.

A routine may be short or long. It usually includes steps that are followed the same way each time the routine is used. Sometimes signals, such as ringing a bell, are incorporated in the routine to help children know when to take certain steps.

Like the schedule, daily routines add a sense of security to children's lives. They

FOCUS ON SCHOOL-AGE PROGRAMS

Because many older children have very structured schedules during school hours, they need a flexible schedule in the child care setting. This age group needs time after school to relax from the demands of studies and extracurricular activities. A healthful snack followed by optional play activities should be offered. Often these children are mature enough to make decisions about what they want and need to do. Child care professionals can give guidance toward making good decisions.

Building Professional Skills

Dependability

WHAT IS DEPENDABILITY?

Dependability is reliability, a "you-can-count-on-me" attitude. You depend heavily on so many things—from alarm clocks and automobiles to friendships—that you may take them for granted. Sometimes it's only when these things don't work as expected—when cars won't start, when friends forget promises—that you realize how important dependability is, in both your personal and professional life.

Dependability in Action

It was almost 9:00 a.m. on Thursday, and Margo had not arrived. Even though the children in the preschool could not yet tell time, they knew when it was time for Margo to appear. "Where is Miss Margo?" one of the children asked. "Isn't she coming?"

Once each week Margo Cummings visited the preschool. She was an accomplished storyteller who always came with books, props, and puppets for story time. This week, however, 9:00 a.m. neared with no sign of Margo. The teacher was about to announce a different activity when Margo burst into the room. She looked flustered and disheveled from hurrying but quickly became composed and smiling when she saw the children.

"Miss Margo's here!" they squealed. "Did you bring your toys? Is it a good story today?"

"Well, of course!" she laughed, and Thursday morning story time went on to be its usual success.

Later, Margo explained her lateness to the teacher. "The water was out in our apartment building, so we had to drive to a friend's house to get ready for work. Then we ran into a construction area, so traffic was backed up."

"You could have canceled," the teacher said. "We would have understood."

Margo smiled, looking at the children. "*Some* of you would have," she said.

Your Analysis

1. What did Margo mean by her last statement?

2. How would you describe Margo's sense of dependability?

3. Did lack of dependability play any role in Margo's lateness? How?

4. Is dependability the same thing as punctuality, or is it something more? What else do the children count on Margo for?

5. What do children learn about dependability when they follow schedules and routines?

"Circle Time or Morning Meeting" is common in early childhood programs. In this center, the children quickly form a circle by sitting around the edges of the rug.

know what to expect and when. They also know what is expected of them. As they adapt to specific routines, children gain confidence and become more independent and organized. Their self-help skills improve. Accomplishing daily tasks introduces them to the good feeling that comes when goals are reached. Moreover, they learn patience and persistence.

Routines are an important tool for teachers. They provide orderliness and discourage conflict, which helps save valuable learning time and contributes to a calm environment. In addition, when daily routines become like habits, children can pay more attention to learning. Skilled teachers integrate learning opportunities into routines.

To be effective, routines should be established according to the age and developmental abilities of children. Presenting them clearly to children enables them to follow the routines with ease. As you will see from the following descriptions of certain common routines, careful thought goes into making them workable.

Arrival Routines

The arrival routine sets the tone for the day. It should be positive and inviting. Those in charge of a program set up a consistent pattern that fits their specific needs. The manner in which children are transported to the facility and the arrangement of classrooms and entryway affect how the arrival routine is structured. The illustration on pages 232 and 233 shows what an arrival routine might be like.

Some children have a hard time separating from their parents during arrival. Leaving a personal item, such as a scarf, may ease the lonely feeling. If separation is difficult, a short parting is usually best. Advise parents to be honest and matter-of-fact with the child. A quick hug, kiss, and wishes for a good day can be shared. The parent should then leave. Discourage parents from disappearing while the child isn't looking. After noticing that the parent is gone, the child will feel tricked. This can cause more fear and insecurity.

If a child cries when a parent leaves, it is usually for only a few minutes. Denying children's feelings by telling them not to cry or to act more grown up is not productive. Instead, show your understanding by saying, "It's hard for you to let Dad go this morning, isn't it?" Offer a tissue to wipe tears. Casually invite distressed children to join an activity whenever they feel better.

Personal Hygiene Routines

When children learn skills that contribute to personal hygiene, life in an early childhood program is simpler. **Personal hygiene** (HI-jeen) is *keeping the body clean in order to promote good health and prevent illness.*

In addition to hand washing, young children can also learn to comb or brush their hair. Teach every child to use a personal comb, not anyone else's. This prevents the spread of such conditions as head lice.

By age two, children can begin to care for their teeth with a toothbrush. Children should routinely brush their teeth after

An Arrival Routine in Preschool

A. Sign in In many programs the arrival routine begins with some technique for monitoring attendance. When parents accompany children, they might use a sign up sheet. ▶

B. Greeting Arrival time is happy and positive when a friendly greeting comes from a staff member. Bend or kneel at the child's level and smile warmly. Use the "treasures" children bring, such as a favorite stuffed animal, to start conversations. You can show interest and respect by asking questions and listening attentively.

breakfast and lunch. When teachers brush along with the children, they act as role models for practicing good dental care. Children can also be motivated to brush by placing a mirror at their eye level. Children love to watch themselves while they brush.

Children should learn to use facial tissues for blowing the nose. Learning to blow out rather than in is not easy for young children. With practice, however, the skill is eventually acquired. Encourage children to blow their own nose by having tissues readily available. After blowing, children should dispose of used tissues and wash their hands.

Teaching personal hygiene routines is one key to controlling the spread of disease. Facial tissues should be used once and thrown away. Why is hand washing afterward so important?

C. Storing Items Include time during arrival to store personal belongings. Cubbies can hold small items. Jackets and coats might hang on hooks. Children learn independence as they perform these tasks on their own.

D. Health Check As children enter the classroom, this is a good time for an informal health check. Pay attention to the appearance of children in order to spot any problems.

E. Conversation Time An arrival routine can end with teachers and children gathered in a group to discuss the upcoming day's activities. A good way to begin this conversation time is to sing a familiar greeting song.

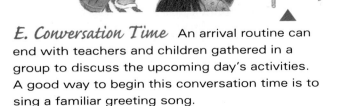

Toileting Routines

Children usually begin to learn about responsible toileting when they reach age two. By this time the **sphincter muscles** (SFINK-tur), *which surround certain body openings and have the ability to close them*, are developed in most children. These muscles enable children to control bowel movements and urination. Because the age of readiness can vary, however, caregivers need to be cautious about pushing children too soon. With close communication between parent, child, and staff members, the learning process goes more smoothly.

Patience is especially useful when children are in the process of learning. They may resist or be upset if toileting becomes a battleground between child and adult. Calm, quiet assistance from caregivers is needed. Accidents do happen and must be handled without hurting the child's feelings or causing embarrassment.

At this stage of development, teachers should assist children in sitting on the toilet (or potty chair). Independent toileting is made easier if pants can be easily pulled down. Clothing that is difficult to remove, such as bib overalls, may contribute to toileting accidents.

Observant teachers notice how children behave when they need to use the restroom—some children may tug at their clothing and others may press their legs together tightly. Clues like these help teachers know when to remind children to use the restroom. Reminders about using toilet paper properly and washing hands thoroughly after flushing should be made.

Even children who have already mastered toileting need frequent opportunities to use the restroom. Regular times should be set aside for this routine. Some schedules include time before the morning snack, after lunch, before and after naps, and following the afternoon snack. In addition, children should feel free to use the toilet whenever necessary.

Dressing Routines

At age two, young children can begin to put on some of their own clothing. Slip-on pants and pullover shirts and dresses are easier to manage successfully in the beginning. By age four, children should require little assistance. For example, if a child needs help with zipping a jacket, you could start the process and let the child finish it. This encourages self-sufficiency. Remember that heavy winter coats and boots are a challenge to put on (even for adults). Children appreciate extra time and patience when learning to manage these garments.

One creative teacher instructed children to lay their snowsuits on the floor before

Marissa has learned to put on her coat by placing it on the floor, finding the armholes, and flipping the coat over her head.

How can children be encouraged to practice routines they learn in child care at home?

els, and bibs for each child. Place protective floor covering beneath feeding chairs.

At age two, children can sit independently at meals, using small chairs at low tables. Their attempts at self-feeding are more successful by this time, but spills are still frequent. Keep paper towels nearby so children can clean up their own spills.

As children develop, they can practice new skills associated with mealtime. If small bowls and utensils are offered, two-year-olds can begin to serve themselves and put food on their own plates. Small pitchers for pouring milk and juice are manageable by age three. Children age two and older can pass out napkins, set nonbreakable plates and drinking glasses on the table, and help with minor cleanup after the meal. Creating centerpieces and placemats is another way children can contribute to the mealtime routine. By complimenting children when they accomplish these tasks, you help boost their self-esteem.

putting them on. The children sat on the snowsuits and put their feet and legs into the legs of the snowsuits. Then they stood up to put on the rest of the snowsuit.

Mealtime Routines

Meal and snack times include hand washing. This is the standard beginning and ending to these routines.

Self-feeding skills develop over time. First attempts begin at about nine months of age, when children begin drinking from a cup. Since young children like to explore their food, and because their aim isn't well developed, this stage of self-feeding is very messy. Be sure to provide washcloths, tow-

Children can help set the table for meals. What other skills can be learned through meal times?

Routines and rituals at nap time help children fall asleep more easily. Even if children can't sleep, the quiet rest time helps restore energy.

Nap Time Routines

Young children need adequate sleep to maintain healthy bodies. A daily schedule usually allows 30 to 90 minutes of nap time. Children age five and older may not need as much sleep as younger children, but they do need at least a short rest period. Most states require a nap time in their licensing laws.

Nap time should be the same each day. It usually follows lunch. While one teacher helps children brush teeth and toilet, another sets up cots throughout the room. Each child needs a personally labeled cot. For familiarity, each cot should be placed in the same place

THE MULTICULTURAL CLASSROOM

Multiculturalism can be incorporated in classroom routines. Here are some ideas:

- **Names.** Names are often linked to culture, making some difficult to pronounce and spell for those who are not familiar with them. Names are a vital part of identity. Arrival time is a good time to greet children by name, making sure that you pronounce them correctly.

- **Greeting Songs.** Add variety to the greeting songs each morning by learning some in different languages. Check music stores and school supply catalogs for tapes.

- **Learning Center Labels.** Identify the learning centers with labels in other languages. Parents can assist with this.

- **Snack Time.** For snack time, ask parents to bring a favorite food in their family that is linked to their heritage.

- **Nap Time.** Nap time can be a "trip around the world" with the soothing sounds of Tchaikovsky, Chopin, Brahms, Beethoven, Mozart, Prokofiev, Ravel, Debussy, Strauss, Bach, Wagner, Segovia, Bizet, Rossini, and more. The library might have classical collections, or parents might loan theirs or provide funds to buy tapes.

- **Departure Time.** At departure, say goodbye multiculturally. Send children on their way with "sayonara," "adios," "ciao," "salaam," "aloha," "shalom," "adieu," and "bonsoir."

every day. For safety, there should always be at least two adults present in the room during nap time.

Nap time can be scary for young children. Teachers should make it as comfortable as possible. Reading a story in a dimly lit room with a ceiling spotlight on the teacher creates a calming mood. After the story, relaxing music can be played throughout the nap.

Rituals often help children fall asleep. Rituals are actions that are repeated regularly. When used at nap time, a ritual becomes a signal for sleep. Some children need a back rub or a foot massage to relax them. Other children want a favorite stuffed animal, book, or blanket to hold.

Departure Routines

At the end of the day, try to plan a calm reunion between children and parents. Schedule the same type of activity for the end of each day. This helps children antici-pate when parents will arrive. Favorite activities include storytelling, working with puzzles, and singing. A good-bye song signals the day's end.

Some children easily leave child care at the end of the day. Others find it frustrating to have their play activities ended. Help parents understand that these children are not really unhappy about going home. They simply need a little more time to "shift gears." You might suggest that parents plan to do a short activity with their children before going home.

At the end of the day, parents should sign their children out on an attendance sheet. While they are doing this, encourage children to put toys away. Personal items, such as art projects, can be collected. Briefly talk to parents about their child's day. This should be a positive experience, not a time to unload all of the day's problems. If there are issues to be discussed more thoroughly, suggest a parent conference.

Why is working with others on a puzzle a better choice for an end-of-day activity than an art project?

LEARNING ACTIVITIES

All of the routines you have just read about are a regular part of the schedule, but they are not the whole schedule. To complete a schedule, play and learning activities are included. These are the theme activities that take place in the learning centers of the classroom. They are the heart of most programs.

While some activities may be scheduled for every day, others are not. Story and music times are likely to be daily events. Such activities as science and woodworking might be rotated into the schedule. An activity can have a routine linked to it, totally or in part. For example, a specific routine helps manage story time. Art, on the other hand, might have variations in routine, depending on the project. You will learn about how to plan and carry out many different kinds of play and learning activities in later chapters.

Trying to pick up objects with chopsticks is more difficult than it looks. Can you identify at least two things children might learn through this activity?

TRANSITIONS

Any time you put a group of preschoolers together, things can easily get out of control. When do you think this might be most likely to occur? One of these times is when children are switching from one activity to another. Just think what might happen if twenty four-year-olds were sent to the restroom all at once to wash their hands. Without guidance, confusion could result. Transitions can help manage situations like this.

A **transition** is *a short activity or technique used to help guide children smoothly from one activity or event to another.* It directs children's behavior so the teacher doesn't have to explain repeatedly what to do. By giving children something to focus on, their minds and bodies are less likely to wander elsewhere. A transition also provides the time young children need to make the mental shift from one activity to another. Good teachers become skilled at using effective transitions.

Transition Signals

Just as you know what it means when the bell rings in your school, young children can respond to sounds and visual cues that tell them what is coming next. No instructions are needed when the same transition signal is used in the same way on a regular basis. Here are some examples:

- Play a simple melody on the piano when it's time to pick up toys.
- Jingle some chimes to signal nap time.

"Let's walk like elephants over to the table for a snack. What do you think elephants would like to eat?" Transitions help children move from one activity to another smoothly.

Why do you think using visual cues or sounds to signal a transition is often more effective than telling children it's time to change activities?

- Flicker the lights off and on to help build anticipation for story time.
- Play a recording of a drum roll to signal a particular activity.

Children in Motion

If you want a large group of children to move from one area to another, you may not be able to let them all go at once. Allowing children to leave a few at a time is a useful technique.

Clay Tucker, a preschool teacher, knew he couldn't send all twenty children to the restroom at once before snack time. Instead, he asked the children wearing red shirts to wash their hands. While he supervised in the restroom, the teacher's aide led the others in a song. As the first group left the restroom and went to the snack tables where a parent volunteer supervised them, the aide asked children wearing blue shirts to wash their hands. This process continued until all the children had been to the restroom and arrived at the snack tables.

To keep this technique fresh, many themes can be used. You might use types of clothing, patterns on clothing, or letters in children's names. Can you think of others? With this method, effective teachers make the transition process a listening and thinking game.

Here's another technique to help children change locations. When asking children to go from outside to inside, ask them to move like gorillas, rabbits, or robots. This method is particularly effective because it focuses children's attention. They are more likely to make it from one place to another without becoming distracted.

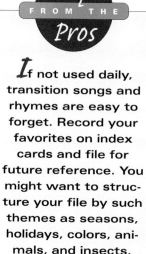

*I*f not used daily, transition songs and rhymes are easy to forget. Record your favorites on index cards and file for future reference. You might want to structure your file by such themes as seasons, holidays, colors, animals, and insects.

Starting Activities

As a new activity begins, doing something special that captures children's interest can draw them in. For example, at the beginning of music time, some teachers use cards that have the title of a different children's song on each one. Children pick a card randomly from a pile, and the class sings the song chosen. Children enjoy the sense of surprise that comes with this transition. Using a prop that catches the eye and arouses the curiosity of children is another possible way to begin an activity.

Cleanup Transitions

Transition techniques can motivate children to clean up at day's end. A job board is one such device. A **job board** *shows jobs that children should do.* A different cleanup activity, such as washing paint brushes or putting away tricycles, is identified on each section of the board. The board is laid flat on the floor. A child tosses a bean bag onto the board and then completes the task indicated by the bean bag's position on the board.

A **job jar**—*a container filled with pieces of paper that show pictures of activities*—serves the same purpose as a job board. Each child draws a piece of paper from the jar and completes the job indicated. Some teachers include special "jobs," such as "hug a friend."

Choice Time

One unique transition activity is choice time. **Choice time** is *a transition technique that lets children decide which activity they would like to participate in next.* This tran-

Using a job jar or job board to determine cleanup responsibilities helps make this part of the routine more interesting. What other ways might cleanup be handled?

sition helps children develop decision-making skills and builds responsibility, independence, and self-direction. It is generally conducted twice each day.

Prepare for choice time by dividing a large board that can hold hooks into areas for each learning center in the classroom. Hang a specific number of hooks in each area according to the number of children that can play in that area at a time. For example, there might be six hooks for the art area and four for the science area.

Before choice time begins, teachers describe the activities that are available in each learning center. In most cases, these activities are **teacher-directed**. That is, *the teacher leads and supervises the children.* Each child selects an activity by hanging a symbol or name tag on a hook in one of the areas. Once the choice is made, the child moves directly to that area.

PUTTING THE PIECES TOGETHER

Within the framework of a schedule, so much goes on. When a schedule works well, you can bet that some thoughtful planning has taken place. Putting the pieces of a schedule together carefully helps insure that children will be happy and better behaved and that adults will be more relaxed and able to do a good job. This is reason enough for taking the time and effort needed to build a schedule that contributes to smooth operation rather than hinders it.

Chapter 12 Review

Chapter Summary

- A well-planned schedule is helpful to everyone in an early childhood program.
- Different programs have schedules that suit their specific needs.
- In creating a schedule, activities should be arranged so that the energy level of children is taken into consideration.
- Routines are established for arrival, toileting, naps, dressing for outdoor play, meals, and departure.
- Child care professionals can make arrival easier for children. A personal greeting for each child helps children get the day off to a good start.
- Nap time is required by the licensing laws in many states.
- Many different ideas for transitions can be used by child care professionals to make the schedule operate smoothly.

Reviewing the Facts

1. When the atmosphere in an early childhood program is calm and orderly, what might this indicate?
2. What is a schedule and why is it useful?
3. List five factors that affect the creation of a schedule.
4. How does the energy level of children affect scheduling?
5. What is a routine?
6. How do both children and teachers benefit from the use of routines?
7. Since some children fear separation from parents at arrival time, what are some suggestions for handling this situation?
8. List four tasks that are incorporated in personal hygiene routines.
9. What are three reminders that caregivers need to make in connection with toileting?
10. What important step should begin and end the routines for meals and snacks?
11. Suggest three ideas for making nap time easier for children.
12. What is a transition?
13. Explain how each of the following could be used as transitions: signals; music; job boards; job jars; and choice time.

Thinking Critically

1. If a five-year-old child asked for help with buttoning a coat, how would you respond? Explain your reasoning.
2. When using a job board, you notice that a few children always manage to land the bean bag on the most desirable activities. What would you do?
3. Predict what could happen in the following situations: nap time is not scheduled at the same time each day; toileting is not scheduled at consistent times throughout the day; time for hand washing is limited; outdoor play is scheduled right before children depart for the day.
4. Do you think it's possible to make schedules and routines too rigid? Explain your reasoning.

Activities and Applications

1. **Developing a Schedule.** Create a daily schedule. Identify routines and when they take place. Where will you need to include transition ideas?

2. **Creating Transitions.** With a partner, create original transition ideas. Share these with other partnerships and analyze the ideas, looking for ways to improve them.

3. **Designing Instructional Posters.** Design three posters to help children remember daily routines, such as washing hands, flushing the toilet, and using a tissue for blowing the nose.

SCHOOL TO WORK

Your Professional Portfolio

What types of transitions work best for you? You will find some that are very effective and others that are not. Develop a card file for transition activities that you like. Use index cards to record each transition idea, specifically describing each one. Organize your file by category, such as choice time and nap time. Place the file in your portfolio.

Observing and Analyzing

Comparing Techniques in Different Facilities

As with many other aspects of early childhood programs, the best way to understand routines and transitions is to visit facilities to see examples of how these techniques are implemented. To see them in action, visit a program that fits each of the following types: family day care, a small preschool (one room), and a large child care center (several classrooms). In observing each, take notes on routines and transitions that are used. Later, compare and contrast what you discovered, using the questions below. Then prepare a written summary of your observations.

Routines
- What routines did you see used in each setting?
- Were any routines shared by all three programs? If so, which ones?
- Why are some routines different and some similar from one program to another?
- Did you see any ways that routines might be improved?

Transitions
- What transitions did you see used in each setting?
- Did any program rely more heavily on the use of transitions than the others? If so, why?
- How effective were the transitions? Which ones worked better than others?
- What suggestions do you have for improvement?

Chapter 13

Food for Young Children

CHAPTER OBJECTIVES

■ Define nutrition and explain its role in development.

■ Identify nutrients required for good nutrition.

■ Plan balanced menus for a young child.

■ Outline important considerations in meal planning for young children.

■ Describe proper food safety and sanitation practices.

■ List meal service guidelines.

■ Plan nutrition education activities.

Terms to Learn

- Child and Adult Care Food Program (CACFP)
- deficiency
- Food Guide Pyramid
- health inspectors
- nutrients
- nutrition
- perishable
- sanitation
- Women, Infants, and Children (WIC) Program

want to stir the batter first!"

"Okay, but I get to mix in the pumpkin."

"Miss Lydia, could I add the cinnamon?"

Lydia Torres knelt at the low table, surrounded by five-year-olds in aprons. She looked at the eager faces, noticing one child who said nothing. "I think it's Michael's turn to help," she said. "We'll let him add the cinnamon."

For a moment, all talking stopped. Six pairs of eyes focused on Michael's trembling hand as he carefully lifted the measuring spoon with the cinnamon in it. Without realizing, Lydia held her breath, hoping that Michael would get the cinnamon where he wanted it to go. A look of intense concentration was on Michael's face as he moved the spoon slowly toward the bowl. Just past the rim, the spoon jiggled, sending the cinnamon streaming into the mixture. "You did that very well, Michael," Lydia said quietly, looking him right in the eyes and smiling.

"Are we going to have the pumpkin bread for a snack?" one child asked as the chatter resumed.

"Can we taste it before we bake it?"

"Look, it's turning orange!"

Lydia responded to each excited comment. "Who can tell me why pumpkin is good for us?" she asked as she looked around the circle. Although Michael still said nothing, she noticed a different expression on his face. There was the hint of a smile and a new brightness in his eyes. It made her feel good inside. "Michael may enjoy this pumpkin bread more than any of the others do," she thought.

FOOD FOR HEALTH, LEARNING, AND FUN

Most children are fascinated by food, especially when they can help prepare it themselves. Wise teachers capitalize on children's interest in food. Exposure to a variety of foods and food experiences helps children develop positive attitudes toward eating properly. In turn, eating properly enhances children's well-being. Those who are responsible for children need to understand how proper nutrition and nutrition education can improve the lives of young children.

THE BASICS OF GOOD NUTRITION

Nutrients are *the substances which are found in food and used by the body to function, grow, repair itself, and produce energy.* **Nutrition** is *the process through which the body utilizes the nutrients in food.*

Some nutrients provide energy for activities, such as running or playing a computer game, and for essential body processes, such as pumping blood and digesting food. Other nutrients help keep the body working smoothly. Without the right balance of many different nutrients, the body cannot produce the energy it needs. It cannot function properly and has less resistance to illness.

Good nutrition is especially important in the early years. It provides the foundation for children's normal physical growth. Proper early growth and development are critical to having a long, healthful life.

Nutrition affects intellectual development as well. To function properly, the brain must receive important chemicals from nutrients on a regular basis. Most of the brain's growth occurs in the first two years of life. Research has shown that well-nourished children learn better.

Children also enjoy better emotional health when properly fed. They feel healthier and have a more positive outlook on life. Their ability to combat fatigue, depression, and everyday stress is enhanced. Healthy, well-nourished children are more likely to feel good about themselves and enjoy life.

Components of Good Nutrition

Evidence of poor nutrition can be observed in many ways. One caregiver, for example, noticed that a child in her preschool seemed tired all the time. In a conversation with the child, she learned that he seldom had breakfast. When the boy's parent's were asked what he typically ate for supper, the response was, "His favorite is a jelly sandwich, potato chips, and a soda." No wonder the child's body did not have energy. It wasn't being fueled properly.

For good health, the body needs six types of nutrients: carbohydrates, proteins, fats, vitamins, minerals, and water. Each plays a unique role in developing a healthy body.

- *Carbohydrates* (car-boh-HI-draytes). These are the body's main source of energy. They also help the body make the best use of proteins and fats. Good sources of carbohydrates include fruits, vegetables, and grain products (such as whole-grain breads and cereals, rice, and pasta).

- *Proteins.* These nutrients help the body make new cells and repair injured ones. They are necessary for growth and to fight off disease. Meat, poultry, fish, eggs, and dairy products provide complete protein—protein the body can readily use. Complete protein can also be obtained by eating the right combination of foods from plant sources. Simply combine dry beans, dry peas, or peanut butter with grains, nuts, or seeds. For example, peanut butter and whole-wheat bread together provide complete protein.

Food provides the nutrients children need for energy, growth, and good health.

- *Fats.* Fats provide energy and carry some vitamins that regulate body processes. They are also needed for healthy skin. Fats are obtained from meat, vegetable oils, whole dairy products, egg yolks, nuts, margarine, mayonnaise, and salad dressing.
- *Vitamins.* These nutrients help keep the body working properly and help other nutrients do their jobs. They include vitamins A, C, D, E, and K, as well as the B vitamins (a group of eight nutrients). Each vitamin has specific jobs to do. For example, vitamin A protects the eyes, contributes to healthy skin, and helps provide resistance to disease. Vitamins are found in varying amounts in a wide variety of foods—grain products, fruits, vegetables, dairy products, meat, fish, poultry, eggs, dry beans and peas, and nuts.
- *Minerals.* Helping regulate body processes is the function of minerals. They also become a part of the body's bones, tissues, and fluids. Many different minerals—including calcium, phosphorus, iron, potassium, and sodium—carry out specific functions in the human body. Eating a wide variety of foods helps the body get all of these important minerals, as well as the other nutrients it needs.
- *Water.* Water is essential for life. You can live for several days or even weeks without food, but only about three days without water. Water is present in every cell of the body. It delivers nutrients throughout the body, serves as the body's cooling system, and helps the body eliminate waste.

Providing Balanced Nutrition

As you have seen, many different nutrients play a role in maintaining good health. These nutrients work as a team. The body needs specific amounts of each.

Too Much of a Good Thing

Concerns about nutrition often focus on whether people get enough nutrients. In some cases, however, getting too much of a nutrient is also cause for concern. Here's why health experts recommend going easy on fat, sugars, and sodium.

- **Fat.** Although fat is an essential nutrient, eating too much fat can lead to overweight. It has also been linked with heart disease and cancer in adults. Health experts recommend that, except for infants and toddlers under age two, people limit the amount of fat they eat.
- **Sugars.** Such foods as candies, cookies, cakes and other desserts, and some breakfast cereals often contain large amounts of added sugars. When children (or adults) fill up on these sweets, they may not eat enough of the other, more nutrient-dense foods they need for good health. The high calorie content of these foods can also contribute to overweight. In addition, eating too many sugary foods can lead to tooth decay.
- **Sodium.** Most Americans get much more sodium than they need. It is found mainly in processed foods and in table salt. Cutting down on sodium may help some children avoid high blood pressure when they become adults.

Food Guide Pyramid
Servings for Children

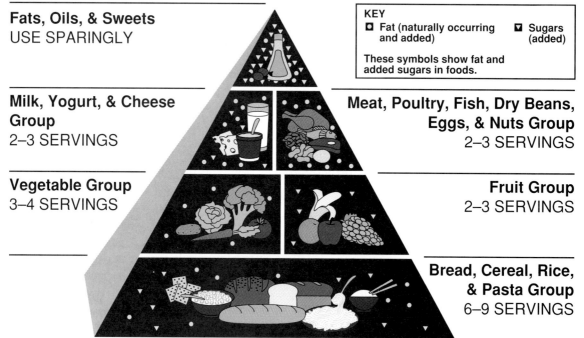

Fats, Oils, & Sweets
USE SPARINGLY

KEY
☐ Fat (naturally occurring and added)   ☑ Sugars (added)

These symbols show fat and added sugars in foods.

Milk, Yogurt, & Cheese Group
2–3 SERVINGS

Meat, Poultry, Fish, Dry Beans, Eggs, & Nuts Group
2–3 SERVINGS

Vegetable Group
3–4 SERVINGS

Fruit Group
2–3 SERVINGS

Bread, Cereal, Rice, & Pasta Group
6–9 SERVINGS

Milk supplies calcium, phosphorus, and vitamin D, which work together to build strong bones. As with other foods, serve a small portion and let children help themselves to more.

If children are lacking in one or more nutrients, especially over long periods of time, they can develop serious health problems. For instance, a **deficiency** *(severe shortage)* of vitamin D can lead to rickets, a disease in which bones soften and may become deformed. A deficiency of iron can cause a type of anemia. Children with this condition are tired, pale, and weak and have poor appetites. Getting too much of some nutrients, such as fat, sugar, and sodium, can also lead to health problems in later life.

For good health, children need a variety of nutritious foods daily. These foods should be chosen with care to insure that they provide the right balance of nutrients.

The Food Guide Pyramid

One way to plan balanced, nutritious meals and snacks is with the help of the **Food Guide Pyramid**, *a guide to daily food choices based on the recommendations of nutrition experts.* The Food Guide Pyramid organizes food into five main groups according to the nutrients they contain. Children and adults need foods from each of the following groups every day:

- Bread, Cereal, Rice, and Pasta Group
- Vegetable Group
- Fruit Group
- Milk, Yogurt, and Cheese Group
- Meat, Poultry, Fish, Dry Beans, Eggs, and Nuts Group

These food groups are shown in the pyramid diagram on page 248. The small tip of the pyramid represents Fats, Oils, and Sweets. Foods in this category are not essential for good health and should be used sparingly. They include butter, margarine, salad dressings, jelly, honey, syrup, pastries, doughnuts, and candy bars.

Although some fats and oils are needed for growth, the amounts required are easily obtained through eating foods from the five main groups. Children under age two, however, are growing very rapidly. The fat in the foods they consume is needed for growth. Milk, especially, should be whole, *not* low-fat, for children at this very young age.

Servings for Young Children

The five main food groups are equally important to health; however, they are not needed in equal amounts. The Food Guide Pyramid shows a range of recommended daily servings for each group. Generally, young children should have at least the lowest number of servings in the range. Older children's needs usually fall in the middle of the range. The needs of adults vary depending on how active they are.

Serving sizes for young children are smaller than those for adults. That's because young children have small stomachs that cannot hold much food at a time. For example, a preschooler might be served half a slice of bread at dinner instead of a whole slice. Some nutritionists recommend serving about one tablespoon (15 mL) of each food choice per year of a child's age. A serving of vegetables for a three-year-old might be about 3 tablespoons (45 mL). One exception is milk. Children need the same amount of milk per day as most adults—at least 2 cups (500 mL). This amount can be divided into several small portions.

A child should not be forced to eat large portions at mealtime. Offer small amounts at first, and then let the child have more if he or she is still hungry. Between meals, offer nutritious snacks. Children need snacks to keep up their energy and provide additional servings from the food groups.

Children's food needs vary from day to day, depending on how active they are and how rapidly they are growing. In general, the important thing is not how much children eat, but what they eat. As long as foods from the five food groups are eaten, the child is probably getting adequate nutrition.

FOOD SERVICE IN CHILD CARE PROGRAMS

*T*he type of meal service provided by a child care program depends on the hours of operation and the age of the children. A full-day program might provide breakfast, lunch, and one or two snacks. If a program is open later hours, an evening meal may also be provided. Half-day preschools might provide one meal and perhaps a snack.

When programs provide full food service, they usually employ a person to plan menus, purchase food, and prepare meals. This person may be a nutritionist or dietitian. In other programs, teachers may take on some or all of the responsibility for planning, preparing, and serving meals and snacks.

Menu Planning

When planning menus for a child care program, three important questions must be considered: Will the meal or snack be nutritious yet within the budget? Will it be easy and safe for children to eat? Will it appeal to children?

Meeting Nutrition Requirements

Most state licensing regulations set minimum standards for meal service in child

Providing food for children goes beyond satisfying their hunger. During the hours they attend a child care program, the responsibility for children's nutritional needs rests with the program's staff.

care programs. These standards insure that menus meet children's nutritional needs.

The U.S. government has developed a set of general guidelines for use in its child nutrition programs. They are shown below.

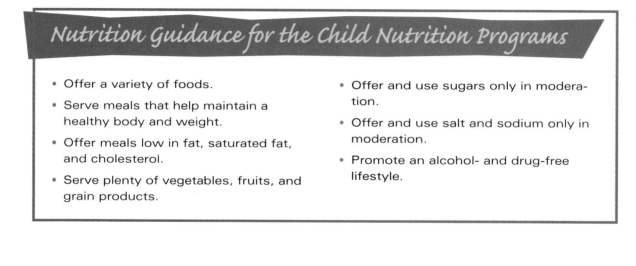

Nutrition Guidance for the Child Nutrition Programs

- Offer a variety of foods.
- Serve meals that help maintain a healthy body and weight.
- Offer meals low in fat, saturated fat, and cholesterol.
- Serve plenty of vegetables, fruits, and grain products.
- Offer and use sugars only in moderation.
- Offer and use salt and sodium only in moderation.
- Promote an alcohol- and drug-free lifestyle.

Meal Pattern for Children

BREAKFAST	CHILDREN 1-3 YEARS	CHILDREN 4-5 YEARS	CHILDREN 6-12 YEARS
Milk, fluid	1/2 cup	3/4 cup	1 cup
Juice or **fruit** or **vegetable**	1/4 cup	1/2 cup	1/2 cup
Bread and/or **cereal**			
Enriched or whole-grain bread	1/2 slice	1 slice	1 slice
Cereal: Cold dry or	1/4 cup[1]	1/2 cup	3/4 cup[2]
Hot cooked	1/4 cup	1/2 cup	1/2 cup
MIDMORNING OR MIDAFTERNOON SNACK (SUPPLEMENT)			
(Select 2 of these 4 components.)			
Milk, fluid	1/2 cup	1/2 cup	1 cup
Meat or **meat alternate**	1/2 oz.	1/2 oz.	1 oz.
Juice or **fruit** or **vegetable**	1/2 cup	1/2 cup	3/4 cup
Bread and/or **cereal**			
Enriched or whole-grain bread	1/2 slice	1/2 slice	1 slice
Cereal: Cold dry or	1/4 cup[1]	1/2 cup	3/4 cup[2]
Hot cooked	1/4 cup	1/2 cup	1/2 cup
LUNCH/SUPPER			
Milk, fluid	1/2 cup	3/4 cup	1 cup
Meat or **meat alternate**			
Meat, poultry, or fish, cooked (lean			
meat without bone)	1 oz.	2 oz.	2 oz.
Cheese	1 oz.	2 oz.	2 oz.
Egg	1	1	1
Cooked dry beans and peas	1/4 cup	1/4 cup	1/2 cup
Peanut butter or other nut or			
seed butters	2 Tbsp.	2 Tbsp.	4 Tbsp.
Nuts and/or seeds	1/2 oz.[3]	3/4 oz.[3]	1 oz.[3]
Vegetable and/or **fruit** (two or more)	1/4 cup	1/2 cup	3/4 cup
Bread or **bread alternate**, enriched or whole grain	1/2 slice	1/2 slice	1 slice

[1] 1/4 cup (volume) or 1/3 ounce (weight), whichever is less.

[2] 3/4 cup (volume) or 1 ounce (weight), whichever is less.

[3] This portion can meet only one-half of the total serving of the meat/meat alternate requirement for lunch or supper. Nuts or seeds must be combined with another meat/meat alternate to fulfill the requirement. For determining combinations, 1 ounce of nuts or seeds is equal to 1 ounce of cooked lean meat, poultry, or fish.

Caution: Children under five are at the highest risk of choking. The USDA recommends that any nuts or seeds be served to them in a prepared food and be ground or finely chopped.

Metric Conversions (approximate): 1 Tbsp.—15mL; 1/4 cup—50mL; 1/3 cup—75mL; 3/8 cup—90 mL; 1/2 cup—125mL; 3/4 cup—175 mL; 1 cup—250 mL; 1/3 oz.—9 g; 1/2 oz.—14 g; 3/4 oz.—21 g; 1 oz.—28 g.

One federal child nutrition program is the **Child and Adult Care Food Program (CACFP).** This is *a federally funded program that helps provide healthful meals and snacks in child and adult care facilities.* In order to receive money and commodity food from the CACFP, programs must serve meals that meet federal nutrition guidelines. The meal pattern established by the CACFP is shown on page 251.

Teachers who plan menus for child care programs should learn about proper nutrition by reading nutrition books and enrolling in an early childhood nutrition course. Here are some tips for making sure the foods served are nutritious:

- Choose fruit and vegetable juices that are 100 percent juice, with no added sweetener.

- Serve fruits and vegetables raw when possible. Valuable nutrients can be lost during cooking. When you do cook fruits and vegetables, choose such methods as microwaving, steaming, or simmering in a small amount of water. Avoid overcooking.

- Choose low-fat dairy products for children over age two.

- Serve only lean meats. To reduce fat, bake or broil meats instead of frying.

- Choose whole-grain breads, crackers, and cereals. Whole-grain products are usually more nutritious, and they provide fiber, which helps keep the digestive tract working normally.

- Encourage children to drink small amounts of water frequently throughout the day. Of course, water is also present in juices and milk, but the best source is plain, natural water from the tap or drinking fountain.

The extra challenge in planning a nutritious menu comes with making it economical too. Since budgets are usually tight in child care programs, a practical approach to planning and purchasing foods is necessary. Buying fresh produce that is in season, purchasing in quantity, and taking advantage of sales are techniques used to keep in line with the budget.

Making Foods Easy to Eat

Young children are just learning to use eating utensils. To make eating easier, include some finger foods, such as carrot sticks or apple slices.

Serve children's food in small pieces. Large chunks of meat, vegetables, or fruit may be difficult for them to chew and could cause choking. Children may need to be reminded to eat slowly and chew food thoroughly.

Avoid serving young children nuts, popcorn, grapes, hot dogs, and hard candies. These foods can easily be inhaled and cause choking. In case of choking, use the Heimlich maneuver (explained in Chapter 10). A poster showing how to perform the Heimlich maneuver should be displayed in every eating area.

Making Meals Appealing

Imagine sitting down to a meal in which every food item is sweet—or everything is tart. You probably wouldn't enjoy it. As do most adults, children like a mixture of flavors in a meal. Their taste buds are sensitive, however, so foods should be only

Tip FROM THE Pros

*U*se your imagination to make food more fun and appealing for children. Cut slices of meat or cheese into stars or animal shapes. Make a boat out of a sandwich, using a toothpick to hold a paper sail. Turn a pancake into a funny face by adding banana slices and raisins to form eyes, nose, and mouth.

Cutting or arranging food into fun shapes can boost children's interest. What else about this snack makes it a good choice for young children?

monotony. For instance, broccoli may be part of a salad for one meal. The next time it is served, it may be steamed as a side dish or eaten raw with a dip as a snack.

A sample child care menu is shown below. How well do you think it fulfills the goals of nutrition, ease of eating, and appeal to young children?

Special Considerations in Meal Planning

Some children may be unable to eat certain foods because of allergies or other medical problems. In addition, religious beliefs may call for avoiding certain foods or food combinations. Be sure to ask parents about any such restrictions that may apply to their child. Keep a convenient record of these restrictions to consult when planning meals.

lightly seasoned. Including bright colors and different shapes on the plate adds eye appeal. For even more interest, serve foods with different textures—soft and creamy, hard and crunchy, chewy, or crisp.

Prepare foods in a variety of ways to encourage new food choices and avoid

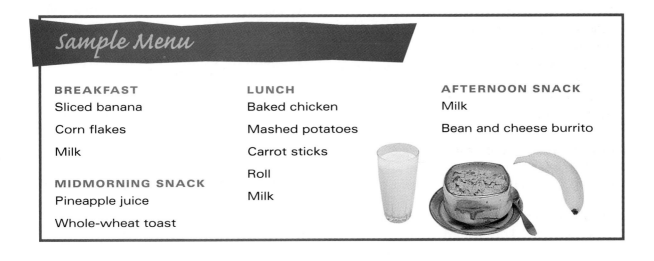

Sample Menu

BREAKFAST
Sliced banana

Corn flakes

Milk

MIDMORNING SNACK
Pineapple juice

Whole-wheat toast

LUNCH
Baked chicken

Mashed potatoes

Carrot sticks

Roll

Milk

AFTERNOON SNACK
Milk

Bean and cheese burrito

THE MULTICULTURAL CLASSROOM

Food offers an excellent way to introduce children to other cultures. Although menus should include foods children are familiar with, introducing those from other cultures broadens their horizons.

One interesting way to ease young children into an appreciation of different foods is to let them smell the seasonings associated with certain foods. The children may recognize cinnamon, basil, oregano, garlic, black pepper, and vanilla, but nutmeg, paprika, chili powder, cilantro, and cumin might not be as familiar. Encourage the children to discuss what these seasonings smell like, and allow tasting. Sprinkle some of the spices into dough or make a spice collage on a paper plate. The next time the children are introduced to a food with an unfamiliar aroma, they may be more willing to give it a try.

Adding ethnic foods little by little during snack time is another good idea. Serving bagels, tortillas, lavosh (Armenian bread), scones, wontons, and pizza is a good start.

Food Safety and Sanitation

Food that is spoiled or tainted with bacteria can cause serious illness in children and adults. Anyone preparing to serve food must be trained in food safety and sanitation practices. **Sanitation** means *practicing cleanliness to prevent the spread of illness and disease.*

Harmful bacteria and other disease-carrying agents can easily spread from unclean hands or equipment to food. To limit the spread of these agents, food handlers must wash their hands with hot, soapy water before beginning food preparation. They must take care not to cough or sneeze on the food. Like all others in the center, they must wash their hands after coughing, sneezing, blowing their nose, or using the restroom. In addition, hand washing is necessary after handling raw meat, poultry, fish, or eggs. Equipment that touched the raw food, such as cutting boards and knives, must also be scrubbed in hot, soapy water before being used for other foods.

All dishes and utensils must be sanitized after each use. This is usually done in dishwashers, using very hot (170°F [77°C]) water to kill bacteria. Eating areas and food preparation areas must be cleaned with a sanitizing solution before and after each use. Serve food on clean dishes, not the same dishes that were used for raw food.

In addition to cleanliness, proper temperatures for storing and serving food are necessary. Many foods are **perishable**, which means *they will spoil if not refrigerated or frozen.* That is because bacteria multiply rapidly at room temperature. Cold temperatures limit the growth of bacteria. High temperatures used in cooking food destroy many harmful bacteria.

To maintain proper food temperatures, follow these guidelines:

- Make sure the temperature inside the refrigerator is between 32°F and 40°F (0°C and 4°C). Keep the freezer at 0°F (-18°C) or lower.
- Never let frozen food sit at room temperature to thaw. Instead, let it thaw in the refrigerator. You may also use a microwave oven to defrost the food, as long as you cook it right away.

Building Professional Skills

Responsibility

WHAT IS RESPONSIBILITY?

People show responsibility by proving they can be trusted with important obligations. Responsible people don't need constant supervision; they carry out their duties without being told. They are also willing to accept the blame when they make mistakes. Responsibility is an important part of maturity.

Responsibility in Action

It was afternoon snack time in the child care center where Nolan and Clarisse worked as aides. Mrs. Andrews, the food service manager, took Nolan aside. "A family emergency has come up, so I can't be here tomorrow. Could you prepare lunch for the children? Since you've helped me in the kitchen before, I think you can handle it."

"Sure," Nolan replied. "I'd be glad to help."

Mrs. Andrews looked relieved. "Good. Here's the menu—hamburgers, vegetable sticks, applesauce, and milk. Remember to put the ground beef in the refrigerator to thaw before you leave tonight. Thanks so much—I'm sure you'll do a fine job." With that, Mrs. Andrews hurried out the door.

The next day, Nolan arrived early. When he checked on the meat in the refrigerator, he realized it wouldn't be enough. "I guess I should have pulled two packages out of the freezer yesterday instead of just one," he told Clarisse.

"You've got hours before you have to start cooking," Clarisse said. "If you set the other package out on the counter now, it might thaw in time."

Nolan shook his head. "No, that's too risky. The kids could get sick, and it would be my fault. Looks like I'll have to make a quick trip to the store."

The rest of the day, including lunch, went well. When Mrs. Andrews returned, Nolan told her what had happened. She smiled and said, "I've forgotten to thaw meat a few times myself. The important thing is that you followed food safety rules. I knew I could count on you."

Your Analysis

1. Why do you suppose Mrs. Andrews chose Nolan to be in charge of lunch? How does this relate to the definition of responsibility?

2. What indications do you have that Nolan is a responsible person?

3. What are some different ways a less responsible person might have handled this situation? Why did Nolan reject those choices?

4. What are some other examples of how people show responsibility on the job?

Health inspectors make regular visits to all food service operations. What do you think this inspector is checking for?

State laws usually require child care programs to be regularly monitored by the local health department. Programs are checked periodically by **health inspectors**, *health department representatives who observe and evaluate a program's health practices.* This protects children by making sure proper food safety is practiced by meal service personnel. Health inspectors check for many things. They check to make sure food is stored and served at safe temperatures. They notice if a food preparer is wearing the required hair net, which keeps hair from accidentally falling into food. They check to see if a food handler's cuts or wounds are covered with plastic gloves when handling food. (Otherwise, disease-causing agents from the wound could enter the food and cause illness.) Health departments also provide the child care staff with training in food safety and sanitation.

- Be sure food is cooked thoroughly. Meat and poultry should be cooked to an internal temperature of at least 160°F (71°C). Leftovers should be thoroughly reheated to an internal temperature of 165°F (74°C). Once you begin to cook the food, continue until it is completely done.

- When serving a meal or snack, keep hot foods hot and cold foods cold. Otherwise, bacteria will grow rapidly as the food reaches room temperature.

- After a meal, refrigerate or freeze any leftovers promptly. If perishable food has been left sitting out for more than two hours (one hour in very hot weather), discard it.

Tip **FROM THE** *Pros*

*W*hen serving beverages to young children, fill cups only half full. This reduces the chance of spills. When spills do occur, there is less to wipe up.

Serving Meals and Snacks

At lunch time in a typical child care program, you might see a scene like this. Three tables are each set with six place settings, including cups, spoons, napkins, and child-size plates. On each table is a platter of sandwiches made with turkey, lettuce, and whole-wheat bread. The sandwiches are cut into quarters. Other serving dishes hold peas, sliced peaches, carrot sticks, and green pepper rings. Milk is served as a beverage. After children and teachers wash their hands, they sit together and begin eating the meal.

Preventing Tooth Decay

*A*n eating pattern of frequent small meals and snacks is fine for nutrition but can be hard on the teeth. Food particles react with bacteria in the mouth, resulting in acid that attacks tooth enamel. For good dental health, encourage children to brush their teeth after meals and snacks.

Getting a meal on the table is only one part of the effort. The other is making meal time enjoyable. To make it so, most programs have basic rules. Typically, children are expected to:

- Help set the table before meals.
- Participate in meal preparation whenever possible. For example, they might make a salad as an activity with the teacher.
- Wash hands before setting the table, helping prepare meals, or eating.
- Begin eating only after everyone has arrived at the table.
- Sit appropriately in chairs while eating.
- Serve themselves reasonable portions of each food choice.
- Say "please" and "thank you" when requesting and passing food.
- Enjoy quiet, pleasant conversation during the meal.
- Use napkins appropriately.
- Clean up their own place setting and spills.

Peeling and slicing fruit for a salad gives these children a sense of accomplishment. In what other ways does helping prepare a meal benefit children?

- Wait to leave the table until everyone is finished.
- Wash hands and brush teeth after eating.

Teachers must also follow certain rules at mealtime. They should set a good example by following the same guidelines that the children are expected to follow. They should never withhold food as punishment, offer food as a reward, or force children to clean their plate. These practices interfere with teaching good eating habits.

TEACHING NUTRITION CONCEPTS

You can provide children with the right foods, but until they learn how to choose them on their own, your job isn't done. Nutrition education should be one of the goals of any child care program.

Through nutrition education, children learn that food does more than just satisfy hunger. This learning process can be extended to the home and parents as well.

Food Experiences for Children

Just because a food is green or has lumps in it doesn't make it bad. Getting children to see that they can enjoy and benefit from all kinds of foods is not always an easy task. A menu with variety exposes children to many foods, some of which may be new to them.

Children should be encouraged to take at least a small taste of each food; however, they should never be pressured or forced to taste a food they dislike or are suspicious of. A new food may need to appear on the menu several times before a finicky child finally accepts it. Putting a new food on a plate with a popular food item is often helpful. Presenting unfamiliar foods in a positive way not only helps children learn about food but also lets them become more comfortable with trying something new.

FOCUS ON INFANT PROGRAMS

Parents usually provide formula for their infants. They may ask you to warm the bottle of formula before giving it to the baby. Do not heat formula in a microwave—parts of the mixture could become dangerously hot while the rest feels only lukewarm. Instead, use a bottle warmer, or heat the filled bottle in a pan of water on the range. Shake a few drops of formula onto your wrist to be sure it is lukewarm, not hot.

When feeding babies, hold them in a nurturing manner. Never leave a bottle propped in a baby's mouth while you attend to other business. This could cause digestive problems, ear infections, or even choking. If the baby wants a sucking device at nap time, provide a pacifier instead of a bottle.

When it is time to offer children solid food (usually after six months of age), follow parent's recommendations for introducing baby cereals, strained fruits and vegetables, and pureed meats. Introduce new foods one at a time. Closely observe children for signs of an allergic reaction, such as a rash or diarrhea.

Most children are interested in learning about different types of food and where they come from.

Preschoolers are not too young to begin learning some basic nutrition concepts. Here are some concepts that can be understood by young children:

- Food is fuel for the body. It helps people grow and gives them energy.
- People should eat a variety of foods every day. This keeps bodies healthy. It helps fight off illness.
- People need to drink several glasses of water every day.
- Food comes from plants and animals.
- People eat different parts of plants, including stems, roots, leaves, and seeds.
- Most food is grown on the farm and then taken to a supermarket.
- People can grow their own food in gardens.
- People from different parts of the world eat different foods.
- Food can be cooked in many different ways.

Nutrition concepts can be taught to children through food experiences. Many teachers conduct food preparation activities with children as young as two years of age. The younger the child, the simpler the food project. Two-year-olds may begin by spreading peanut butter on crackers. As children gain experience in food preparation, more complex recipes can be prepared. They might like to make granola or vegetable soup. Conduct the activity at a child-size table over an easily cleaned surface. Talk about the smell, taste, and appearance of the food while preparing it.

Other activities, such as reading books, can often be linked with nutrition education. Reading the story "Goldilocks and the Three Bears" in the morning can be followed by preparing porridge with the children in the afternoon.

Puzzles and matching games about food are also worthwhile activities. They help children identify and label food choices. Table games encourage older children to

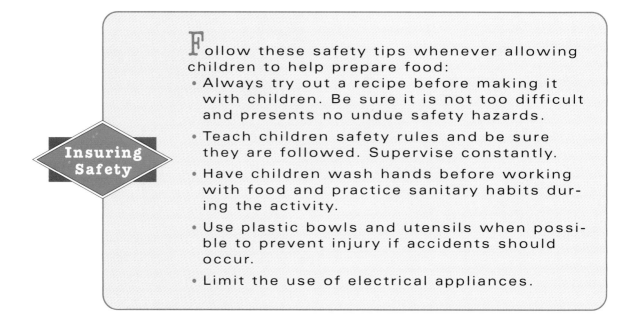

Follow these safety tips whenever allowing children to help prepare food:

- Always try out a recipe before making it with children. Be sure it is not too difficult and presents no undue safety hazards.
- Teach children safety rules and be sure they are followed. Supervise constantly.
- Have children wash hands before working with food and practice sanitary habits during the activity.
- Use plastic bowls and utensils when possible to prevent injury if accidents should occur.
- Limit the use of electrical appliances.

Insuring Safety

classify food into food groups. Some teachers have younger children sort pictures according to food and nonfood.

Field trips are another method of nutrition education. The class might visit a pizza parlor, supermarket, orchard, farm, restaurant, vegetable stand, farmer's market, or ice cream store.

Puzzles and other activities can help reinforce what children have learned about food.

FOCUS ON SCHOOL-AGE PROGRAMS

School-age children want more freedom of choice in their food selections. Offer nutritious options so that any choice is a healthful one.

Allow school-age children to help plan, purchase, and prepare some of their daily snacks. These projects help them feel important and responsible. Most school-age children enjoy preparing food. They can become very creative and develop new recipes of their own.

Creative teachers use songs, records, finger plays, poems, flannel board stories, bulletin boards, and puppet shows to teach good eating habits. The public library is generally a good source for these materials.

The U.S. Department of Agriculture funds agencies called Nutrition Education Training (N.E.T.) centers. These N.E.T. centers provide a wealth of activity ideas for nutrition education, usually free of charge.

Nutrition Education for Parents

Parents are role models for their children's eating habits. The more parents know about nutrition, the more likely they are to provide healthful meals at home and to set a good example when it comes to food choices. Child care providers can look for opportunities to educate parents on nutrition. For example, they might:

- Ask parents to join the class for a snack or lunch.
- Send home nutritious recipes in newsletters.
- Host a potluck meal featuring healthful foods.

- Invite parents on nutrition-related field trips.

Some parents may need extra assistance with nutrition. These parents may be referred to a federally funded nutrition program called the **Women, Infants, and Children (WIC) Program.** *This program provides nutrition advice and low-cost food, including infant formula. It is available to low-income pregnant and breast-feeding women, infants, and children up to five years old.*

FOOD FOR THOUGHT

Nutritionists believe that eating habits learned in early childhood continue into adulthood. If children learn to choose wisely and moderately from the food groups, they are likely to add quality and length to life. By providing nutritious meals and snacks plus food-related learning activities, a child care program can help foster good eating habits now and in the years to come.

Chapter 13 Review

Chapter Summary

- Good nutrition is important to physical, intellectual, and emotional development.
- The body needs these nutrients: carbohydrates, proteins, fats, vitamins, minerals, and water.
- To plan meals and snacks that provide the right amounts of all necessary nutrients, use the Food Guide Pyramid.
- Children's meals should have variety and appeal in addition to being healthful and nutritious.
- Proper food safety and sanitation practices prevent food-related illness.
- Guidelines should be set up for mealtimes to help insure enjoyable meals.
- Children benefit from nutrition education. Parents should also be educated about nutrition.

Reviewing the Facts

1. Explain the importance of good nutrition.
2. What is the function of carbohydrates?
3. Give three examples of foods that supply carbohydrates.
4. What is the role of proteins in nutrition?
5. Why is it important to eat a variety of foods daily?
6. Name the groups in the Food Guide Pyramid.
7. Should children be served the same quantity of food that adults are served? Explain your answer.
8. What is the CACFP and what is its role?
9. Give three examples of foods that could cause young children to choke.
10. List three ways a meal can be made appealing to children.
11. Briefly describe four procedures meal preparers should follow when working in the food area.
12. When serving meals, why is it important to keep hot foods hot and cold foods cold?
13. Describe three educational food experiences for children.

Thinking Critically

1. Why might children be more willing to try new foods if they have helped prepare them?
2. What link might there be between good nutrition and good self-esteem?
3. What might be some advantages of using plant food combinations, such as beans and rice, as a source of protein?
4. Suppose a parent or teacher regularly tells a child, "No dessert until you eat all your vegetables." What does this teach the child about the relative value of desserts and vegetables? What problems might this cause in the long run?
5. As a caregiver, suppose you discover that several children are not eating breakfast. Some are eating inappropriate foods for breakfast. What steps could you take to encourage families to have a nutritious breakfast each morning?

Activities and Applications

1. **Parent Interview.** Ask the parent of a young child about the child's eating habits. What techniques has the parent used to introduce new foods?
2. **Recipe File.** Collect at least ten nutritious snack recipes for preschoolers. Be sure to include finger foods and "fun" foods.

Chapter 13 Review

3. **Supermarket Visit.** Take a young child with you to the supermarket. Which foods catch the child's eye? Why are the foods attractive to the child? Are they nutritious?

4. **Activity Planning.** Create an activity that could help preschool children learn about food and nutrition. For example, you might make a set of food flash cards or write a puppet show.

Your Professional Portfolio

Imagine that you are in charge of food service for a child care center that operates from early morning through evening hours. Plan one day's menu for preschool children, including breakfast, lunch, dinner, and two snacks. Also write an explanation of why your menu is nutritious and appropriate for preschoolers. Place the completed menu and explanation in your portfolio.

Observing and Analyzing

Looking at Lunches

The lunches that children have in a child care program are usually either prepared at the school or sent from home. Some lunches, however, are cooked at another school or in a central kitchen for delivery to several sites. Occasionally programs contract out to community restaurants or caterers for daily deliveries.

When convenience is a concern, a parent may appreciate having the lunch provided or available for purchase at the school. To save costs or to control what is eaten, a parent may prefer to send lunch from home. If you ask children which they prefer, most would choose the lunch that tastes best, regardless of the source. The most important issue for all, however, should be making sure the meal is a nutritious one. Try the observation ideas below to explore this thought.

- **Public Programs.** Observe a public school or government-subsidized program for school-age children and record what is served, what is eaten, and what is thrown out barely eaten or untouched. Was the food prepared in an appetizing manner? Also record the children's comments. Were they favorable or unfavorable? What suggestions, if any, would you make?

- **Private Programs.** Visit two private programs, one that provides lunch prepared in the program's kitchen and another where the children bring their lunches from home. Make the same observations mentioned above.

- **Nutritional Value.** After observing the lunches served in the two activities above, analyze them for nutritional value. Which was the most nutritious? Which looked the most appealing? Which foods were the best liked, and which were the least popular?

- **Commercials.** Observe commercials shown during Saturday morning television programming for children. Make a list of the food-related items shown. Which items are wholesome, healthful choices? Which are not nutritious? Which commercials are shown more, the healthful choices or the less nutritious? Why? How do you think exposure to these commercials affects children?

Meet Consuella Martinez, child care program director. As director, Consuella manages a staff of twenty people. Together they tend to the various needs of ninety children ages six weeks to ten years.

Why did you choose this career?

"I've always liked children. I babysat often during junior high school. During high school I volunteered in a child care center. The center's director suggested I attend college to become qualified to work in the child care profession. Thanks to her interest and encouragement, here I am today!"

What education and skills do you need?

"After high school I studied two years to obtain an associate's degree in child care. After working several years as a child care teacher I completed two more years of college to obtain my bachelor's degree in early childhood education. That qualified me to be a child care director.

"Directors need lots of different skills. Some days I feel pulled in ten directions at once. Good communication and problem-solving skills are essential. It's also important to work well with all kinds of people.

"As director, I use management skills like any other businessperson. I manage our budget and maintain records on staff and children. A role I take very seriously is insuring a safe and healthful environment for our children and staff. In addition, I'm expected to maintain good relationships with parents. Last, but not least, I have to operate our program legally at all times. It's very important to abide by state laws and to cooperate with state officials."

What is a typical day on the job like?

"No day is really typical for me! Directors have to be flexible. We do whatever it takes to keep the whole program running smoothly. Most mornings I greet families as they arrive. Later I visit each classroom to observe teachers and offer a helping hand. After lunch time I take kindergartners to school. Later I return phone calls and do billing or payroll. Around three o'clock I pick up school-age children from their schools. When it's needed, I also care for an ill child, substitute for a teacher, purchase supplies, or interview someone for a position."

What is most challenging about your job?

"Working with people can be the best and the worst part of my job. For instance, it's hard telling an employee her work is poor. It's even harder to fire someone. Reminding parents to pay overdue bills is never fun. Interviewing and training new employees is time consuming. I wish we could pay people more than we are able to, but fortunately, enough people put a high priority on their desire to work with children. After all, caring for children is an important job!"

What is your favorite part of the job?

"Actually, I have many favorites. I love to see how children mature and grow. I enjoy conducting staff training workshops. Organizing parent programs is a creative part of my job. We offer 'family nights' where children, parents, and child care staff get together for fun and games. This helps build a partnership between parents and the child care center staff."

SHARE YOUR THOUGHTS

1. What personal qualities might help a person be an effective child care director?
2. Identify one of the challenges Consuella mentioned. Offer suggestions for making the task less difficult.
3. What part of being a director sounds most rewarding to you? What part would you like least?

Appendix

CDA Competency Goals and Functional Areas

Candidates for the CDA credential are assessed according to CDA competency standards. These national standards are the criteria used to evaluate a caregiver's performance with children and families. The standards are summarized in the chart below. The chart shows six competency goals that are subdivided into 13 functional areas. Each task or function described must be carried out by the caregiver in order to accomplish the competency goals. Additional information on these standards can be obtained from The Council for Early Childhood Professional Recognition, 1341 G Street, NW, Suite 400, Washington, DC 20005-3105.

CDA COMPETENCY GOALS	FUNCTIONAL AREAS
I. To establish and maintain a safe, healthy, learning environment.	1. Safe: Candidate provides a safe environment to prevent and reduce injuries. 2. Healthy: Candidate promotes good health and nutrition and provides an environment that contributes to the prevention of illness. 3. Learning Environment: Candidate uses space, relationships, materials, and routines as resources for constructing an interesting, secure, and enjoyable environment that encourages play, exploration, and learning.
II. To advance physical and intellectual competence.	4. Physical: Candidate provides a variety of equipment, activities, and opportunities to promote the physical development of children. 5. Cognitive: Candidate provides activities and opportunities that encourage curiosity, exploration, and problem solving appropriate to the developmental levels and learning styles of children. 6. Communication: Candidate actively communicates with children and provides opportunities for support for children to understand, acquire, and use verbal and nonverbal means of communicating thoughts and feelings. 7. Creative: Candidate provides opportunities that stimulate children to play with sound, rhythm, language, materials, space and ideas in individual ways and to express their creative abilities.

III. To support social and emotional development and provide positive guidance.	8. Self: Candidate provides physical and emotional security for each child and helps each child know, accept and take pride in himself or herself and to develop a sense of independence. 9. Social: Candidate helps each child feel accepted in the group, helps children learn to communicate and get along with others, and encourages feelings of empathy and mutual respect among children and adults. 10. Guidance: Candidate provides a supportive environment in which children can begin to learn and practice appropriate and acceptable behaviors as individuals and as a group.
IV. To establish positive and productive relationships with families.	11. Families: Candidate maintains an open, friendly, and cooperative relationship with each child's family, encourages their involvement in the program, and supports the child's relationship with his or her family.
V. To ensure a well-run, purposeful program responsive to participant needs.	12. Program Management: Candidate is a manager who uses all available resources to ensure an effective operation. The Candidate is a competent organizer, planner, record keeper, communicator, and cooperative coworker.
VI. To maintain a commitment to professionalism.	13. Professionalism: Candidate makes decisions based on knowledge of early childhood theories and practices. Candidate promotes quality in child care services. Candidate takes advantage of opportunities to improve competence, both for personal and professional growth and for the benefit of children and families.

Glossary

A

accessible. Easily used by those with disabilities. (28)

accident log. A written record of all injuries as they happen. (10)

accident report form. A form used to record specific information about any accident involving a child. (10)

accommodation. A change in thinking that makes new information fit into what a person already knows and understands. (5)

action verses. Songs for which children act out the motions described in the lyrics. (22)

active listening. Responding with a description of what you think another person is feeling, and why. (15)

active play. Activities that are primarily physical. (24)

advisory board. A group of people, often parents, community members, or people in early childhood careers, who help directors develop and implement center policies. (8)

anecdotal record. A written description that focuses on a particular incident. (16)

antibodies. Substances produced by the immune system that when released into the blood help destroy disease-causing organisms. (11)

art. The use of skills and creative imagination to produce something pleasing. (18)

assimilation. Taking in new information and trying to make it fit with what is already known and understood. (5)

attachment behavior. When an infant shows signs of pleasure at the appearance of a caregiver and signs of distress when that person leaves. (4)

attention span. The ability to focus on a specific activity for a period of time. (5)

au pair. (oh PARE). A person who comes from one country to live with a family in another country, exchanging housework and child care for room and board. (1)

autonomy. (aw-TAHN-uh-mee). Independence. (5)

B

beat. The recurring pulse that gives a song rhythm. (22)

bias. Any attitude, belief, or feeling that results in unfair treatment of an individual because of his or her identity. (17)

bilingual. Ability to speak and understand two languages. (19)

body language. Gestures, body movements, and facial expressions that help convey meaning in conversation. (15)

bonding. Forming a strong attachment to, and preference for, the primary caregivers. (4)

burnout. Physical and emotional exhaustion from too much time and attention spent on the job. (30)

C

CDA advisor. An individual who counsels candidates and provides specific training for the CDA (child development associate) credential. (2)

call-and-response songs. A song in which an adult sings questions and children sing back the answers. (22)

cardiopulmonary resuscitation (CPR). (CAR-dee-oh-PULL-muh-NAIR-ee ree-SUH-suh-TAY-shun). A life-saving technique used when the heartbeat and/or breathing has stopped. Gentle puffs of air are given to the person while forcing the heart to pump blood by applying gentle pressure to the chest. (10)

career path. A plan for each step that will lead to career goals. (30)

Caregiver Report Form. A form used to organize and record the provision of routine care. (25)

centration. A term coined by Piaget to refer to how children in the preoperational period can focus on only one characteristic at a time when they sort objects. (6)

cephalocaudal. (SEF-uh-luh-KAWD-ull). A principle of development in which children master body movement and coordination from the head downward. (3)

character. A quality exemplified by moral strength. (30)

checklist. Specific information that an observer looks for while observing children. (16)

child abuse. Nonaccidental injury inflicted on a child. (11)

Child and Adult Care Food Program (CACFP). A federally funded program that helps provide healthful meals and snacks in child and adult care facilities. (13)

child care. A broad term that describes any situation in which children are provided with supervision, support, and sometimes training by individuals outside the child's immediate family. (1)

child care resource and referral specialist. An individual who works mainly on the telephone to assist parents in making child care arrangements. (2)

child development. The pattern of change that occurs as children grow from birth to adolescence. (3)

Child Development Associate (CDA) credential. Awarded to an applicant after the person demonstrates competency skills in specific areas of child care. (2)

child development consultants. Individuals who give child development advice to people who create children's products. (2)

child neglect. Failure to provide a child with the basic necessities of life, including food, clothing, shelter, and medical care. (11)

choice time. A technique used to let children decide which activity they would like to participate in next. (12)

chronological grouping. Placing children of the same age together. (17)

classification. Mentally grouping objects into categories according to similarities. (6)

close-ended materials. Items that are meant to be used in primarily one way, with an expected result. (17)

cognitive development. Intellectual development that occurs as children think, understand, reason, and use language. (3)

collage. (kuh-LAHZH). A picture or design made by gluing or pasting separate pieces of material to a background surface. (18)

communicable diseases. Infectious diseases that are passed from person to person. (11)

compassion. Recognizing when others are having problems and wanting to be of help. (2)

concepts. General ideas formed from other information. (5)

concrete operations period. A period of intellectual development identified by Piaget during which children (ages seven to eleven) think logically and relate logic to actual objects and experiences. (7)

conferences. Large gatherings at which members of a profession exchange information about the latest findings, developments, and practices in their field. (30)

confidentiality. Maintaining the privacy of others. (14)

confirmation letter. A letter that is sent to a potential employer in order to verify an agreement to meet at a certain time and date. (29)

conscience. (KAHNT-shunts). Attitudes about right and wrong that guide behavior. (6)

consequences. Events that occur as the result of a particular behavior. (15)

conservation. The understanding that an object's physical dimensions remain the same even when its appearance changes, a concept Piaget linked to the preoperational stage of intellectual development. (6)

continuing education. Acquiring new knowledge and experience, even after obtaining a career position. Continuing education refines and updates job skills. (30)

cooperative play. Playing together and agreeing on play themes and activities. (6)

cover letter. A letter of application that accompanies a resumé. (29)

creative movement. Responding to music through physical movement. (22)

criminal background check. An investigation to determine if an applicant has been convicted of a crime. (29)

cubby. A small space for storage of personal items. (9)

curriculum. A long-range plan of activities and experiences for children. (1)

custodial needs. Physical needs, such as toilet-ing, hand washing, eating, napping, and resting. (9)

D

deficiency. Severe shortage. (13)

depth perception. The ability to judge distance and see objects in perspective. (7)

developmental grouping. Placing children together according to their ability. (17)

developmentally appropriate curriculum. Activities that are geared to different levels of ability and development in order to accommodate all children in a program. (1)

dioramas. (DY-uh-RA-muhs). Three-dimensional pictures made with small, cut-out designs. (18)

director. A key person in most child care settings. The director may work with children but has the primary responsibility of management. The director manages daily operations and guides the staff. (2)

diversity. The term often used today when talking about all the qualities people have that make them different from one another. (7)

dramatic play. The imitation of real-life situations during play. (6)

dress codes. Rules for dress in the workplace. (14)

E

early childhood. The years between birth and age eight. (1)

early childhood education. Child care programs that promote development through formal teaching and learning experiences for children up to age eight. (1)

early childhood professionals. People who work in early childhood programs. (2)

echo method. A method of teaching songs in which the children first listen as a line or verse is sung and then repeat it. (22)

egocentric. (ee-go-SEN-trick). Seeing everything from a person's own point of view. (4)

emergency treatment waiver form. A statement that is signed by a parent or legal guardian and gives permission to secure emergency medical treatment for a sick or injured child. (10)

emergent literacy. The gradual process of learning to read. (19)

emotions. Feelings about self, others, and the world. (3)

empathy. The ability to recognize and understand the feelings of others. (6)

entrepreneur. (AHN-truh-pruh-NUR). Someone who owns and operates a business. (30)

environment. Everything—objects, conditions, atmosphere—that makes up the surroundings. (1)

event record. A record that identifies a specific situation and describes what happens each time that situation occurs over a period of time. (16)

extended family. A description of family that includes relatives other than parents and children. (1)

eye-hand coordination. The ability to move the hands and fingers precisely in relation to what is seen. (4)

F

facilitate. To help bring about something without controlling it. For example, teachers facilitate children's play. (17)

family grouping. Placing children of a certain age range (including several different ages) in the same classroom or group. (17)

fine motor skills. Skills that require use of the small muscles, as in the fingers, wrists, and ankles. (5)

finger plays. Specific hand motions that accompany a song or chant. (19)

flannel board. A piece of cardboard or wood covered with flannel or felt and used to tell a story by attaching fabric pictures. (19)

focus object. An item that is related to an activity and helps introduce it. (17)

Food Guide Pyramid. A guide to daily food choices based on the recommendations of nutrition experts. (13)

frequency count. A record of how many times a particular behavior or situation occurs during a specific period of time. (16)

G

gender identity. The awareness of being male or female. (6)

gender role. The behavior and responsibilities expected of a man or woman in the family and society. (1)

gifted children. Children who are extraordinarily talented or excel in one or more areas. (28)

grand mal seizure. A complete loss of consciousness, with stiffening, jerking, or thrashing of the body. (11)

gross motor skills. Skills that use the large muscles of the back, legs, shoulders, and arms. (5)

growth plateau. A period of relatively slow and steady growth. (7)

H

health inspectors. Health department representatives who observe and evaluate a program's health practices. (13)

Heimlich maneuver. (HIME-lick muh-NOO-vur). A technique used in response to choking by applying pressure on the body to dislodge an object that is blocking air through the windpipe or throat. (10)

home visitor. A parent educator who goes into the child's home to teach the parent how to guide the children's learning and to answer parents' questions. (2)

hormones. Growth-regulating chemicals that are produced by the body and carried in the blood. (7)

hypothesis. A possible explanation based on observable facts. (23)

I

I-messages. An honest description given by a person in order to say how he or she is affected by and feels about certain behavior. (15)

immune system. A bodily system that produces antibodies that resist disease. (11)

immunization. A vaccine given orally or through a shot to protect the person from a particular disease. (11)

improvisations. Creating a melody and lyrics as the mood strikes. (22)

inclusion. Combining children with average abilities and children with special needs in the same classroom. (28)

Individualized Education Plan (IEP). A written plan that outlines how to encourage development in a child with special needs. (28)

industry. The desire to perform skills, succeed at tasks, and make social contributions. (7)

infancy. The time between birth and twelve months of age. (4)

infectious diseases. Illnesses that are caused by organisms that enter the body and damage tissue. (11)

inferiority. A feeling of not having met expected standards. (7)

initiative. (ih-NIH-shuh-tiv). Motivation to accomplish more. (6)

interview. A meeting between a job applicant and a potential employer. At this time the employer learns about the applicant and the applicant learns about the job. (29)

invented spelling. Spelling a word the way it sounds. (19)

isolation room. A separate, cozy, comfortable place to rest when children become ill while attending a child care program. (9)

J, K

job board. A device that shows jobs that children should do. (12)

job jar. A container filled with pieces of paper that show pictures of activities or jobs. (12)

L

language arts. Activities that teach children to listen, speak, read, and write. (19)

language chart. A large paper where children's verbal responses are recorded. (19)

latchkey children. Children who stay home alone before and after school. (27)

learning centers. Areas that are clearly defined for specific types of play and are organized around a theme or curriculum topic. Examples are music, science, and language arts. (9)

learning disability. A disorder that affects the way the brain processes information. (28)

lesson plan. A detailed, written explanation of an activity, including the purpose, any materials needed, and the step-by-step method for carrying out the activity. (17)

letter of application. A letter sent to a potential employer to apply for a job. (29)

letter of inquiry. A short letter sent to a potential employer to ask about job openings. (29)

liability insurance. An insurance policy that covers costs involved in any resulting lawsuit if a program is found responsible for an injury or damages that occur at the center or in connection with center activity. Medical costs for injury can be included in this insurance. (8)

liable for negligence. Held accountable in a court of law if found negligent in preventing an accident or handling an emergency in a responsible manner. (10)

licensing laws. Rules and regulations that early childhood programs must follow as outlined by individual state laws. (8)

literate. Able to read. (19)

lyrics. Words to songs. (22)

M

manipulatives. Toys and materials children operate and change with their hands. (17)

mathematical vocabulary. Words that express numbers and quantities. (23)

mathematics. The study of numbers and their functions, and of shapes. (23)

maturation. The gradual process of growth as each stage of development unfolds. (3)

maze. A deliberately confusing series of pathways. (24)

melody. The tune of a song. (22)

mobile. An art project made with a collection of items or pictures suspended on a wire by string. (18)

motor skills. Abilities that depend on the use and control of muscles. (3)

mural. A long, continuous painting or drawing on one very large piece of paper. (18)

N

nanny. Someone trained in child care and employed to go into the home to care for children. (1)

native language. The language spoken in the home and first learned by children. (19)

naturalistic observation. Observing children as they behave naturally in their everyday environment. (16)

negativism. Refusing to do, or doing the opposite of, what is asked. (26)

networking. Making and maintaining contact with others in order to exchange information and services. Within a profession, people network to find and fill jobs. (29)

noncommunicable diseases. Infectious diseases that do not pass from person to person. (11)

nontoxic. Not poisonous. (9)

nuclear family. A family consisting of a mother, father, and their children. (1)

numerals. Written symbols that represent numbers. (23)

nurture. (NUR-chur). To provide love, support, attention, and encouragement. (4)

nutrients. The substances that are found in food and used by the body to function, grow, repair itself, and produce energy. (13)

nutrition. The process through which the body utilizes the nutrients in food. (13)

O

object permanence. The understanding that an object continues to exist even when out of sight. (4)

occupational briefs. Summaries that describe specific jobs. (30)

on demand. According to individual needs. Feeding schedules of infants are on demand. (25)

one-to-one correspondence. The understanding that, when counting objects in a group, each item is counted once and only once. (6)

on-site. Located on the premises. (27)

open-ended materials. Items that can be used in a variety of ways, with no single "correct" outcome expected. (17)

open-ended questions. Questions that require more than a yes or no answer. (17)

origami. (OR-uh-GAH-mee). A special Japanese paper folding technique in which squares of tissue paper are folded into representational forms, such as birds. (18)

P, Q

parachute play. An active play activity in which a group of children participate in games based on the use of a large circle of nylon fabric. (24)

parallel play. Children playing near each other but not with each other. (5)

Parent Report Form. A form that details a child's activities and behavior before arrival at the center. (25)

participant observer. Someone who interacts with children while observing. (16)

pathogens. Disease-causing organisms, such as bacteria and viruses. (11)

perceptual motor skills. Skills that require the coordination of vision, intellect, and movement. (4)

perishable. Foods that will spoil if not refrigerated or frozen. (13)

personal hygiene (HI-jeen). Keeping the body clean in order to promote good health and prevent illness. (12)

petit mal seizures. (puh-TEE mahl). A few seconds during which consciousness is clouded and possibly a few muscles twitch. (11)

philosophy. General beliefs, concepts, and attitudes an early childhood program has about how children learn and how the program should serve and educate young children. (8)

pitch. The highness or lowness of musical sounds. (22)

policy. A statement of rules or guidelines that guide the actions and decision making of an organization. (8)

portfolio. A collection of actual samples of a person's work, put together to show his or her capabilities, often to a potential employer. The examples are assembled in a binder, folder, or some other type of container that allows for simple, attractive presentation. (2)

positive discipline. The process of teaching children acceptable behavior without harming them physically or emotionally. (15)

positive reinforcement. A response that rewards a particular positive behavior, making it more likely to be repeated. (15)

preoperational period. Piaget's second period of intellectual development that covers ages two to seven. In this period children start to think symbolically and imaginatively, relying less on motor skills and more on thinking to direct behavior. (5)

preschoolers. Children from three to five years of age. (6)

prevention. Taking action to keep something from happening. (10)

print making. Placing an object in paint and then pressing the object onto paper or another base material. (18)

print-rich environment. A setting in which printed materials are used throughout the classroom in meaningful ways; promotes language skills in children. (19)

process versus product. The belief that what children learn through the process of creating art is just as important, if not more important, than what they produce. (18)

productive language. The ability to use words to express yourself. (26)

professional. A person who possesses the education and training to perform a job well and has skills and qualities admired and respected by others. (14)

professional ethics. Standards of right and wrong that apply to a person's behavior as a professional. (14)

professionalism. A sense of commitment, enthusiasm, and responsibility associated with a career. (30)

program goals. Basic skills, concepts, and attitudes to be developed and encouraged in children; these are developed from an early childhood program's philosophy. (8)

prop box. A container for storing items used in a specific dramatic play theme. (20)

proportion. The size relationship of an object's parts. (18)

props. Items that suggest themes for dramatic play. (20)

proximodistal. (PRAHK-suh-MOE-DISS-tull). A principle of development in which children develop from the center of their body outward. (3)

puberty. A stage when boys and girls undergo a series of physical changes and develop into men and women who are able to reproduce. (7)

R

rating scale. A verbal or numerical evaluation of listed items; may be used as a technique for observing children. (16)

rational counting. The understanding that the last number counted in a group represents the entire number of objects. (6)

rebus recipe. A recipe that illustrates ingredients and directions with picture symbols. (23)

receptive language. The ability to understand words spoken by others. (26)

recruit. To actively seek, as when employers recruit candidates for a job. (29)

redirection. A guidance technique that steers a child who is misbehaving to a different, more acceptable activity. (15)

references. People who know you well and can provide a potential employer with information about your character and work habits. (29)

reflexes. Instinctive, involuntary reactions to a stimulus, such as a noise or a touch. (4)

resourcefulness. An ability to find the ways and means to do something. (2)

resumé. A written summary of education, work experience, and any special talents or skills; often prepared for a potential employer. (29)

rhythm instruments. Musical instruments, such as maracas and drums, that allow children to experiment with making their own rhythms. (22)

role model. A person whose behavior and attitude are imitated by others. (5)

role play. To assume the identity of someone else; may be part of dramatic play activities. (20)

rote counting. Reciting numbers in order without understanding that each number represents a specific amount. (6)

routine. A regular, expected procedure that is followed in order to accomplish something. Arrival, mealtime, and nap time, for example, are regular routines within a child care program. (12)

running record. A sequential record of anything that happens during a specific period of time; often used as a technique for observing children. (16)

S

safety hazards. Items, conditions, and situations that could cause physical or emotional danger. (10)

safety policy. A policy that states the rules and procedures to follow to insure physical and emotional well-being. (10)

sanitation. Practicing cleanliness to prevent the spread of illness and disease. (13)

sanitized. Cleaned in a way that will kill the organisms that can cause illness. (9)

schedule. A plan for how time will be used, placing events in the order that they will occur and indicating how long each event will last. (12)

school-age children. Children from the ages of six to twelve. (7)

science. A system of knowledge covering general truths and laws about the physical world. (23)

self-concept. The picture individuals carry in their mind of who they are, what they can do, and what they are like. (3)

self-control. The ability to react to difficult situations in a calm, productive manner instead of an emotional one. (14)

self-correcting. Educational materials that are designed to provide immediate feedback after a child correctly or incorrectly finishes the task. (8)

self-directed. When children respond on their own without having to be told what to do; leading to independence. (12)

self-discipline. The ability to guide your own behavior without help from others. (15)

self-esteem. How people feel about the image they have of themselves. (3)

self-help skills. Skills that allow children to help take care of themselves and their personal needs, such as self-feeding. (5)

sensorimotor period. (sents-ree-MOH-tur). Piaget's first stage of intellectual development, which describes the period from birth to age two when infants and one-year-olds learn by using their senses and motor abilities to gain information about the world. (4)

sensory table. A table with a boxlike, hollow top that can hold water, sand, beans, or other substances to play with. (23)

separation anxiety. A child's fear or stress at being separated from familiar people. (26)

sequence. A step-by-step pattern. (3)

seriation. Organizing objects according to increasing or decreasing size. (6)

social responsibility. The practice of making a positive contribution to the community and obeying community laws. (21)

social studies. The part of a curriculum that teaches children about themselves and their family, community, and the world. (21)

solitary play. Engaging in play alone rather than with other children. (5)

special needs. Circumstances that cause development to vary significantly from what is considered average. (28)

sphincter muscles (SFINK-tur). Muscles that surround certain body openings and have the ability to close them; control of such muscles is needed for toileting readiness in children. (12)

spontaneity. (SPAHN-tuh-NAY-uh-tee). Acting impulsively, or without taking time to use thinking and reasoning skills. (2)

spontaneous dramatic play. When children engage in dramatic play without the suggestion or direction of adults. (20)

staff-to-child ratio. The number of personnel in relation to the number of children in a classroom or group. (8)

staff turnover. The rate at which employees leave their jobs, creating the need for new employees to be hired. (25)

stereotype. A preset idea about a person or group of people based solely on one characteristic, such as gender, nationality, race, or religion. (6)

storytelling. A skill in which a person tells a story from memory instead of reading from a book. (19)

stranger anxiety. The fear of unfamiliar people, usually expressed by crying, that many infants develop. (4)

stress. Mental and physical tension and strain caused by problems, pressures, fears, or unsettling changes. (7)

syrup of ipecac. (IH-pih-kak). A substance given to cause vomiting in poisoning situations; it should only be used when vomiting the poisonous substance will not cause further internal damage. (10)

T, U

teachable moments. Unplanned opportunities for learning. (17)

teacher-directed. Activities in which a teacher leads and supervises children. (12)

temperament. A person's inborn style of reacting to the environment. (4)

temper tantrum. An episode in which children show anger or frustration in an aggressive or destructive way. (26)

tempo. The speed at which a song is sung. (22)

texture quilt. A quilt made from scraps of fabrics of different textures; infants use their sense of touch with these. (25)

thematic unit. A curriculum segment that is based on one central topic, or theme, about which children will learn. (17)

three-dimensional. Having height, width, and depth. (18)

time management. Planning to use time well in order to accomplish goals. (14)

time out. A short period of time in which a child must sit apart from other children and activities. (15)

toddler. A child between the ages of twelve and thirty-six months. (5)

toxic. Poisonous. (9)

traffic pattern. The direction of movement that children take as they move from one part of the classroom to another. (9)

transition. A short activity or technique used to help guide children smoothly from one activity or event to another. (12)

tutor. Someone who provides individual instruction on a regular basis. (27)

V

vaccine. A small amount of a disease-producing organism that is introduced into the body, usually by injection, so the body can build a resistance to it. (11)

values. Beliefs and attitudes about what is important. (3)

visual discrimination. The ability to notice similarities and differences in colors, shapes, and designs. (19)

vocalizations. Sounds infants make that imitate adult language. (4)

W, X, Y, Z

whole language. The practice of including language skill development in all classroom activities. (19)

Women, Infants, and Children (WIC) Program. A federally funded program that provides nutrition advice and low-cost food, including infant formula to low-income pregnant and breast-feeding women, infants, and children up to five years old. (13)

Index

Credits

Cover & Interior Design: William Seabright & Associates

Cover Photography: Robert F. Kusel

Illustrations:

Circle Design
Carol Spengel: 174-175, 195
Morgan-Cain & Associates: 70-71, 203-204, 232-233
PALS Preschool & Kindergarten: 357
Jordan Parker: 175 t
Liz Purcell: 397

Photos:

Arnold & Brown: 51 t
Roger B. Bean: 20, 25, 29, 31, 40, 61 b, 64, 65 t, 67, 74 l, 81 l, 83, 85, 88, 89, 93, 97, 100, 101, 103, 106, 113, 118, 125, 136, 151, 155, 157 t, 159, 165, 166, 168, 169, 170, 173, 178, 186, 190, 194, 202, 207, 209, 211, 220, 223, 226, 228, 233 t, 234, 235, 236, 237, 238, 239 t, 246, 290, 294, 296, 298, 305, 315, 321, 327, 338, 343, 344, 346, 347, 349, 360, 363 t, 376, 377, 379 b, 381, 386, 392, 394, 406, 421, 424, 434, 437, 440, 441, 450, 452, 453, 455, 470, 471, 473 b, 474, 476, 477, 479, 480, 486 t, 487, 488, 490 b, 495, 496, 497, 499, 500, 503, 507, 508, 516, 521, 522, 523, 524 t, 525, 546, 560
Marshal Berman Photography/Design Office: 348, 379 t, 562
Keith Berry: 37, 38, 46-47, 51 b, 79, 95, 107, 112, 153, 160, 174 t tc b, 175 ct cb b, 192, 197, 200, 213 b, 224, 250, 268, 275, 316, 336, 359, 365, 372 t, 374, 378, 388, 389, 420, 423 t, 426 br bl, 427 t, 433, 436, 442, 458, 520 b, 539 b, 547 t, 553, 557 t, 559
The Bettmann Archive: 60
CLEO Freelance Photography: 80, 117, 128, 132, 134, 157 bl, 191, 514, 529

Constructive Playthings, U.S. Toy Co., Inc.: 174 cb, 448, 468, 472, 490 t, 491 b
Gail Denham: 116, 131, 135, 137, 188, 231, 248, 364, 403, 432
EF AuPair: 23
Fisher-Price: 473 t
FPG International Corp.
Telegraph Colour Lib: 164
Cliff Gardiner, Jr.: 41 b, 121, 122, 355
Ann Garvin: 54-55, 90, 142-143, 163, 199, 244, 245, 253 t, 264-265, 271, 284, 306, 313, 330-331, 340, 353, 356, 384, 401, 402, 415, 429, 464-465, 469, 481, 532-533, 551, 568-569
Hasbro/Playskool: 176
John Hopkins: 177
Human Issues Collaborative
Ron Chappel: 72
The Kids on the Block Inc.: 517
Robert F. Kusel: 1, 2-3, 14-15, 56-57, 144-145, 266-267, 332-333, 466-467, 534-535
Lakeshore Learning Materials, Carson, CA: 297, 368, 457
Mishima: 22 t, 65 b, 70 r, 71, 152 t, 243, 280, 299, 418, 454, 501, 506, 515, 537, 555, 565
Armando F. Mola: 380
NAEYC
Melanie Rose White: 561
Nasco: 94, 167, 371, 404 t, 417, 426 t, 427 br
Little Tikes®: 393
Omni-Photo Communications, Inc.
Ann Hagen Griffiths: 98, 148
Brent Phelps: 110, 184, 241, 253 b, 259, 272, 325, 411
Photo Researchers, Inc.
John Carter: 87
Tim Davis: 133
Patrick Donehue: 70 l
Will McIntyre: 61 t
Will & Deni McIntyre: 44 t

Special thanks to the following individuals, schools, businesses, and organizations for their assistance with the photographs in this book:

In Peoria, Illinois:
    A Child's World
    Bylerly Music
    Central Illinois Hearing Aid Centers, Inc.
    Early Intervention Services—PARC
    Friendship House
    Greater Peoria Family YMCA Child Care
        Center
    Kroger Co.
    Lakeview YWCA
    Little Friends Learning Center
    Montessori Children's House of Peoria
    PALS Preschool & Kindergarten
    Proctor Hospital New Horizons Employee
        Child Care Center
    Rogy's Gingerbread House
    St. Patrick's Day Care Center
    Thomas Jefferson School
    Valeska Hinton Early Childhood
        Education Center

In Chicago Area, Illinois:
    McGraw YMCA/Evanston
    Murray Language Academy
    New City Child Development Center

In Normal, Illinois:
    Illinois State University Child Care
        Center

In Denton, Texas:
    Azlann Montessori School
    Denton Christian Preschool
    Learning Curve Academy
    McNair Elementary
    University of North Texas Child
        Development Lab

In Southern California:
    Grant Elementary School
    Hill & Dale Pre-School
    The Oberon-Levoff Family
    Martin Minkardo
    McBride Special Education Elementary
        School
    Mt. Olive Pre-School
    Will Rogers Elementary School
    Richland Child Care Center
    Santa Monica College Child Care Center
    Santa Monica High School—SAPID
        Center
    Natalie, Michael, and Andrew White
    Windward School

Models and fictitious names have been used to portray characters in the stories and examples in this text.